INFERNAL TRIANGLE

ALSO BY PAUL McGEOUGH

Manhattan to Baghdad: Despatches from the Frontline in the
War on Terror
In Baghdad: A Reporter's War
Mission Impossible: The Sheikhs, the US and the Future of Iraq
Kill Khalid: Mossad's Failed Hit . . . and the Rise of Hamas

PAUL McGEOUGH

INFERNAL TRIANGLE

Conflict in Iraq, Afghanistan and The Levant
Eyewitness reports from the September 11 decade

ALLEN&UNWIN

First published in 2011

Copyright © Paul McGeough 2011

Allen & Unwin
Sydney, Melbourne, Auckland, London

83 Alexander Street
Crows Nest NSW 2065
Australia
Phone: (61 2) 8425 0100
Fax: (61 2) 9906 2218
Email: info@allenandunwin.com
Web: www.allenandunwin.com

Cataloguing-in-Publication details are available
from the National Library of Australia
www.trove.nla.gov.au

ISBN 978 1 74237 563 2

Set in 12/16 pt Minion by Bookhouse, Sydney
Printed and bound in Australia by Griffin Press

10 9 8 7 6 5 4 3 2 1

MIX
Paper from
responsible sources
FSC
www.fsc.org   FSC® C009448

The paper in this book is FSC certified.
FSC promotes environmentally responsible,
socially beneficial and economically viable
management of the world's forests.

For Judy Ewing

A belated appreciation,
to you and to your late father Pete,
for pointing the way to a career in journalism

CONTENTS

THE LEVANT

PEOPLE ARE CRYING IN THE STREETS

Six blocks from what is left of the World Trade Center, the streets are full of crying people. The city is totally shocked. Hundreds of emergency vehicles and paramedics are massing on street corners. Jet-fighters circle Manhattan. A great mushroom cloud hangs overhead. People are on rooftops and in tearful crowds on the pavement. The entire lower end of the island is gridlocked. Car radios are at full blast. Papers that a few minutes ago were on people's desks now litter the streets and float in the air like a blinding white snowstorm. It is 10.30 a.m. The second tower has collapsed, for a time numbing the city and the world to what the consequences might be.

Smoke and zero visibility, even six blocks away. Smoke and dust. It's just like in the movies when a building collapses and all you see is a cloud of dust in the shape of the missing building; only now the streets are more eerie and more tense than the wildest depictions Hollywood might dream up. A great cloud of smoke, dust and building debris belts up Church Street, driven by the force of the explosion. There are more explosions from within the cloud. Hundreds of police and firemen are charging uptown, racing ahead of the explosion as the cloud punches its way after them. I'm running with them—I can feel it behind me.

Mothers with children are holding bandanas to their faces, trying to get away, evacuating their apartment buildings. Businesses have closed. Every vehicle in the area is covered in a thick layer of dust. Dazed and injured firemen wander the streets aimlessly. I wipe the blood off the stunned face of one of them and take him to a temporary medical post. Dozens of these posts are being set up on street corners as hundreds of paramedical vehicles arrive in the area.

Later, I get closer, to within two blocks. It is like a moonscape; the dust on the ground is so thick, so heavy. It is almost impossible to breathe—all the emergency services personnel are wearing face masks. They give me one.

Now there are more explosions. I presume it is the buildings around me. The whole of Manhattan is enveloped in a ghostly cloud of dust. Another explosion goes off—I don't know what it is. Cars in the street are exploding—have they been booby-trapped? The smoke from the car explosions is black. Everyone walking around this side of town looks like a ghost—covered from head to foot in grey dust.

Kenny Johannsenn, who works in the World Trade Center, is almost in tears: 'I was in the number one tower. I was waiting for the elevator in the basement. This is the time of day when the building is most crowded. There are thousands of people because it is shift-change time, and also the subway under the building is pushing peak crowds. The lift door exploded open. There was a man inside, half burnt. His skin was hanging off. I dragged him out of the lift and somebody helped me get him out of the building. The explosion hit the building at about level 80. I counted at least seventeen people jumping from that height. What choice did they have? It was either be burnt alive or jump.'

Mike Derby, 30, was attending an economics conference in the Marriott Hotel, which is part of the World Trade Center. His hands shake as he describes what he saw. 'A man was giving a boring speech about securities when it happened,' he tells me. 'The building shook. I didn't think much of it, but all the economists in their grey suits started running. They knew it was a terrorist attack. I got out into the street. I watched maybe 30 people jump. It was surreal. The people who jumped didn't just flop. They were carried, spread-eagled on the wind. I was surprised when the bodies did hit the pavement. I didn't think they would make so loud a noise. I was looking up at the second tower when the jet came in like a black flash.'

Now it is more than two hours after the first explosions and—very disturbingly—no injured people are coming out. The ambulances are all lined up but no one is being put into them. Literally thousands of emergency personnel have arrived. All the streets from the World Trade Center up to 17th Street, more than 36 blocks, are bumper to bumper with emergency-services vehicles. And a team of about 400 surgeons, doctors, nurses and volunteers is mustering at Chelsea Piers on 17th Street, setting up an emergency field hospital.

It is still impossible to see anything. The whole site remains blanketed in a cloud of dust. And smoke. The emergency teams have been told to expect tens of thousands of injured people. But a doctor I speak to says he doesn't expect many survivors to come out of that mountain of wreckage. The air force continues to circle the city. They are pushing us back uptown. There is another explosion. It doesn't look good.

Washington DC, USA

1 March 2011

Almost ten years on, it still doesn't look good. In the immediate aftermath of the attacks, the sense of crisis was such that it was difficult to anticipate the geopolitical landscape weeks ahead, much less years ahead. But those brave enough to make a prediction would not have expected the world's pre-eminent military and economic power to be the somewhat diminished world force that it is today.

President George W. Bush's first initiative was to go to a war against Afghanistan after the Taliban regime refused to give up Osama bin Laden—the terrorist leader whose Al-Qaeda organisation pulled off what would be called the September 11 attacks.

But the collapse of the Taliban in a matter of weeks came too easily. If American power was to be projected around the world, the White House rationale went, it needed to vanquish a more substantial enemy—and that enemy, they decided, would be Iraq.

Huge military and financial resources that might have helped to stabilise Afghanistan were redirected to Iraq, where they were never quite enough for an invasion and occupation that was based on lies and half-truths. The occupation of both countries was badly managed, costing more than a trillion dollars and the combat deaths of more than 7000 troops for the countries that made up the US-led coalitions—most of them American.

Inflicted on any Western society, the cost of liberation borne by the people of Iraq and Afghanistan would be considered catastrophic. In Iraq, the civilian toll was more than 100,000 according to Iraq Body Count; more than 650,000 according to a more controversial survey by the highly respected *Lancet* magazine in 2006. In Afghanistan, estimates of the civilian body count exceeded 24,000. Significant infrastructure in Iraq was destroyed in the war of invasion and by subsequent looting and insurgency. On the collapse of central authority in Kabul, Afghanistan quickly fell back on drugs and corruption as warlords and tribal chiefs reasserted their control in the face of a weak and corrupt central government that survived only because Washington propped it up. All of that was a perfect environment for the Taliban and other insurgents to regroup to go on the warpath—with vengeance.

When both occupations spiralled out of control, American generals coined a new military term—the 'surge'. This meant doubling down to confront the crisis by pouring in tens of thousands more troops in a bid to quell anarchic violence. In Baghdad there was a fall-off in the blood-letting, but some observers cautioned that the warring parties had merely opted to sit on their hands pending the departure of US troops— particularly as Washington paid them to not fight each other. In Afghanistan, the surge made little lasting impact on a fractured and war-weary society.

Distressingly, nearly a decade on from the terror strikes that prompted the two invasions, neither country has become the model of democracy envisaged by their American architects, and elsewhere in the region there was a renewed sense of crisis.

In Lebanon, there was an uneasy sense that another chapter of civil war loomed; and, to the south, another round of so-called peace talks between the Israelis and Palestinians—sponsored by the Obama White House—collapsed.

Bin Laden's Al-Qaeda went to ground in the wilds of nuclear-armed Pakistan, which, despite the pouring in of billions of dollars by Washington, seemed to move closer to the brink of Islamist chaos with the passing of each month. A repeat of the September 11 attacks seemingly was beyond Al-Qaeda's reach, but its offshoots and wannabes around the world continued to mount smaller yet brutal attacks that were sufficient to wreak havoc locally and to prompt increasingly tighter and more costly security measures in the West.

As the end of the September 11 decade loomed, introspection was inevitable in Washington and in its allied capitals. The question hanging in the air, replete with the appropriate local expletives, was: 'How did it all come to this?'

Then, a bolt from the blue. After years in which their autocratic and dictatorial leaders sold themselves to Washington and the West as partners in a war on terror, getting arms, aid donations and a blind eye to the oppression of their people, hundreds of thousands of protesters turned on the regimes of the Arab world.

It was complex indeed, but the glimmer of hope was this— instead of opting for Osama bin Laden-style suicide bombs, or spraying bile and invective at the West, they took to the streets of their cities, with their own 'We the people . . .' demands for a say in their day-to-day lives and their destiny.

AFGHANISTAN

THE FUTURE FOR AFGHANISTAN'S WOMEN

Kabul, Afghanistan
6 October 2004

The alleys of crumbling mud brick and fretted timber get narrower as we arrive back in the Stone Age. Climbing a steep hillside, they twist and turn away from the noise of the bazaar—to a dead end where the war widows of Kabul eke out a living. Barefoot and sweating, they squat on a flour-strewn floor, kneading and rolling dough, which they shape and fire as pizza-like loaves of bread for others among the 60,000 war widows who are fringe-dwelling in the Afghan capital.

There is no power or water. The dusty ceiling is head-high and the whitewashed walls have been blackened by a fire that still burns as a tail-end reminder of the Taliban. Adhering to its strict reading of Islam, the fundamentalist regime barred the widows from working, even as it used their men as cannon fodder. But it relented in a rare concession to humanitarian pressure, agreeing that widows could work to feed other widows.

Three tumultuous years after the Taliban were driven out by the United States, as balls of dough hurled by the kneaders land with a thump before the rollers, these widows have little time for Kabul's debate on women's liberation. Stabbing the dough with her fingers to create the detailed pattern that will decorate the cooked bread, 30-something Shuraya was blunt: 'Nothing's changed for me—I still wear a burqa and my boy sells plastic bags in the market to cover the rent hikes in the new Afghanistan.'

For Kabul's educated female elite, however, there is change—the dreaded blue burqa is gone, they can go to college and work, and their daughters are welcome at school. And when I visited a city business this week, the receptionist sat beneath a poster-sized copy of the Universal Declaration of Human Rights—wearing dangling earrings, jeans and a fitted jacket for which, three years ago, she would have been flogged. People stopped to stare as her female boss, with a gorgeous bob-cut and no scarf, drove her own four-wheel drive off the premises.

The government's commitment to women is a glass half-full, half-empty argument: only two of President Hamid Karzai's 30 ministers are women; only about twenty public management posts are filled by women; and 21 per cent of all state employees are female. But there is little joy for the widows and the 90 per cent of Afghan women who are uneducated, especially those who live in the provinces, in a country where most men cry 'tradition' to circumvent the fine words of constitutions and treaties.

Enter Dr Massouda Jalal, a broad-faced, broad-shouldered paediatrician with nerves of steel. She has stared down the warlords, threats of a legal challenge by the government, criticism by the clerics and the public humiliation of her philosophy-professor husband to sign on as the only female candidate in this Saturday's presidential election. Her campaign office is in a bullet-raked block of flats built by the Russians, and her platform is simple: power for the people. 'I don't have military, media or financial power, but I will not be intimidated,' she said. 'The people back me—41 per cent of the voters are women—and they know that most of the other candidates are criminals, or the candidates of criminals.'

Dr Jalal has a following—at the post-invasion national conference to select an interim leader, she ran second to Mr Karzai. But observers here say that her best hope this weekend is to consolidate her role as a low-wattage beacon for the rights of women.

Dr Jalal has been blocked from appearing on state television, which will not name her, referring to her only as 'a woman'. She has been barred from campaigning at colleges and, as a woman, she is not allowed to speak at mosques. In desperation, she decided to campaign at the women's bakeries, which were her idea as a United Nations staffer during the darkness of the Taliban years. Which is why I met a new bakery manager this week—her predecessor was sacked for allowing politics among the loaves.

The predicament of rural women in Afghanistan is especially dire. This year in Herat, in the far west, there have been more than 80 cases of self-immolation or the attempted murder of women in domestic crises. Rape, often by the warlords' fighters, is not taken seriously by the police or the judiciary; most provincial girls are forced into marriage anywhere between the ages of ten and sixteen; and often they are traded in settlement of tribal disputes. And on voting day a good proportion of them will be told how to vote.

Complaining of impunity for violence against women on a vast scale, Amnesty International last year declared that Mr Karzai's interim regime had proved itself unable to protect women. The organisation cited the case of a woman who was murdered by her father for refusing his choice of husband—attempts by the district governor to have the case prosecuted were frustrated when the alleged killer was given sanctuary by a militia group of which he was a member. Most rural women are not allowed to leave their home without a male chaperone and Amnesty says it was told in discussion groups that divorce is rarely allowed because 'It is not an Afghan tradition.'

Activists like Dr Jalal believe that their best argument in a very conservative, religious society is to convince society that all the reforms the activists demand are in the Koran—if it is read properly. Shukria Barakzai, who carried the torch for women as a member of the committee that drafted the new Afghan constitution, agrees. 'The constitution gives us equal rights and Islam gives us rights in work, business and marriage. But Afghan tradition closes all these doors. Most Afghan men are brutes, so we have to change their mentality; and we have to educate the women.'

But, sitting back as she sipped her tea, wearing a pants-suit a few shades paler than burqa blue, she volunteered a very personal story that revealed that even as a member of the educated elite she was not immune from the male Afghan cry of 'tradition'. 'This sounds like a joke, but it's not. Last year, while I was slaving for women's rights in the constitution, my husband took a second wife without consulting me—which he should have done under Islam. I found out a month after the wedding. For the first twenty minutes I thought I had failed; but then I was happy, because I could feel the pain of the hundreds of thousands of other Afghan women in the same position.'

Another presidential candidate, Abdul Latif Pedram, last week called for family law reform to be debated during the campaign, especially the right of men to take multiple wives. But the response included demands by no less a figure than the chief justice that Pedram be struck out—and total silence from the women's movement. Even Dr Jalal would not buy in, telling me that reform had to be step by step and that education was her priority. 'Put too much water on the grass and it will die.'

The women's movement has made security a key issue and is demanding that the country's powerful warlords be defanged. Those women who have dared to speak out have been so threatened that Sima Samar, chairperson of the Afghanistan Independent Human Rights Commission, now travels with three armed bodyguards. And Malalai Joya, 25, a prominent activist, is in hiding with an armed United Nations bodyguard.

Dr Jalal, who does wear a loose-fitting scarf but refuses a guard, is undeterred. But a couple of final questions from me seemed to throw her: Did she drive a car? Did she want to? 'Why would I want to do that? Women don't drive here; they don't know how to and I'm too busy.' But the politician's survival instinct then kicked in. 'Besides, presidents don't drive cars.'

DUST TO DUST

Bamiyan, Afghanistan
20 November 2004

The farmer Zahir Mohamedi lives in the folds of the Foladi Valley. When he wants to forget the past, he retreats to the baked earth of a hilltop threshing floor, on which he and his family have just finished the autumn ritual of separating wheat from chaff. But as the village of Qafela Bashi rises to a smoky Ramadan morning, he agrees to relive the horror of his forced role in the destruction of the colossal Buddhas of Bamiyan. Often this experience comes back in nightmares, and distress darkens the 42-year-old former fighter's smooth features as he shares with me a rare account of the destruction of the priceless statues that were the legacy of a fabulous fusion of Persian, Greek and Indian art more than 1500 years ago.

It was 2001 and Mohamedi was one of thirteen Bamiyan men being held prisoner by the fundamentalist Taliban, the Islamic diehards who had wrested control of Afghanistan from its squabbling warlords but ultimately became the pawns of the September 11 mastermind, Osama bin Laden.

'They had guns on us all the time,' the farmer says, staring ahead. 'They strapped explosives to our backs and made us walk over the hills to the top of the big Buddha. Then they rushed us down and locked us up again. They brought us back up the next day. They tied ropes around our waists and hung bags of explosives from us—red and blue wires were attached to the bags.'

Mohamedi, who was fifth in the line of conscripted demolition men, shook with fear. 'But one of them put a pistol to my head and yelled, "You go down on the rope, or I shoot and you'll fall down." They slung a steel bar across the niche of the Buddha and dangled us over it as though we were already dead. As we dropped down I saw that drums of explosives were already placed on the Buddha's shoulders. Our bodies were torn open as we bashed against the stone chest of the statue—one of the prisoners died on the rope. We were ordered to insert the bags among the pigeon nests in the big holes where the Buddha's arms had been broken off at the elbow. They dragged us back up, tied our hands again and drove us back to our cells. Later we heard a massive explosion.'

Bamiyan is a place of sublime beauty. Maybe it's the thin air in the high Hindu Kush, or perhaps it's my sense of elation at not feeling—after more than three years of post-September 11 reporting—constantly under threat from some of those around me; but the Buddhas' eye view of this sweeping valley is intoxicating.

The river flat meets hills that are autumn-brown and so smooth that surely they are tidied each night with a heavenly clothes brush; beyond them, rocky razorbacks wear winter's first snow as they cut a jagged edge in a sapphire sky. In the middle distance, the crumbled remains of Shahr-e Gholghola—the City of Screams—glow as a golden echo of the marauding Genghis Khan, who destroyed the hilltop citadel in 1221. And cut into the crimson cliffs further out are the decorated fortifications of Shahr-e Zohak, where the Shansabani kings ruled until the thirteenth century.

The neatness of the valley is extraordinary. Lines of thin golden poplars etch the snow-fed irrigation channels that are the valley's lifeblood. Tiny figures—men dressed in grey, dun and putty—tread well-worn paths to the bazaar. A family hefting pitchforks works with a circling ox in a threshing tableau from biblical days; and there's a man heading for the hills—he carries a teapot.

All that remains of the Bamiyan greatness that drew the luxury-laden caravans of the old Silk Road and the dope-fired Kombis on the hippie trail in the 1970s is a faint outline on the back wall of each niche, a graceful shadow of statues which had stood for centuries as the world's biggest depictions of the Buddha.

A treacherous staircase winds up through the pink stone to a platform about 100 metres above the valley floor. It lies behind where the Buddhas' gilded heads had watched out reassuringly for centuries in the name of a creed that, appropriately enough, preaches detachment from the transient pain of daily life.

One statue stood at 55 metres; the other at 38 metres. At their finest, the taller was draped in robes of red; the smaller in blue. The vaults above their golden faces were adorned with exquisite renditions of a chariot-borne Sun God and of the Buddha, surrounded by bare-breasted maidens plucking strings.

Vandalism over the centuries had robbed the Buddhas of their faces and their gilded hands and feet. Afghan warlords had used the space between the legs of the taller as an ammunition dump; and the Taliban used the groin of the shorter for target practice, but the statues still expressed what the historian Nancy Hatch Dupree describes as 'the embodiment of cosmic man'.

In the morning sun, the pink wall around the niches is tattooed with black dots. Come closer and they are revealed as the mouths of hundreds of caves that centuries ago were the cells of Buddhist monks and pilgrims. Some are bricked and boarded up, to thwart the looters who have made off with hundreds of exquisite murals from chambers that have been carved like wedding cakes turned inside out. What the vandals have left in some of the caves is tantalising—decorative panels from which dozens of fist-sized Buddhas have been smashed; and the remnants of wall paintings in all the classic colours of an Afghan carpet.

Smoke issues from a cave to the right of where the small Buddha stood. It is one of six rock holes on a 40-metre ledge that are home to 22-year-old Mohamed Ali and seventeen members of his extended family . . . along with their chickens and donkeys and a loom on which they weave Afghan rugs, their only source of income.

The view is stunning. They have enclosed the yawning cave entrances with walls of mud bricks, doors fashioned with discards from a timber mill and windows of plastic sheeting. Ali's wife's one handbag hangs next to her burqa on a spike driven into the moist wall of the cold chamber in which they sleep.

The drop is 35 metres. But as his tiny children negotiate the edge with the sure-footedness of mountain goats, Ali sits on his haunches and explains: 'We have nowhere else to go—the Taliban drove us from our village.'

Surprisingly, he doesn't elaborate on the brutality of the Taliban assaults in which hundreds of Toyota pick-ups swept through villages and valleys, spraying fire from mounted machine-guns— a crude but effective mujahideen battle tactic borrowed from the civil war in Somalia. Or of the callous mop-ups that followed; before September 11, I interviewed a quaking refugee from this area who had watched as the aged baker in his village had been shoved head first into the burning coals of his bread oven.

The women of the caves huddle shyly, quietly embroidering handkerchiefs amid a scatter of cooking pots and water cans. Ali recounts how he hid in the mountains as an explosives-laden Taliban convoy pulled up to the Buddhas early in 2001: 'We watched through binoculars. They started by firing tanks—but they weren't strong enough.'

In 1999 the Taliban's one-eyed leader, Mullah Omar, had declared the Buddhas to be rare ancient monuments. They predated the ninth-century arrival of Islam in the country and as there were no longer any Buddhists to worship them, he exempted them from the Taliban claim that the Koran decrees all idols must be destroyed. But in February 2001, the Mullah did a spectacular backflip. In the face of a wave of international protest, he declared the Buddhas to be 'shrines of the infidels' that, along with other non-Islamic shrines in Afghanistan, would be demolished. United Nations officials, attempting to keep ajar what they called Afghanistan's humanitarian window, had already concluded that Osama bin Laden's Al-Qaeda had won a bitter power struggle gripping the Taliban. This explains Omar's radical change of heart.

The farmer Mohamedi claims to have seen a tall bearded figure in Arab dress among the official party cheering the demolition of the statues. He and his cellmates would conclude that this was none other than Osama bin Laden, whom they recognised from photographs. These claims add to a theory among archaeological and other observers that the destruction of the Buddhas may well have been a first strike in bin Laden's September 11 master plan.

Virtually the entire town of Bamiyan had fled, so eyewitness accounts of the destruction of the Buddhas are rare. But the extent of that demonic engineering challenge is revealed when Mohamedi's account is meshed with reports based on interviews with two other locals who were dragooned into the demolition parties, and with the work of archaeologists attempting to understand the process of destruction.

First, the ridge above the niches was bombed from the air and then the T-55 tanks were wheeled in. But, like the burning tyres the Taliban teams had attached to the Buddhas' heads, these war machines only chipped and blackened the surface. Then the Taliban tried packing charges around the base of each statue—but this technique had little effect until they piled an outer circle of sandbags around the explosives, directing the blast up into the monuments. Finally, amid much celebration, they brought down the smaller Buddha. But the larger one seemed to cheat gravity, though its feet were blown away. Willed on by thousands of locals hiding in the mountains, it defiantly held its gaze across the Bamiyan Valley.

Originally, Zahir Mohamedi had been kept in what had been his Hezb-e Wahdat militia's headquarters in the heart of the town, away from the statues. But after his first mission to haul explosives to the ridge above the big Buddha, his captors had locked him in the Bamiyan Hotel, on a 70-metre rise just in front of the Buddhas.

He remembers: 'We could see through a window—there was a terrifically powerful explosion and a great cloud of dust. All the officials danced and cheered and ran away. But they came back and most of the big Buddha was still there.' The next morning, he says, an even bigger party assembled. 'When we got there, there were 300 or 400 pick-ups with many foreign fighters, and about twenty trucks. We could see that the feet of the big Buddha were gone and when we got to the top again, the head was destroyed.'

Claims by archaeologists that many of the Afghan Taliban fighters were reluctant to participate in the cultural vandalism add to the view that, essentially, this was a job by the Al-Qaeda foreign fighters who had swarmed to the Afghan jihad. Mohamedi supports this with his observation that few of his captors could speak his language. 'They kept waving their guns and just pointed, indicating what we should do,' he recalls.

Forty-year-old Mirza Hussein identified himself to a French reporter as a prisoner held by the Taliban in one of the nearby caves, who was ordered to stash the explosives that the farmer Mohamedi saw on the shoulders of the bigger Buddha. And Said Qyam told a British reporter that he, too, had dangled on a rope, with orders to stuff explosives into holes that the Taliban had drilled deep into the head of the bigger Buddha.

Someone had a video camera and the footage now circulates in Kabul: first, the drums of explosives on the shoulders of the Buddha create a fireball that crushes the shoulders and what was left of the head. The footage then cuts to a merciless second detonation, so powerful that it shakes the entire valley and cloaks it in a blanket of smoke and dust as the Buddha's chest collapses. Mullah Omar, who like Osama bin Laden is still on the run from American pursuit squads, was well pleased. He told a visitor: 'All we are breaking are stones.'

At the end of the Foladi Valley is the village of Pai Kotal (which translates literally as 'end of the road'). Here I found 86-year-old Haji Abdullah, one of the more respected religious authorities in Bamiyan. The old man rises irritably from a mat on which he has been snoozing in the sun at the edge of a field worked by his sons. He declares that, as a Muslim, the fate of the Buddha statues is none of his business. But he ponders, running his ringed fingers through a wispy beard, and then he gives a little ground: 'They were symbols of tolerance.'

His 40-year-old son, Mohammed Mousa, is more forthcoming. 'If they remain destroyed we suffer from the emptiness of the niches . . . Rebuild and maybe we forget the misery of the Taliban who burnt down our village.'

The Afghan director of the Buddhas' site, the spiky-haired Modabir Mohamed Nasir, is thoughtful on the fate of the Buddhas, which, in their current sad state, pull only $US300 a month in ticket revenue, compared with as much as $US6 million a year in the past: 'Rebuilding is an international decision. It would be easy enough with modern technology, but we can't let it happen. There will be no historical value in what we rebuild. And it's a part of our history that the Taliban destroyed them; to rebuild would be to cleanse that history.'

The entrance to Haji Feda's office compound is a chilling reminder of Afghanistan's past wars. Set into the high mud walls are solid metal doors that have been sliced from the end of a shipping container—the warlords used to literally fry their prisoners to death by locking them in these steel boxes in the heat of summer. Feda is the secretary of the Hezb-e Wahdat, a political party that has morphed from the militia of the same name that included Zahir Mohamedi in its ranks. Haji Feda seems capable of a politician's compromise: 'There is an idea to rebuild just one of them. That would give us a sense of what we had lost, but we'd still have an empty niche to tell the world of this attack on its cultural history.'

The biggest business name in Bamiyan is Sultan Ali—there is his family's fuel station, its construction firm, pharmacy and hardware store. Sultan Ali's handsome 24-year-old brother, Karim, is in charge of hardware. Surrounded by mountains of guns, clocks, glassware, radios, flasks, teapots, shoes, cooking pots, Irish coffee glasses, televisions and meat-mincers, he recalls how the Taliban behaved like duck shooters as they hunted the locals. For him, the Buddhas were a bridge between any people and any god. He tells me: 'We know that Buddha was not a god, but he was a connection and we have lost that. It was just rock and mud—like Mecca is. But both are places where God sees us.'

Young Karim and Zahir Mohamedi are the only locals who address the question of guilt—did people do enough to try to save the statues? 'We believed Mullah Omar's promises that the statues and our homes would be safe,' Karim says. 'Now we are filled with remorse. We should have fought for our town and for the Buddhas.'

The morning after the final demolition, Mohamedi and his group of prisoners were driven out of Bamiyan, east through the Ghorband Valley. Drained as he ends his story, he says that seven of the twelve disappeared on that drive and that the rest were held separately in rural houses. 'I was freed in a prisoner exchange and now I stay in my village. I've tried a couple of times to find the others—no success,' he adds.

Asked about the Buddhas, he becomes the most emotional of all to whom I spoke. 'I was a witness. As a mujahideen, I was stationed near them—I knew how beautiful they were,' he says before rhapsodising on the power of the murals in the caves and niches, which he seemed to know in some detail. 'It upsets me too much. The memories are terrible, but I want people to know what happened—even though I was a part of it. I'm not afraid to tell of the disaster. I'm proud to be able to give this information.'

Finally, would he rebuild? Mohamedi thinks long and hard, looking out at the remains of an ancient watchtower atop a nearby hill. 'Maybe if we did, we might get our honour back. We are proud of our history . . .'

Since the Taliban fell in 2001, much work has been done to stabilise the two great niches, to stop their wounded walls caving in. There are metal trusses and steel slings to hold loose slabs of the conglomerate rock in place, and wire mesh has been draped down the back of each niche. The statues have been reduced to huge piles of rough boulders and sand mixed through with unexploded ordnance that spew from each niche, taunting all the king's horses and all the king's men of the archaeological world.

One of them is the silver-haired Edmund Melzl, a retired German restorer, who is awed by the task: he has never worked on anything bigger or older than an eight-metre-tall, fifteenth-century stone crucifix in Bavaria. He says a final Taliban touch was to lay anti-tank mines on the ground around the Buddhas, to smash to smithereens the boulders that might have survived their fall.

Melzl has known these Buddhas for 45 years and he'd like to see them put back together. Surely this is an impossible task. The boulders are a crumbling conglomerate rock, a mass of stones of varying sizes, pressed together in clay and mud. But in the nearby mosque that serves as his office, Melzl assures me that geologists can tell the depth at which each rock and bucket of sand should be placed in any reconstruction. He chooses his words carefully: 'It would be nice to see them rebuilt. There is much documentation from Indian and Japanese restoration projects in the past, but we still can't say if they can be rebuilt.'

There is an awe-inspiring moment during my visit to Melzl's office when he pulls out trays filled with the fragile, layered, surface fragments of the statues that have already been recovered. He hands over a small box: it holds perfectly preserved, 1500-year-old straw, grain and animal hair that helped bind the mud-plaster finish onto the statues. He fingers centuries-old wooden pegs that were driven into the Buddhas to hold the folds of their garments. But for their colouring, these pegs might have been carved yesterday.

There has never been a restoration project like this. Afghanistan's President Hamid Karzai has spoken for and against reconstruction—for now, he's against. The provincial government is all for it, and has the backing of significant archaeological voices in Switzerland, Sri Lanka and China. Experts and governments in Japan, Germany, Italy, Switzerland and France have weighed in as UNESCO does a delicate dance, attempting not to offend locals by spending millions to stabilise the fractured cliff face and nurse piles of rubble in the midst of an ongoing humanitarian crisis.

In the meantime UNESCO has declared that Bamiyan will be struck from the World Heritage List if there is any attempt to rebuild the Buddhas. This stance is supported by Afghanistan's foremost archaeologist, Professor Zemaryalaï Tarzi, who is vehemently opposed to what he dismisses as a Walt Disney re-creation. Others argue that the Buddhas must be replaced to provide structural integrity for the niches. Last year, Swiss scientists produced a model of the bigger Buddha, which they say is a basis for rebuilding in new materials. And Mohammed Rahim Ali Yar, a warlord turned local governor, is adamant that he and the locals will rebuild—in concrete, if necessary.

There is another possible outcome that most locals don't dare countenance. This is the serious search that is under way for an elusive and huge third Buddha. Such are its reputed beauty and dimensions that, if it were found, the world would still come to Bamiyan without the dubious drawcard of either of the upright statues being rebuilt.

The challenge is in finding this enormous reclining figure. There are clues are in the fastidious diaries of the seventh-century Chinese scholar, Hiuen-Tsiang. During a pilgrimage to Bamiyan, he wrote: 'To the east of the city, 12 or 13 li [6 or 6.5 kilometres], there is a palace in which there is a figure of the Buddha lying in a sleeping position, as when he attained nirvana. The figure is in length about [300 metres] or so.' That is an enormous Buddha. The accuracy of Hiuen-Tsiang's diary detail has been proved elsewhere, but some archaeologists insist his estimated length has to be an exaggeration.

Professor Tarzi and Kazuya Yamauchi, a senior researcher with Tokyo's Centre for the Preservation of Cultural Property, are on the case. Given what is at stake, their reported confidence is breathtaking, though both men are looking in different places and refusing to concede that the other might be right. They will face off next month at a conference in Tokyo. Convened by UNESCO and Japan's National Research Institute for Cultural Properties, this three-day gathering will bring together more than 30 Afghan and international experts on the Bamiyan Buddhas.

The conference organiser, Christian Manhart of UNESCO's Division of Cultural Heritage, is sceptical about the third Buddha. In a phone interview from his Paris office, he told me: 'We don't know if it survived because it is likely to have been made of mud bricks. Everyone is 100 per cent convinced of their theory of where it is. I was at a French workshop and there were three different researchers who refused to bend on their conflicting theories. Tarzi and Yamauchi can't agree—but I hope they will be collegiate at the Tokyo meeting.'

For now, back at Bamiyan, Melzl the restorer and his colleagues are packing up to head for Tokyo. Much of the gallery of shelves for recovered statue fragments in Melzl's office is disappointingly empty, and with this northern summer's work season about to end, his three-man team is unlikely to achieve their immediate objective—that of clearing both niches of all rubble.

The restorer potters around the mosque in his socks as his excited colleagues, the curly-headed Greek architect Georgios Toubekis and the lanky German sculptor and art historian Bert Praxenthaler, supervise the activities of a mobile crane that has just taken three days to come over the mountains from Kabul—a distance of a mere 230 kilometres. Afghans working with shovels and wheelbarrows put down their tools to watch—it is the first crane they have seen. A huge boulder is moved into a covered store area, but disaster strikes as the crane manoeuvres a slightly smaller specimen, one which Praxenthaler estimates to weigh 12 tonnes.

The crane's arm is not fully extended but the ground under one of its hydraulic supports gives way; it topples precariously and the driver jumps for his life. The 12-tonner crashes into the already positioned bigger boulder, shearing great clumps off both specimens. Exasperated, Praxenthaler exclaims: 'It would happen when the press is here!'

The Greek is resigned. 'Some days this country is magical; on others it's a nightmare.' Triage on the big Buddha stops for first aid on the crane-driver's foot—he twisted it as he landed in the dirt.

A message from the gods, perhaps?

SEEDS OF DESTRUCTION

Kabul, Afghanistan
15 January 2005

It was early last year when a Western diplomat finally identified a certain something that seemed to hang in the air during his regular visits to the US embassy in Kabul. It was smugness, he concluded. Sure, his American counterparts in Afghanistan dealt with a crisis a day. But compared with the nightmarish dramas of security, diplomacy and policy endured by their colleagues at the Washington bunker in Baghdad, things were going pretty well. Or were they?

'It was in April,' the observant diplomat recalls. On his fingers he ticks off developments in Afghanistan as seen through American eyes at the time: 'The US military—doing great. New democratic institutions—getting off the ground. First presidential election—planning well under way. Women's rights—good things happening there, too. But then somebody said, "Holy shit! Will you look at the drugs mess?"'

Three years after the US-led invasion of Afghanistan, that mess could wreck George Bush's hope of ever finding a sure democratic footing in Central Asia. As Afghans went to the polls in October, Bush's ambassador to Kabul, Zalmay Khalilzad, warned darkly that Afghanistan was on the verge of becoming a 'narco-state'. The envoy's alert got little traction; it took a damning report by the United Nations Office on Drugs and Crime to reveal the extent to which the US-led coalition has failed utterly to contain Afghanistan's all-important role in a global heroin trade now worth more than $US30 billion a year.

The issue wasn't just that drugs were still a mess. In the preceding twelve months they had exploded into a more threatening, more complex mess. The poppy fields of Afghanistan now produce almost 90 per cent of the world's opium—a stupefying 4200 metric tonnes of high-grade opiates last year alone. Like a rampant cancer, the illicit acreage metastasised across all 32 provinces—up 64 per cent to more than 130,000 hectares. The number of households producing drugs rose by more than a third to 356,000—or one in every ten Afghanis—and, at $US2.8 billion, opium's contribution to the Afghan GDP was about two-thirds the value of the legal economy.

In the Iraq crisis, two early US mistakes are cited frequently as the cause of the security disaster that now confronts Bush in Baghdad. These are the failure by the US occupation forces to stop rampant looting and, weeks later, their disbandment of the Iraqi military. Similarly, two early mistakes in Afghanistan are being identified as the cause of a security crisis that many observers now believe is putting Kabul in its own paralysing headlock. These are the failure to tackle drugs from Day One, and the turning of an American blind eye to the activities of the powerful and corrupt warlords running the industry.

Suddenly the United States is desperate for action. At first glance, all other parties in Kabul are also demanding the abolition of an industry that, in many ways, is a more insidious gift from Afghanistan to the world than terrorism. But there is no agreement on a counter-narcotics strategy, so the debate is a war zone—with diplomats, NGOs and Afghan officials trading insults and abuse while the drug barons make merry in the mountains. A measure of the narco-bitterness is that, with few exceptions, those approached by me would speak only if they were allowed to hide behind the *nom de guerre* of 'a Western diplomat'.

In the allocation of post-Taliban turf in Afghanistan, the Americans fought hard to get responsibility for the remnants of Al-Qaeda and the Taliban; the Italians were given justice; and the Germans, the police force. The British got the poisoned chalice—drugs. Now they are so sick of hearing the word 'failure', and of being reminded of Prime Minister Tony Blair's 2001 pledge to eradicate the scourge of opium along with the Taliban, that they barricade themselves behind a wall of no comment.

But the reality is that they are being elbowed aside by the Americans, who themselves are split as to how best to approach the task. Their biggest worry is the use of drug revenue to fund terrorism, so Washington makes loud demands for more hectares to be eradicated more quickly. And having so firmly fixed eradication on the agenda, there is anxiety now that the United States is pushing the Afghan authorities to 'request' assistance in the form of Colombia-style chemical spraying of opium poppies—and anything else that might grow or breathe nearby.

Farmers in two villages near Jalalabad told me of their crops wilting within days of their hearing the sound of low-flying aircraft in the night. Their claims have been officially denied, but I have been reliably informed that American officials and others in Kabul are actively debating the need for spraying. The Afghans are divided—President Hamid Karzai has said that he won't have it, and he has appointed a commission of inquiry to investigate the complaints of the villagers near Jalalabad. But last month one of his senior counter-narcotics officers argued that 'as a last resort, chemical spray could be useful to frighten people'.

The Pentagon also doesn't want to damage the deals it has with the drug kingpins who are supposed to be helping in their search for the elusive Osama bin Laden and Mullah Omar—the fugitive leaders, respectively, of Al-Qaeda and the Taliban. So, while the US military makes all the right noises about doing its bit in the war against drugs, the reality lies in a comment by the Pentagon's chief policy adviser, Douglas Feith, to the *Washington Post*: 'The key to success is not turning this into an American military mission. It's the Afghan government trying to enforce its own laws and what we're interested in doing is building up their capacity so they can do it.'

The British have been more measured, because their response to the crisis in Afghanistan is driven by what to do about the junkies of London and Luton. They drafted the ten-year counter-narcotics plan that the Afghans follow, but now the United States is demanding 'real' results as early as one to two years from now. Any sense of civility in the Washington–London debate went out the window early last year during a US congressional hearing provocatively titled 'Afghanistan: Are the British Counter-narcotics Efforts Going Wobbly?' During the hearing, Robert Charles, a senior state department anti-narcotics official, asked if the British had become squeamish, before promising a 'very aggressive, very proactive' US campaign which would show that if 'the penalties are high enough, the [farmers] will not grow heroin poppies. We need to show the people that we are serious.' And in doing so, the livelihoods, indeed the lives, of thousands of Afghans come into play.

The range of tactics that might be used against Afghan opium is not in dispute—harass the smugglers and heroin refiners, eradication, alternative livelihoods and a muscular judicial system. But the disagreements flare over the order in which, and the weight with which, each should be applied to get sustainable long-term results. The British tended towards alternative crops and livelihoods; key American voices—but not all—have become champions of eradication. And, despite all their pious words, the Afghans sometimes seem to be paying lip service to everything as they try to figure out which option will give them a better long-term return—the drugs or the donors.

Some diplomats in Kabul worry that opium's economic horse-power is not understood outside the country, despite the fact that its 2002–03 earnings were $US4.8 billion, 70 per cent more than the $US2.8 billion paid to Afghanistan in foreign aid in the same two years. One of them directed me to a September assessment of the Afghan economy by the World Bank: 'A reduction in opium production would have very significant macroeconomic implications . . . a $US1 billion shock for the economy; adversely affect government revenue . . . reduction in imports . . . reduced foreign exchange inflows . . . the equivalent of a credit crunch . . . a real depreciation of the currency . . . and deflation due to lower demand for goods.' The diplomat concluded, 'That's a recipe for disaster.'

Opium is the currency in much of rural Afghanistan. Loans to farmers that used to be advanced in cash now come as opium (the quantity repaid takes into account price fluctuations), and those who default on opium loans are jailed. Government teachers in remote areas are said to be paid in raw opium; there is a chunk in some brides' dowries; and, in many bazaars, traders accept tiny amounts of the drug in exchange for a household's winter supplies of tea and sugar.

There is a whole class of Afghan businessmen for whom opium is just another commodity to be traded—electronics one week; drugs or firewood the next. Their dirty dollars fund burgeoning imports and are laundered through a ferocious construction boom in Kabul and elsewhere. Office towers, hotels and the very aptly named 'narco-villas' are rising in the best streets in the best suburbs.

Assessing opium's performance, the report by the World Bank notes in its po-faced way: 'Afghanistan now has a strong comparative advantage . . . durable commodity . . . commands a high price . . . guaranteed market . . . credit and other inputs available . . . non-perishable . . . easy to transport . . . market organisation is excellent . . . ample potential for further increased production . . . more closely resembles a competitive market than a criminal cartel . . . constitutes an enormous injection of income into Afghanistan's battered rural economy.'

Just as Brent crude is traded in London and pork bellies in Chicago, opium futures are sold in Jalalabad and Kandahar, with impoverished farmers selling their output at ridiculous discounts long before the harvest so they can feed their families through winter. Growers have taken to using satellite phones to monitor weather conditions and crop quality so that they can pitch their own pricing and acreage accordingly; smugglers are equipping themselves with night-vision goggles and bullet-proof vests. In Dushanbe, capital of neighbouring Tajikistan, anti-narcotics agents complain of brazen new marketing—heroin in smart packages showing a map of Afghanistan and an arrow driving up into the former Soviet republics to the north to indicate the source and the intended market. In some cases, even the name and address of the processing laboratory is provided.

As a cottage industry, opium is cheaper to extract than gold; it is moved around the world more easily than oil. And the returns are exceptional—some diplomats attribute a significant strengthening of the afghani against the US dollar in August to the rate at which narco-dollars were flooding into the country at the time.

The World Bank uses measured language in its Afghanistan report. It tends to suggest rather than recommend; it uses phrases like 'The government might like to . . .' instead of 'Kabul must . . .' But when addressing the fast-narrowing US focus on eradication as a long-term solution to the opium crisis, it talks straight: 'A key lesson [from other countries] is that eradication alone will not work and is likely to become counterproductive.'

The bank warns that farmers will be forced to grow more opium, not less; they will simply move to remote areas, as they did in Colombia; and that there will be even more violence and insecurity, as there was in Peru, Bolivia and Colombia. And the bank sides with the NGO argument that the plight of poor growers must be considered and that success in the fight against opium will probably take decades, not years. It warns: 'Abrupt shrinkage of the opium economy or falling opium prices without new means of livelihood would significantly worsen rural poverty.'

In the gentlest possible way, the report then shreds the Karzai government's drugs strategy as a lot of good intentions that are overly ambitious but under-resourced. Instead, it urges the pursuit of the kingpins over impoverished farmers, and enduring alternative livelihoods ahead of eradication.

There are no easy answers in this debate. In post-Taliban Afghanistan, circumstances have conspired massively against authority and good sense. Farm-gate opium prices skyrocketed in 2001, on the back of market manipulation by the Taliban, and held near a dizzying $US300 a kilogram for three consecutive harvests. This year they have tumbled, but the return to farmers is still twelve times better than what they would earn growing wheat.

An added wrinkle is that grain prices have plummeted in the same three years—so the bazaars are filled with plentiful supplies of cheap grain, much of it trucked in by the likes of the World Food Programme. A country that was virtually self-sufficient in cereals last year now has its hand out to the world for about half of its cereal needs this year, even as its farmers forgo sowing legal grain so that their best land is free to produce the majority of the world's opium—illegally.

In hindsight, some of Britain's early attempts to curb the crop did have a John Cleese touch to them. First, they tried to take a leaf from the book of the European Community and offered as much as $US1500 a hectare for growers not to plant opium. This scheme was abandoned because farmers saw it as an incentive to plant bigger crops in the belief they would get the current harvest and a British payout the following season. Next, local governors were paid hundreds of thousands of dollars to eradicate poppy crops and compensate the growers. But most were accused of pocketing the money and enlisting local labour to 'eradicate' crops that were either diseased or had already been harvested. Videos of these sham exercises were sent to Kabul to verify that eradication had taken place.

Haji Din Mohammed, governor of Nangarhar province, is one of those whom farmers accuse of withholding their compensation. But at his office in Jalalabad, with a look of sweet innocence, he points the finger of blame elsewhere: 'The growers were promised they'd be paid, but nothing happened. So they don't believe their government and they don't trust the international community. But is the world really serious? You can't just come along, eradicate a few jeribs [five of these make a hectare] and send a video to NBC!'

After the dismal failure of the first three years, a deep sense of frustration is discernible among the thousands of foreign diplomats, soldiers, economists, anthropologists, agronomists and other specialists as they strive ineffectually to achieve what the Taliban's Mullah Omar did in a five-line fatwa that took him only a minute to write and a single growing season to enforce. Fearful that limited foreign aid would be cut further in the year 2000, he ordered that no opium be planted. It was a cynical but effective exercise. None was planted, but the Taliban was sitting on huge inventories from bumper crops the preceding two years and, because of its widely publicised ban on growing poppies, prices jumped tenfold.

When Omar issued his edict, Afghan poppy growers complied because they understood too well the Taliban practice of getting its way by execution and amputation. By contrast, growers today are fearless of the foreign-backed authority in Kabul and they have not been deterred in the slightest by armed US patrols roaming their villages in search of bin Laden and the Taliban. Hearing conflicting messages from international and national authorities, the growers ignore new fatwas from the mosques while traders, laboratory operators, smugglers and the drug lords laugh in the face of authorities who regularly submit to them.

Searching for a well-placed 'Western diplomat' who might make sense of where this debate was going, I find a tweed-jacketed expatriate who is among the best placed to observe the cut and thrust in Kabul. Deeply troubled by the growing American fixation on crop eradication—and even more so by the failed efforts to draft an attack plan that could win the support of all—he resorts to a technical term: 'It's an absolute shit fight.'

'The Afghan power circle is too vicious and way too strong to do just eradication.' Without naming Washington, he goes on: 'There's a naive short-term approach that eradication means eradication—it doesn't. When Pakistan and Iran "eradicated" poppy cultivation, all they did was force it over the border into

Afghanistan; if you eradicate in one province, it'll simply move into the adjacent province. This whole country is in play and the warlords and drug lords have the funds, the force and the incentive to make sure that they keep the national state just as they like it—weak and insecure.'

This man is of the view that any assault on drugs has to be pragmatic because, despite inordinate pressure on the Kabul government to be seen to be doing something, the reality is that its capacity to act is greatly limited.

'I think a lot of people are being very naive,' he says. 'For how long do you reckon Kabul can sustain such a campaign and, in particular, establish alternative livelihoods for the growers? Wouldn't they get a lot more mileage if they went after the ten biggest dealers instead of bashing down the crops of 1000 poor farmers? You have to understand, opium is a coping mechanism for the poor—but it doesn't mean they're getting rich.' He finds more to worry about in what lies ahead: 'The industry has not been criminalised, as it has in Latin America—but if we start driving people out, what sort of hard core will remain and will that mean even greater insecurity? If you eradicate, who'll control the opium and heroin inventories? What will happen to prices—and will the net result be any different?'

The coming months should reveal how serious Afghanistan's newly elected president is about confronting the opium crisis. Hamid Karzai's dependence on warlords and drug barons in the three years between the US invasion and Afghanistan's 9 October presidential election made nonsense of his pious rhetoric. His election commitment to end corruption prompted wan smiles in the expatriate salons of Kabul, but another 'Western diplomat', a man known to have an intimate knowledge of the formulation of US policy and tactics, is confident: 'If Karzai acts as he says he will, he has a real chance of pulling this off. The warlords are so deeply involved and we know who most of the major players are, so it'll serve a lot of purposes if he can take them head-on. The growth in drugs has been exponential, so we face a watershed year ... Karzai does, too.

'Provincial governors, people in the cabinet and in the bureaucracy are up to their necks in drugs.' Asked to name names, he snaps, 'Everyone is corrupt. Pick any name you like ... but there's a list of particular names that I expect the Americans will make a lot of noise about if Karzai includes any of them in his new cabinet.'

Asked about a warlord triangle that dominates public life in Jalalabad—as well as the provincial governor, Haji Din Mohammed, it includes his son Zahir and Hazarat Ali, the governor's security supremo—the diplomat says simply, 'Big-time crooks.' What do the Americans make of Hazarat Ali, who took them for a ride to the tune of millions in the 2001 search for bin Laden? 'Some of them say he's a bad guy, but he's our bad guy.'

Yet, when Ahmed Shah Himat, Jalalabad's remarkably relaxed police chief, is asked about high-level miscreants, he is deadpan: 'We don't have warlords in our area and we haven't found anyone from the government involved in opium.'

Staunch allies of Karzai, one a minister and the other a provincial governor, have been named as big-time drug dealers. Even his politically active brother, Ahmed Wali Karzai, has been linked to the trade. Both US and Afghan authorities have been accused of merely going through the motions of arresting big drug players. In the northern province of Balkh there was a ruckus in July when the police chief busted a local warlord for drug trafficking—but it was the warlord, not the policeman, who was later appointed provincial governor.

Citing half-a-dozen such cases, the Afghanistan scholar Barnett Rubin observed in an October paper published by New

York University's Centre on International Cooperation: 'Most of the [warlords] had worked closely with the US; several of them appeared on television with Defence Secretary Donald Rumsfeld. When members of the US cabinet meet publicly with commanders tied to traffickers while the US orders the destruction of the poppy crops of poor farmers, Afghans can only conclude that the US commitment to counter-narcotics is not genuine.'

NATION-BUILDING
AT GUNPOINT

Kabul, Afghanistan
15 July 2006

As a warlord with all the backing of his Alokozai tribal elders, Dad Mohammed Khan did not stoop to campaigning for his seat in Afghanistan's infant parliament. Suspicious electoral officials disallowed several ballot boxes in which the heavy-set candidate scored 100 per cent. But Khan still topped the vote in Helmand province, a parched southern wasteland that local opium farmers and smugglers call the Valley of Death.

These days, newly minted MPs tiptoe through sensitive security and make way for work parties feverishly refurbishing the building in which the Shura-e Milli (National Assembly) and the Meshrano Jirga (Council of Elders) are the laboratories for a daunting experiment in democracy.

Some of the MPs I canvassed were upbeat about the prospects for the effectiveness of the first US attempt to export democracy in the post-September 11 world, but more were scathing. Diplomatic and human rights observers raised questions not just about the parliament's membership and conduct during its first session, but also about the limits of its constitutional architecture. And most were disturbed by the seeming contempt of the president, Hamid Karzai, and his crony government for these representatives of their people having the temerity to find their voices—and to speak their minds.

The MPs rightly obsess about their security. Few travel back to their electorates and many move around Kabul in heavy vehicles, with armed guards fore and aft. They face an avalanche of threats and the Taliban has announced a $US25,000 reward for the body of a parliamentarian and, ominously, twice that for an MP delivered alive.

Fariba Ahmadzai, a woman whose campaign posters in Kandahar were defaced by the gouging of the eyes in her picture, is troubled by the price on her head. She is energised by what she describes as a battle with 'the enemies of peace' but she cannot leave her Kandahar office without donning her burqa and whistling up her guards.

For her own protection, the MP Raazia Baloch was presented with an AK-47 when she was elected. But like so much else in today's Afghanistan, when she first attempted to fire the gun, it backfired.

The diminutive and—it must be said—utterly fearless Malalai Joya worries about intimidation from outside the parliament, but she is even more affronted by threats of defilement and injury hurled across the chamber by her colleagues in the assembly. Just 28 years old and from the northern province of Farah, she garnered the second-highest vote in the province for her relentless opposition to the warlords and local commanders who trashed Afghanistan and killed tens of thousands of their countrymen during its serial civil wars.

She is a slip of a thing and, dressed in patterned black, was almost lost in a big armchair as she told me: 'Most of these MPs should be in the courts for war crimes, not lining their pockets in the parliament. They are drug barons and warlords; jihadis and Taliban. When I spoke against them, one yelled "Take her! Rape her!" and another told me that I'd soon learn to respect them if I was cut with a knife. They threw water bottles at me. Three other women MPs even came to my seat and threatened to throttle me. And the international community thinks these are delegates of the people?' Joya now stays on the move. For her protection, she sleeps in a different house in a different quarter of the capital every night; she stays away from her provincial home; and she refuses to telegraph her movements.

She had in mind the likes of Mullah Salam Rocketti, a repentant Taliban strongman and former provincial governor who earned his last name through his deadly proficiency with a rocket-launcher. When he spoke to me, he swore in hushed, husky tones that he had swapped his weapon of choice for two government-licensed pistols. But he remains miffed about three ageing but powerful US-made Stinger missiles which he handed to the Americans as a price for being allowed to come in from the cold: 'They didn't pay the reward I was supposed to get . . . and I could have sold them to Pakistani arms dealers for $US150,000 each.'

Another in Joya's sights is Sher Mohammed, a warlord and former governor of Helmand, who was sacked under international pressure after the discovery of nine tonnes of raw opium in the basement of his office. But even that was not enough to stop President Karzai appointing him to the Council of Elders. And a cause of bemusement for all in Kabul—Afghans and foreigners alike—is the presence on the benches of the National Assembly of Haji Farid, a former personal driver for Osama bin Laden.

This parliament is a bold attempt to supplant traditional Afghan horse-trading, in which leaders who hold the aces use complex deal-making to play off tribal, ethnic or religious groups against each other. The artistry lies in keeping all parties satisfied—or enough of them sufficiently satisfied to unite them against the losers. It may sound like a crude version of politics the world over, but it's based more on patronage than on transparency or accountability. And when the deals collapse in Afghanistan, the guns are drawn.

Back-of-an-envelope analysis by foreign diplomats breaks the elected assembly into three broad groups of about 80 MPs each. There are generally pro-government warlords and local strongmen, whose internecine wars in the past are proof of an underlying inability to get on; there's a mixed bag that is generally anti-Karzai, which includes more than 30 former communists; and there are those who float between these two camps.

The Afghanistan Independent Human Rights Commission cuts the pack differently—it estimates that more than 80 per cent of provincial MPs and as many as 60 per cent of the Kabul representatives either are, or have ties with, warlords, drug dealers or human rights violators. Some of the MPs were elected by more than 50,000 voters; others arrived in the parliament with as few as 1500 endorsements.

But for all the criticism, this is not the president's pocket parliament. The MPs approved the meagre national budget after reallocating more funds to public-service salaries, pensions for war veterans and more funding for the disabled. They rejected five of Karzai's cabinet nominees and they swiftly dispatched his candidate to head the judiciary—a wizened fundamentalist whom a diplomat described to me as 'corrupt, incompetent, unqualified, senile . . . and reactionary'.

One of the more intriguing parliamentarians is Dr Ramazan Bashardost, a minister in the first interim administration who was sacked for urging the government to run thousands of aid agencies out of the country in the belief that Afghans were the better judges of how to spend billions in donor dollars. He has concluded that most of his parliamentary colleagues worry more about vested ethnic and tribal interests than the all-embracing good of the nation. And despite the rejection of Karzai's nominees and the rewriting of the budget, he said: 'The parliament refuses to ask the hard questions and it can't operate checks and balances on this government.'

Bashardost, who shocked his colleagues by refusing to accept a $US10,000 car allowance and by distributing all his MP's salary to the poor, believes Karzai makes clever use of parliament, finding backers for most of his positions and using it to effectively make the decisions that he doesn't have the courage to announce himself—like sacking the chief justice, which was demanded by his foreign chaperones. Bashardost fears parliament is destined to become Karzai's rubber stamp because 'most MPs think it's in the national interest to go along with Karzai. They don't hold to the idea that parliament has separate—and different—powers to exercise'.

Just as the politicians struggle to find their way, so too does the nation which, suddenly, the world realises is a mess. Against the daily grind of bad news from Baghdad, Kabul had been a more optimistic beachhead for Washington. New roads cut through man-eating deserts and leapt treacherous mountains; girls were joyfully back in the classroom. The luxury $US250-a-night Serena Hotel opened with fanfare and a Kabul taxi firm imported a stretch limo for wedding parties. Mobile phone sales and new email accounts are surging. Millions of refugees have come home to a new constitution and there have been heroic election turnouts. And through it all, President Hamid Karzai strutted the globe like an elegant starburst, greeting fellow leaders in an array of tribal hats and colourful coats that earned him a place on magazines' best-dressed lists.

But as Afghan households count their meagre gains in this new dawn, a troubling sentiment is emerging. Afghans now openly criticise their leader and, during riots in May, wild mobs burnt his image in the streets. The wealthy have become exceptionally so, but the poor languish as their homes are bulldozed to make way for poppy palaces and narco-villas.

There is still the stench of raw sewage in the streets; power is rationed because the electricity ministry cannot pay its fuel bill; there is little running water. Teachers and the police complain of insufficient and erratic pay. Kabulis grumble furiously about the aggression and arrogance with which the armoured convoys of US and NATO forces and foreign security contractors have taken over the streets.

Unemployment is chronic and, with average wages just $US60 a month, all struggle against rocketing prices in the bazaars and a wild property market—a house that fetched $US20 rent a month under the Taliban now pulls more than $US3000 from a foreign aid agency.

Despite 14 per cent growth last year, the economy is essentially drugs and donations. Virtually no taxes are collected. Big dollars are doled out for reconstruction. But after crippling security costs and profit-taking, as contracts are sold from one company to the next, there is often little left to build roads or public facilities.

In the shade of a tree near the hut from which he rents out big cooking pots for wedding feasts, 45-year-old Khalilullah ventured that life was better since the fall of the Taliban. But then he reconsidered. 'Nothing is really changed. There are no benefits for the people . . . our expectations have not been fulfilled. We can move around more than we did under the Taliban. But with insecurity and higher prices people are losing faith in Karzai and the US.'

International support for Karzai's government is also slipping. The European Union's envoy in Kabul, Francesc Vendrell, told *Newsweek*: 'Karzai has not been able to act firmly—many provincial governors are incompetent and corrupt and many police chiefs are linked to the drug trade and criminal groups.'

In the face of a stinging Taliban resurgence in the south this summer, there is a disturbing number of villagers expressing the same sentiment that allowed the Taliban to snatch Afghanistan from the mujahideen in the 1990s—they don't care which side wins, just as long as the fighting stops.

Simmering uncertainty about the fate of the Afghanistan venture has exploded in rancour to become an unseemly blame game. A conspiracy of events began in May: anti-US and anti-government riots in Kabul resulted in sixteen deaths and more than 100 injured after a US military vehicle collided with a civilian vehicle; and there was anger over claims that more than 30 civilians died in a mistaken US air strike in the south.

A crisis of confidence among diplomats and the foreign military brass in Kabul is also fuelled by other developments: expectations of a record opium crop, confirming five years of Western failure to tackle the Afghan narco-menace; and the Taliban's links with drug smugglers, gaining it support from the poppy-growing regions across the south.

Running operations from Pakistan, the Taliban now claim to have more than 12,000 men under arms and to be in control of more than twenty districts across their old southern heartland provinces of Kandahar, Zabul, Helmand and Uruzgan. The total poppy crop is worth almost $US3 billion a year. Local government and police chiefs are rolling over for the Taliban to the extent that a local MP told me: 'It's a Taliban government down south now—the Afghan and foreign military can move only by aircraft; Kabul controls only 5 to 20 per cent of the southern provinces.'

Dad Mohammed Khan, the warlord who served as a local intelligence chief before he was elected to parliament, said: 'People listen to the Taliban now because they are afraid, and that keeps them silent about the movement of the Taliban. They believed there would be a lot of help when the Americans came, but they are disappointed at getting nothing and they are turning against the foreigners. Increasingly, they doubt that the US can defeat the Taliban.'

Afghanistan is a clash that can still go either way. A beleaguered army of foreign forces, diplomats and aid workers fights for the concepts of democracy to take root. The willingness of millions of Afghans to vote in the face of violent threats revealed hunger for a new life. But they are up against an amoral, self-serving elite that operates with a reckless sense of impunity as it divides the spoils of power in backroom deals that have little to do with democracy.

Kabul's fledgling press is in revolt over attempts to curb reporting. A United Nations report that implicates much of the political elite as brutal war criminals is being suppressed and, at the last minute, Karzai brazenly added thirteen warlords with links to drugs and private militias to a list of 100 new police chiefs. One of the worst is Kabul's new top cop.

As it prepares to quit the south, the United States rejects accusations of policy failure. But the fact that 6000 Afghani troops are replacing only 3000 Americans is an implicit acceptance that on the US watch the Taliban regained control of much of the same region from which they snatched Afghanistan in the

1990s. And that while the Taliban reduced poppy cultivation to virtually zero in 2001, Washington and its allies are watching over the mother of all opium harvests this year.

One of Karzai's old allies, the sacked governor of Helmand, Sher Mohammed, warns: 'It would be a dreadful mistake if the international community cannot give our president unified support, because Afghanistan and the world will not find another Hamid Karzai.'

Just as the United States rejects comparisons between Iraq and Vietnam, it bridles at a growing tendency to compare Afghanistan with Iraq. But a Kabul-based human rights observer just back from Washington said, 'They're scratching their heads, asking "How did it come to this?" and "What are we going to do now?"'

THE SEVEN-YEAR STITCH

Kabul, Afghanistan
25 October 2008

These years have been so wasted. The depth of the crisis gripping Afghanistan almost a decade after its supposed liberation is a frightening measure of hubris in the capitals of the world.

Reports stacked high on decision-makers' desks from Washington to London, from Brussels to Canberra, reveal the steady march of the Taliban and the other insurgency groups that now have Afghanistan by the throat. But it is only as they embark on the eighth year of conflict that political and military leaders are belatedly searching for an adequate response.

Groping in a policy vacuum, it's almost as though anything is worth a try: peace talks with the Taliban and the other insurgent movements; more foreign troops for an Iraq-style 'surge'; even a return to the warlordism of Afghanistan's sorry past. And for all that, in the eyes of some of the recognised experts on the region, Washington still does not appreciate the enormity of the challenge in Afghanistan and the region.

In the first years, 2002 to 2004, there were disquieting aspects of the whole enterprise, particularly Washington's paranoid pursuit of Osama bin Laden and his Al-Qaeda cohorts; the Taliban was allowed simply to melt away before circling back to whack the whole international effort in Afghanistan. But in the absence of clear proof to the contrary, and in such uncertain times, Washington's blustering about how it knew what it was doing was taken at face value.

In those vital first years, troop numbers were kept absurdly low and global assistance to Afghanistan ran to just $US57 per citizen—compared with $US679 in Bosnia. More recently, a British commentator rudely observed that Washington had spent ten times more on each sea otter affected by the 1989 Exxon Valdez oil spill than it gave in 'condolence payments' when its forces accidentally killed Afghan civilians.

But the spiky upward climb of every measure of chaos since 2005 is enough for the parents of tens of thousands of young soldiers from around the world to question the sanity of leaders who sent them to fight a war with their hands tied. Likewise, ordinary Afghans can only shake their heads in wonder at the morality of the West's indifferent delivery on endless promises, implicit and explicit, which were made when Taliban-controlled Kabul fell late in 2001.

And to make matters worse, as governments around the world now spend hundreds of billions in an attempt to rescue their economies, savvy military families in the West, and Afghan families, might reasonably conclude that the chances of a better, more responsible deal in Afghanistan have shrivelled in the past few weeks. Washington's pleas for other countries to offer up more men and machines to fight this runaway war fell largely on deaf ears, even before the global economic meltdown. And a United Nations appeal for a paltry $US404 million, which was launched in July to help stave off hunger in Afghanistan this winter, is not even half subscribed.

Washington confronts double jeopardy. The tactic of fighting short-handed has failed and so has the strategy of going after Al-Qaeda first.

As early as July 2006, the British general running NATO's Afghanistan mission, David Richards, vented his anger at the managerial madness of the international intervention, describing as 'close to anarchy' a mishmash of more than 30 separate military operations—the 'summer camp' limits that some imposed on their troops engaging in actual combat and NATO's wondrous decision-making process which, on average, took 80 days to respond to field commanders' urgent requests for equipment. Overlayed on all that were endless and well-meaning NGOs and aid groups.

In February 2007, the outgoing US commander in Afghanistan, Lieutenant General Karl Eikenberry, revealed the surprising depth of his own pessimism when he told the US Congress: 'The long-term threat . . . is the potentially irretrievable loss of legitimacy of the government of Afghanistan.'

A few weeks later a Dutch NATO commander, General Ton van Loon, fixed me with a steely gaze, claiming: 'The Taliban's spring offensive will not happen because we are going to take the initiative—we'll go wherever we can to make sure that the Taliban can't stop progress.' But the following months were the war's worst, surpassing the violence and mayhem of 2006, which, in turn, has been surpassed by the data for this year. Attacks on Afghan and coalition forces this year are already up 44 per cent on last year; more than 240 American troops are dead; more than 1400 Afghan civilians have been killed by coalition fire; and more than 140 attacks on humanitarian operations were carried out in 29 of the country's 34 provinces. In one six-month period this year, more than 700 policemen were murdered.

All coalition countries are guilty of missing the big picture, of perceiving all of Afghanistan through the tiny turf they command and the warm inner glow of the latest school or clinic they have opened. But NATO takes the cake. A report prepared for a NATO summit in Bucharest in April this year reads as an ode to untrammelled joy: 'military success . . . significant strides . . . space and opportunities for economic and political progress'. It trumpets the capture of districts held by the Taliban, but is silent on those taken or still held by the insurgents. It celebrates the building of new highways, but says nothing of the Afghans who have been abducted or murdered, or the supply convoys that are being ambushed, on these roads.

NATO hides behind equivocation, with statements like 'Although the security situation in the region is still fragile . . .' or 'As the Taliban extremists suffered a series of tactical defeats, their ability to conduct sustained activity is limited geographically . . .'

Then six months later, out of the blue, the consensus among Washington's sixteen intelligence agencies is that Afghanistan is going down the drain. A 'downward spiral' was the leaked sound bite from a highly classified National Intelligence Estimate being prepared for the US president, George Bush.

One of the most powerful voices to cast doubt on the allies' grand strategy in Afghanistan was no less than Admiral Michael Mullen, the chairman of the US Joint Chiefs of Staff. 'I'm not convinced we're winning in Afghanistan,' he told Congress last month. Warning that time was tight for the coalition, he added: 'We cannot kill our way to victory.'

That comment was the signal for an outpouring of official anxiety. But as others vented, the US defence secretary, Robert Gates, insisted 'there's no reason to be defeatist'. And as the chorus of doubt from senior military and diplomatic figures on both sides of the Atlantic grew, the British foreign secretary, David Miliband, denied the allies were failing.

US General David Petraeus, the architect of the Iraq surge, takes over next week as head of the US Central Command—which puts him in charge of Afghanistan. Petraeus comes to the job predicting that the lack of development and the rising violence will make Afghanistan 'the longest campaign of the long war'. Already he has ordered a 100-day review of the conflict, which will go to troop numbers and the prospects for reconciliation between the floundering government in Kabul and the insurgency movements. Given that no foreign-led force has won a war in Afghanistan, precisely how many troops are needed to win is a moot point.

During the failed Soviet occupation in the 1980s, Moscow had up to 140,000 of its troops and another 300,000-odd Afghan forces. More recently, a former NATO commander, Dan McNeil, estimated that the United States and its allies would need 400,000 foreign and local troops to win in Afghanistan—about three times more than he had.

But it is a much more modest 4000 new American troops who are due to land in Afghanistan in January. And though the top brass insists Afghanistan is not conducive to an Iraq-style 'surge', they are calling for an additional 15,000 men—a request that is unlikely to be met in the short term.

In light of its massive and continuing commitment to Iraq, Washington is unable to free up troops in numbers that might make a difference in Afghanistan. Its pleas for troops and funds from countries outside NATO suggest it has given up on the likelihood that its European allies will put more boots on the ground.

Afghanistan's president, Hamid Karzai, has made impassioned pleas to the Taliban leadership to engage in a process of reconciliation—remarkably, with Washington's blessing. But who among the fractious insurgency movements might take part in such talks and on what terms seems a long way off resolution.

Saudi Arabia confirmed this week that it had hosted exploratory talks between the Afghan government and Taliban representatives in the holy city of Mecca last month. Pakistani officials, including the former prime minister Nawaz Sharif, also reportedly took part and an intriguing Saudi attendee was Prince Turki bin Faisal, formerly a powerful head of Saudi intelligence who was close to the Taliban in the 1990s.

Taliban spokesmen were quick to deny that anybody who went to Mecca had travelled with the movement's blessing, insisting loudly that there could be no such talks while foreign forces were in Afghanistan. Former Taliban figures have also said the demand that the Taliban denounce Al-Qaeda as a prerequisite to any mediation would abort the process.

Even if the Taliban could be defanged, there are other powerful insurgency groups to be reckoned with—such as former mujahideen leader Gulbuddin Hekmatyar's Hezb-e Islami movement and the Taliban renegade Jalaluddin Haqqani. And, of course, there is Al-Qaeda. On the other hand, there is no certainty that Afghanistan's Uzbek and Tajik minorities would tolerate peace talks without resorting to arms.

Notwithstanding the many hurdles to such talks, the top United Nations official in Kabul, Kai Eide, is enthused by the mere prospect. 'If you want to have relevant results, you must speak to those who are relevant,' he told reporters earlier this month. 'If you want to have results that matter, you must speak to those who matter.'

Despite, or perhaps because of, speculation that the insurgency movements have little interest in talking—seeing themselves well-placed in a conflict in which chaos plays to their advantage—the American generals are enthusiastic too. 'I think you have to talk to enemies,' Petraeus said last week.

Fixing on the right policy mix to rescue Afghanistan is a daunting task, which neither Barack Obama nor John McCain has addressed in any substantive manner in their race for the White House. Two experts who have are Barnett Rubin and Ahmed Rashid, two of the most acknowledged analysts on Central Asian affairs. Unfortunately, their prescription, set out in great detail in the current issue of *Foreign Affairs*, is more an Everest-like diplomatic challenge, with a timeline that would run for years, than it is a quick fix.

But that's the Afghan catch-22: all the tinkering imaginable in Afghanistan would have no effect without the kind of long-term regional diplomacy these experts propose. Truly, it is a daunting task. More foreign troops, a flash new Afghan national army, billions for reconstruction, a crackdown on drugs or more pressure on Pakistan to curb its Taliban-leaning military and security services, they say, will not work alone.

Urging the United States to break out of a diplomatic paralysis induced by its so-called war on terror, Rubin and Rashid urge a diplomatic and political process that requires Washington to work with its enemies to isolate Al-Qaeda, thereby reducing the threats faced by Afghanistan and Pakistan as well as the terrorist threat to the rest of the world.

The spreading of the Afghan conflict into Pakistan has created a regional crisis that risks more terrorism and even the collapse of a nuclear-armed state—but there is no international framework to deal with it. Drawing on the imagery of the Great Game, they argue that the crisis has morphed from a game of chess into the unruly Afghan game of *buzkashi*, in which horsemen fight for possession of a dead goat. In the current Great Game, they say, Afghanistan is the goat.

Solutions now on the table require a generational commitment by the United States in Afghanistan—but no countries in the region will tolerate that. Pakistan sees Afghanistan through its conflict with India; Iran sees the US presence as a bid for regime change in Tehran; China, India and Russia have no desire to keep the United States or NATO in their backyards.

Rubin and Rashid argue that the crisis calls for a grand diplomatic initiative that addresses Afghanistan's and Pakistan's security needs and the rampant conspiracy theories that have stoked mutual distrust in the region and of the United States. There has to be a role for both China—it was an ally of Islamabad and potentially a big investor in Pakistan and Afghanistan—and for Saudi Arabia, an Islamic power that is also an ally of Pakistan and formerly of the Taliban. Moscow has to be involved and Tehran would need guarantees.

Acutely aware they are setting out a painfully slow process, Rubin and Rashid urge the next American president to put aside the past, Washington's keenness for 'victory' as a solution to all problems, and its reluctance to involve competitors, opponents or enemies in diplomacy. 'A successful initiative will require exploratory talks and an evolving road map,' they say. 'Today, such suggestions may seem audacious, naive or impossible, but without such audacity there is little hope for Afghanistan, for Pakistan or for the region as a whole.'

A casual observer might be forgiven for concluding that Petraeus had the advantage of reading a draft of the Rubin-Rashid paper before he formulated the objectives for his 100-day review of the Afghanistan crisis. Unnamed sources briefing the *Washington Post* said the general was focusing on two major themes—government-led reconciliation with the Taliban in Afghanistan and Pakistan, and 'the leveraging of diplomatic and economic initiatives with nearby countries that are influential in the war'.

The Spanish diplomat Francesc Vendrell departed Afghanistan last month, feeling sorry for Karzai, the hapless Afghan president. Washington and its allies had put too much faith in him while not doing enough for him at the same time, Vendrell said at the end of a gruelling six-year term as the European Union's man in Kabul.

But Vendrell's warning about Karzai applies also to Petraeus. 'We thought we'd found a miracle man,' he said of Karzai. 'Miracle men do not exist. Too much responsibility without power was vested in this person.'

Great expectations and the combination of insufficient resources and a failure to see Afghanistan as part of a vastly bigger and more complex regional dynamic will cruel the pitch for the general too.

A WOMAN'S LOT

Kabul, Afghanistan
22 November 2008

Who would be a woman in this godforsaken country? There are no meaningful statistics but anecdotal evidence of sexual and domestic violence—and the widespread use of rape as a weapon—indicates that hopes for the emancipation of Afghan women, which were high in 2001, now hang by a slender thread.

International human rights officials in Kabul are privately explosive about what they see as a marked slide in human rights generally and for women in particular—especially in light of demands by officials that they must play the glad game. 'Can't be all doom and gloom,' a senior foreign official regularly exhorts his frustrated staff.

Amid the many mistakes in Afghanistan, there have been two constants. One is the Western obsession with winning a war while forgetting the welfare of the Afghan people, most notably the women. The other is reducing the equation to a simplistic contest between the 'good' President Hamid Karzai and the 'bad' Taliban.

American generals demand thousands more troops to protect the population in the south and in the east from the Taliban. But little is said about a dire need to protect the population from bullying local powerbrokers who are beholden to Karzai. The Taliban make big sections of the country ungovernable. But in the areas in which Kabul at least has nominal control, the social default is to a tribal-fundamentalist ideological mix that is enforced as much by people the president supports as by those he fears.

For women, this pincer grip has knocked their rights to the bottom of the agenda. 'Karzai operates like a mafia crook. His regime is corrupt, brutal and repressive and it is based on the president's umpteen deals with the devil—fundamentalists, warlords and criminals,' a senior human rights figure told me privately this week. 'But Karzai never acts alone. His regime was supposed to be different to the Taliban . . . and the Australian and the French and all the other governments [still] back him.'

Karzai lurches from one crooked or corrupt power base to the next—one day pardoning brutal rapists and saying nothing about it, the next celebrating the execution of small-time criminals while the Mr Bigs of the criminal and political worlds remain untouchable.

When eighteen-year-old Firishta's arranged marriage became unbearable, she ran back to her father's home in Samangan, a province in the north of Afghanistan. But the young woman was pursued by her father-in-law, who was enraged by the dishonour she had brought on his name. He took to Firishta with an axe, murdering her as her family looked on. Later he told the police: 'I am not sorry.' In this case, at least, the police intervened as might be expected.

When they acted in the case of a thirteen-year-old boy who was among the victims of a spate of rape cases in adjacent Sar-e Pol province, it was not quite as the boy's uncle Ali Khan had envisaged when he complained in the local press about a lack of police action. 'The police chief beat us up, threatened us with death and insulted us in the presence of my sister and her paralysed husband,' Ali Khan said.

Each such case is ignored or provokes hand-wringing about the cultural complexities of Afghanistan, about endemic corruption, and about the indifference of local authorities either because they are hostage to warlords and the mosque or because they share an ingrained Afghan notion that women are second-class citizens. But none of that quite explains the conduct of Karzai or those around him in a horrific gang-rape case, which has been playing out in the north since the 2005 presidential and parliamentary election campaigns and, more recently, in Kabul.

The victim, 45-year-old Sara, is now too scared to emerge from her home in tiny Moho, in the Roydoab district of Samangan province. Dilawar, her 50-year-old husband, who also goes by a single name, has fled the village, fearful that as the head of his household he will be targeted for daring to challenge the might of the local warlords. But at the same time, the wispy-bearded Dilawar refuses to succumb to the silence that usually envelops Afghan families for whom rape brings shame and dishonour. Instead, he has enlisted human rights activists and officials to back a fight that he is taking to the gates of the presidential palace, armed with only his courage and the tattered, pink carry bag in which he holds his precious documents.

Dilawar and Sara's son, Islamuddin, then aged 22, had not been seen since he was pulled from their home by a man they identified as Commander Karim, a local warlord who they claim attempted to frame their son for an affair that he—the commander—was having with the wife of another commander in the district. Sara twice challenged the commander in public on the disappearance of their son. For that, she was brutally punished.

Karim and three of his militia lieutenants—who were brothers—took her from her home and dragged her to an animal pen about 200 metres away, where they raped her in front of more than a dozen witnesses. Sara was then mutilated with a bayonet before being chased naked through the village and finally left to find her way home alone.

Laying out his documents on a conference table in the Kabul office of the Afghanistan Human Rights Organisation this week, the farmer Dilawar told me that local authorities refused to act against the men until he had petitioned the parliament, the president, the United Nations and other human rights organisations.

Commander Karim had enough political and militia clout to avoid conviction despite the evidence of seventeen witnesses, says lawyer Lal Gul, the chairman of the human rights organisation. But in 2006 the three brothers were convicted and each was sentenced to eleven years in jail. Subsequently, this decision was upheld by an appeal court and later confirmed by the Afghan Supreme Court.

One of the brothers died in jail. But when Dilawar returned briefly to the village in May this year, he was unnerved to see the other two—Noor Mohammed and Khair Mohammed—swaggering in the village bazaar. They had been released after serving little more than two years of their sentences, apparently in response to a petition to Karzai from their mother.

Sara and Dilawar have complained loudly and publicly since May; in August they won the backing of senior United Nations officers in Kabul, who firmly denounced the rapist brothers' early release.

In the face of local indifference, Karzai's office might have been expected to be jealous of the president's international reputation when it came to kid-glove treatment for rapists. But his staff has been inordinately slow in explaining how his distinctive signature was appended to the brothers' pardon documents.

The pardon papers misrepresent a key fact. They state that the brothers deserved mercy because they had already served four years in jail, twice as long as they actually had been behind bars. And reflecting the absence of any distinction between rape and adultery in Afghanistan's sharia law, they cite the brothers' crime simply as adultery.

When challenged, the initial response from Karzai's office was to fob off senior human rights officials, claiming that the pardons related to a different rape—not that of Sara. In the face of persistence, they promised an investigation.

That was in August. In the interim there has been only silence while the human rights lawyer Lal Gul represents the case as an example of the ability of warlords and their political patrons to act outside the law as they influence the highest levels of decision-making in the land.

In the pardon process, Gul and his foreign counterparts in Kabul detect the hand of a member of one of the Samangan warlord families who is on Karzai's staff. 'But,' one of the internationals added, 'Karzai knew exactly what he was doing when he signed the papers.' The official added: 'Sara's case so illustrates how power and leverage work in this country. Some can protect themselves and their families but if you are at the bottom of the pile you are totally exposed.'

Arguing that Karzai has no genuine commitment to women's rights, 28-year-old Sabrina Sagheb, an MP, snapped: 'The president does not believe in democracy—he uses its elements to defeat democracy. How would he respond if one of his family were treated like this? How can he do it?'

Dilawar has already sold half of his small plot of land to raise funds for the case. But why press on in such a hostile environment? 'This was an animal crime and the men who raped my wife must be properly punished,' he said resignedly. 'I want justice.'

More than 80 per cent of Afghan women are illiterate. Three out of four girls under sixteen are forced to marry, often to settle family debts. School attendance in Afghanistan has risen impressively to about 5 million, but the World Bank says girls comprise just 35 per cent of this figure.

An average 60 per cent of girls under eleven—more than a million—still do not attend classes and in five of the country's 34 provinces, at least 90 per cent of school-age girls are kept away. Schools for girls in areas where the Taliban is active are torched and teachers are intimidated. In Kandahar last week, eight exuberant teenage girls on their way home from school were sprayed with acid by two men who came alongside them on a motorcycle. One of the girls was blinded and, despite its denials of responsibility for the attack, a Taliban objective was achieved: the next day, local families pulled all 1500 girls from the Mirwais Minna school.

Much is made of the reach of public-health facilities, which are improving slowly. But when French military medics this year opened a clinic at Dawalat, just 60 kilometres north-east of the capital, there was just one woman among the first 1000 patients. The all-enveloping burqa remains a common sight in Kabul, as women move through the markets like anonymous shadows and those who dare to be role models run the risk of being gunned down.

At the end of September, Malalai Kakar, who was celebrated for her gun-toting courage as the chief of the women's police in

Kandahar, was assassinated by the Taliban as her fifteen-year-old son drove her to work. The head of the local Department of Women's Affairs suffered the same fate two years earlier. In 2005, the 24-year-old Shaima Rezayee, who shed her burqa for the glamour of hosting a popular TV music show, was murdered in Kabul.

In the western city of Herat, a female prosecutor has had so many threats she has been lumbered with eight bodyguards and is too scared to allow her children to attend school. The father of a doctor who has received threats disguises himself as a woman before daring to visit international human rights officials in Kabul—and the only useful advice they can offer is that he and his family should join the middle-class and professional exodus from Afghanistan.

It is sickening to sit through an interview with Sabrina Sagheb, the youthful female MP. Initially she wants to celebrate the equal rights granted to women in Afghanistan's new constitution and the gift of 25 per cent of seats in the parliament. 'We are free,' she declares. Then, between long, pensive silences she volunteers that women remain a lesser gender; that violence is a great challenge; and that rape, especially of children, is on the rise. 'It's horrible,' she says. At the end of 30 minutes' conversation, she denounces Karzai as a criminal: 'He is one of those who break the law.'

The fear among foreign human rights activists here is that the weight of constant attack will wear down local women's groups. 'I worry that their ability to hold on to their ideals and objectives is diminishing all the time,' a foreign official told me.

WHISKER FROM OBLIVION

Paktika Province, Afghanistan

13 December 2008

U S Army Captain Dave Conner was still preparing his convoy for the bone-jarring ride into a hornet's nest when the first hint of trouble came—a report that twenty known Taliban fighters had disappeared from the remote village of Gayan.

Conner's mission was to distribute aid to villages along the border splitting Afghanistan and Pakistan—and to send a signal to the Taliban that they did not have the field to themselves. But the insurgency was no longer a low-tech rabble. Armed with satellite phones, Taliban spotters could report his every move. It was a game of cat and mouse—one wrong step spelled catastrophe for either side.

The Taliban had thousands of fighters the length of the frontier and an armoury of home-made bombs to unleash. Conner, 30, had the might of US military technology and 36 men in his patrol—he wanted to bring them all home alive.

From bases far away, the Americans were tracking the Taliban even as it tracked them. Hugging valleys through the barren brown hills to Gayan, in a convoy with outriders from a local security group and the Afghan National Army, the US captain was kept abreast of the Taliban talk. But now he was more exposed because he was leading his men on foot patrol between villages. A Taliban spotter had already reported to his own controller the numbers, weapons and direction of the US patrol and gloated chillingly: 'Oh, if only we had a suicide bomber ready.' Then, in a momentary slip, the spotter carelessly gave away his position, revealing he was on the highest point over the valley. Captain Conner moved fast, splitting the patrol. He ordered half his men to remain in the hamlet of Azura, and led the others to the camp at Gayan to order a mortar strike on a plateau on the stubbled mountain spine to the west, where the Taliban spotter lurked.

But further up the US chain of command, Captain Conner's request was denied because satellite imagery had revealed two buildings on the plateau, which meant the potential for civilian casualties. After years of air strikes gone awry, it was a critical problem for the United States—and a propaganda triumph for the Taliban.

The Americans were to leave Gayan the next morning, but not before a last aid distribution near the open space reserved for cattle traders in the bazaar. 'If they are giving stuff out, I'm going down for some boots and a warm coat,' a Taliban spotter laughed into his satellite handset.

Whichever way the Americans turned, it seemed the Taliban were there too. No sooner did Conner dispatch an Afghan security detail to check the bazaar before the US convoy drove through than another Taliban spotter was reporting their moves. As the convoy eased to a halt in the bazaar, furtive movement around a rocky outcrop on a slope above suggested the presence of even more Taliban watchers.

Captain Conner ordered men to the high ground. Worried by the risk of a suicide bomber, he set the rest of his unit in a tight cordon around the convoy as it stopped to distribute blankets and shoes to a near-riotous crowd of locals. The trailer in which the aid had been hauled was empty in a flash. And then it was time to go.

As the convoy bumped and crashed over rocks in the riverbed that would lead them back to their main base at Tillman, the head of the Afghan security group, Anar Gul Satani, rode part of the way. The men of his ragtag militia could be seen on the ridges, waving the convoy on with their weapons.

Satani would leave the patrol at a place called Walawas, where two rugged valleys intersect to carve the district into its fractious tribal regions. It was the boundary of his turf. 'Then they will be on their own,' one of the Taliban spotters reported even before the convoy had arrived at the drop-off point.

Suddenly, the track was eerily empty of traffic. Captain Conner tightened up, conscious of the common Taliban tactic of shutting down traffic to spare the locals when a hit on an American target was imminent; they too need to worry about collateral damage.

Conner had a good idea of just where the attack would come. A few kilometres on, the track dropped down from a steep spur, sweeping to the east as it forded a dry riverbed that wandered aimlessly across a splayed, rocky apron. Two weeks earlier, an American convoy returning from Gayan had rounded this same spur to meet a wall of rocket-propelled grenades and small-arms fire—forcing it to halt where a small roadside bomb had been buried.

Ordering a halt well before the spur, Conner issued orders for most of his troops to climb the scrabbly hills and for the remainder to go on foot ahead of, and alongside, the lead vehicles in the convoy.

'I knew they knew we were on our own,' he said. 'If it was to be a small-arms attack they'd have the high ground, so we had to get up there too, hopefully to see them first to better protect ourselves.' By taking the high ground, he would also be able to look over a good kilometre or more of the track on which his convoy was most vulnerable.

But from up the ridgeline, there was nothing to see. The only movement below was a meandering herd of goats. The valley was silent. The Taliban had stopped talking. Conner knew it was too quiet. He moved to a hump on the spur to watch the convoy approach the river crossing below.

And then came the blast. An improvised explosive device—known as an IED—blew up with a noise that slapped the hillside. Billowing smoke enveloped the lead vehicle. Men scattered, taking cover as they scanned the ridges and slopes, expecting rocket grenades and gunfire.

But again, there was nothing but eerie silence. Two of the Americans nearest to the explosion would suffer brief hearing loss but the driver had survived without injury. The only damage to his machine was a ruptured oil line—minor, but enough to disable it.

Conner and half-a-dozen others tumbled down the hill towards the crossing. Beneath the vehicle the broken shell of an RPG lay in a small crater that was perhaps 50 centimetres across, maybe 30 centimetres deep. This bomb was so small that Conner deemed it to be a decoy—its more deadly companions had to be nearby.

Patrolling with the Americans was a unit of the Afghan National Army. The commander, Jawad, ordered a dozen of his men to comb the area for another bomb. Walking the shoulders of the track, they found it just 200 metres further along. The trigger was a near-invisible length of fishing-line stretched taut across the track. On one side it was tied to a peg driven into the dirt; on the other, it was tied to a buried detonator.

Jawad opted for a low-tech approach to defusing it. He tied 100 metres of string to the end of a tree branch, backed up the track and tugged the branch against the fishing line to activate the bomb. As he pulled, the fishing line broke. But there was no explosion. Jawad, who goes by a single name, then had his men hurl rocks on the track. When that failed, he ordered them to spray it with AK-47 fire. Again, nothing.

In this war between the most powerful army in the world and a ghostly Taliban force armed with the crudest weapons, the dust-cloaked mountains seem to have become a level playing field.

Captain Conner moved one of his machines to the shoulder of the track. The turret-mounted 50-calibre machine-gun raked the track with lethal force. First a single burst of fire and then eighteen more, but the only thing raised was dust and grit.

It was the twentieth spray of bullets that finally found the target. The track heaved as it erupted in a massive blast that was intended for the convoy. Rocks and dirt spat at the sky.

When the dust finally settled the Americans strapped themselves back into their $US1 million mine-resistant, ambush-protected (MRAP) vehicles. The hardy Afghan soldiers travelled alongside in open-backed Ford pick-ups; the bomb would have blown them sky high.

Captain Conner called his convoy to move slowly forward. It had travelled barely 200 metres before a third bomb thundered behind them. Another billowing cloud of smoke and dust filled the golden light of the late afternoon.

An Afghan truck—known as a jingle truck for the rows of bells dangling along its sides—had detonated the third bomb. It was smack in the middle of the road where many of the Americans had stood not long before as they pondered how to detonate the second bomb. I had been lying on the ground next to it, taking photographs. All ten vehicles in Captain Conner's convoy had driven over it but, by some fluke, they had failed to trigger the device.

The jingle truck was destroyed. Remarkably, the driver survived and he fled instantly. His load of flour and cattle-feed was sprayed on the shoulders of the track. His fuel tank had been thrown a good 25 metres.

'Holy shit, sir,' exclaimed Sergeant Danny Fisher, from Tennessee. 'We just survived the big one.'

As we all drew breath by the roadside, the Americans and Afghans laughed the nervous laughter of men who were still alive after detonating the two biggest roadside bombs planted in the province by the Taliban. When Captain Conner placed his M4 in the craters of the second bomb to indicate its size, the gun looked like a toy. When he stepped into the crater of the third bomb, he was almost waist deep.

The trigger devices, buried at a distance from the explosives, had survived the blasts. The paper between the pressure plates in the trigger for the third bomb bore childlike drawings of a US helicopter shooting at Afghan traffic. Beside these drawings was a single, chilling notation: *Al-Qaeda*, it said.

By the crude calculus of war, the Taliban had lost this round. It was to their advantage to attack an American convoy after it had distributed its aid supplies—that way the villagers received much-needed boots and blankets before the Taliban got its targets. The bombs had not inflicted any casualties on the convoy, but a plus for the Taliban was the disabling of a valuable vehicle and pinning down 50-plus US and Afghan soldiers for much of the day. However, the jingle truck destroyed by the third bomb was locally owned, and for that the Taliban would be condemned in the valleys and villages.

As Captain Conner considered the day's events and the good fortune that seemed, at least on this day, to have held for the Americans, his customary deadpan expression was unaltered. 'We were just trying to get from one place to another . . . but someone was looking out for us,' he said. As his men began the drive back to base, towing the damaged MRAP vehicle, he told them: 'Tonight, you all better say an extra Our Father.'

DOING THE BIDDING
OF ORGANISED CRIME

Kabul, Afghanistan
22 August 2009

Buried in the wastes of south Afghanistan, Oruzgan is a lost-cause province often invoked as a decorative footnote because it is the birthplace of Mullah Omar, the founder of the Taliban. But this dustbowl on the road to nowhere is taking on new significance for some of the analysts searching for a key to unlock the corrosive crisis that is modern Afghanistan. They call Oruzgan the 'laboratory province'.

As home to the bulk of Australian forces in Afghanistan, Oruzgan has also become the military parking lot in which Canberra spins its wheels, at the edge of a nation-building black hole consuming hundreds of billions of dollars coughed up by the international community.

Less often, Oruzgan is cited in another context: it was the carefully chosen springboard for Hamid Karzai's uprising against the Taliban in the days after the September 11 attacks on New York and Washington. That, and the absence of muddying factors such as cross-border infiltration, drugs and a multiplicity of tribes—say the analysts—makes Oruzgan unique to understanding the political and social dynamic at the heart of Karzai's Afghanistan.

Fix Oruzgan, they say, and you might have a template for fixing all of this corrupt, failing narco-state in which a hapless 30-odd million Afghans—and their would-be Western saviours—have been hurled into a void between bottom-up notions of modern democracy and a tradition of top-down patronage politics that has shaped Central Asia for centuries. But the 'laboratory province' argument poses profound questions for Canberra: What if its 1500 troops are fighting the wrong enemy? What if Australians unwittingly are a part of the problem, not the solution?

In Kabul this week for Afghanistan's second major democratic poll, I came to the 'laboratory' theory obliquely. It had gone midnight, the summer air was cool and the city pin-drop quiet as two diplomats—who cannot be named—sat in one of the capital's prettier walled gardens, slicing and dicing the election.

The televised candidates' debate had taken place the previous evening and now one of the diplomats seized on a comment by the maverick intellectual candidate, Ramazan Bashardost: 'He said that the guys he talks to in Oruzgan say that Karzai has brought back to power the people who lost against the Taliban and they have been going after the people to take revenge.'

Locked in the central south, Oruzgan does not have the complication of Taliban cross-border movements. It does not have the levels of narco-cultivation and gem trafficking that bedevils neighbouring Helmand, and it is too remote and removed to have had its tribal mix complicated by internal migration. 'You don't have any of the issues that cloud thinking in other places,' one of the diplomats argued. 'What you do have [are] some of the major tribes who have been cut out of the party.'

Karzai planned the 2001 uprising against the Taliban from his base in the Pakistani city of Quetta. But because key members of his Kandahar-based Popalzai tribe initially remained loyal to the Taliban, his search for foot soldiers took him to Oruzgan, where an island of Popalzai pushed up into the province from Kandahar, says the Dutch author and journalist Bette Dam, who did not join the midnight sojourn in the Kabul garden.

A towering and much-feared figure in the provincial capital, Tarin Kowt, was Jan Mohammed Khan. He had a reputation that was built on his fierce resistance to the Russian occupation of Afghanistan in the 1980s—when he came to know Karzai—as much as on his role as a local strongman and pre-Taliban governor.

The bond between these two was sealed in the 1990s when there was an attack on Karzai in the centre of Tarin Kowt. Jan saved his life. In the Taliban years, Dam says, they worked as a team, at times travelling to the Pakistani capital, Islamabad, to appeal to the US embassy for funds to resist the Taliban. However, a local tribesman betrayed Jan and he spent the last of the Taliban years in jail.

Karzai personally freed Jan from prison in 2001 and one of his first presidential decisions was to reappoint him governor of Oruzgan, thereby co-opting Jan's local networks as his own. 'This,' Dam says, 'is where the problems began. To Karzai, Jan was the great warrior ally who saved his life. But to some of the locals, he was the thuggish cause of the anarchy and corruption that had ruled their lives before the rise of the Taliban.'

In this new order, people's true allegiances no longer mattered. Jan decided who was and who wasn't Taliban, all based on his old rivalries—and that's the information that was fed to American and other forces coming to Afghanistan. 'He disqualified a lot of people in this way,' Dam says.

•

Days after I met the two diplomats and had spoken with Dam, I was invited to another Kabul garden to meet another analyst who has advised various elements of the international machine in Kabul on the basis of almost two decades' experience in the region. She explained that the Oruzgan tribal elders had been reluctant starters in Karzai's uprising—'but they were drawn by the promise of American firepower'.

'Now,' she explained, 'they complain that they have been neglected despite being among the first to help. They were not rewarded and they are not appreciated.' Her assessment of Jan is not pretty: 'Violent and vile, foul-mouthed, particularly cruel—a model of the leadership type Afghans do not like.'

In any Afghan upheaval, locals understand that 'the whole constellation' changes. But with the demise of the Taliban, the imposition of a new local order was skewed massively by the might of American guns. 'It was a major imbalance of local power,' says Dam. 'And Jan Mohammed immediately used his new links to go after rivals and old enemies. He's Popalzai, like Karzai, and he used the power of the US to go after the Ghilzai tribes, branding them as Taliban. There are lots of stories of counter-terror and anti-narco operations that went horribly wrong. People got killed and their homes were bombed—it alienated a population that was not hostile. Jan Mohammed went after people who were sitting at home, doing nothing. Some had been with the Taliban, but they had handed in their weapons and they were not a threat to anyone.'

But while Jan hunted the Ghilzai, he also had a score to settle with lesser sub-tribes associated with his Popalzai tribe. 'One of his tactics is to manipulate pre-existing tensions. When a district police chief was killed, he lied, telling the dead man's brother that the killer was the district governor who came from a different family. Jan then appointed the brother to replace the dead police chief—who then turned around and killed the district governor. Jan knew he was dealing with two big families, who represented two sub-tribes, that could be easily pitched into conflict,' Dam says.

It was made clear to the sub-tribes and families on Jan's hit list that there was no place for them in the new Karzai order. They were humiliated—their young men were made to watch while the elders were dragged off with bags over their heads. Afghans have a word for the position into which Jan forced them. *Majbur* means they were backed into a corner; they had no choice.

The Taliban have a knack of reaching out to tribes that are of local substance but have been marginalised by the likes of Karzai's Popalzai. Jan made Oruzgan fertile ground for the Taliban, creating a whole marginalised class who were motivated more by the loss of tribal honour than any Islamist or anti-Western ideology.

'In this environment,' Dam says, 'the Taliban is very good at responding to grievances and capitalising on them. They provide an umbrella and resources for those who want to fight back. And when Jan defines his enemies as Taliban and tells the Americans that they are, the problem is that a lot of them become Taliban.' Her point is: if the likes of Jan are not exploiting their position—Jan is no longer governor, but he continues to be a powerful local presence—then the Taliban cannot make a purchase.

There is not much to fight over in Oruzgan. It is not of great interest to the government or to the Taliban, which 'means there is potential to make Oruzgan right,' she says. 'But the government is the biggest obstacle to solving local problems so that people might lay down their weapons. It's local government and its close links to Karzai that allows them to maintain this little war,' Dam says. 'The people read the signals when they are bypassed in every local appointment—so they keep fighting. Solve these local conflicts and the Taliban would go elsewhere . . . a lot of the Taliban would go home. What you have here is a very strong dynamic of exclusion and inclusion. It has to be fixed.'

This is patronage politics Afghan-style. Powerbrokers include their friends and tribe and exclude others, reflecting their strength in displays of violence, cruelty and greed. 'This dynamic has to be toned down,' Dam says. 'The alienated tribes have to be included and for that the government must behave differently. Local government won't do it because it is scared, and the national government won't insist on it because it depends on the networks of local government,' Dam says. 'Hamid Karzai doesn't draw red lines for the behaviour of his allies in Oruzgan and across Afghanistan. Basically, he uses the system instead of trying to set the limits he needs to set.'

Several analysts who have spent time on the ground in Oruzgan told me that they discerned a sharp policy difference between the Dutch and the Americans, more often than not backed by the Australians. The Dutch understood the need to map the conflict. 'It's not a simple question of good and evil,' one said. 'But the Australians just want to go after "bad guys". The Americans work with Jan Mohammed—they fight together and the US uses Jan's militia. The Dutch don't work with them. The Australians are not so nuanced—they seem to take their lead from Jan Mohammed on what are local problems and who is or isn't the Taliban. The Australians are a military force and that's how they see the conflict.'

All this needs to be seen in the historical context of central government in Afghanistan. It has rarely worked and when it did—from the 1930s to the 1970s—the regimes understood the vital role for local power and a genuine sharing of resources at that level. To that extent, Washington's strategic belief in a strong, central government in the new Kabul is flawed.

Explaining the tribal view of central government as a foreign entity, the RAND Corporation political scientist Seth Jones recently quoted a Kandahari tribal elder who was explaining that Kabul played no meaningful role in his life: 'My allegiance is to my family first. Then to my village, sub-tribe and tribe.'

Running with the local strongmen and failing to effectively reach out to the marginalised—a failure of the Australians and Dutch in Oruzgan—misses the point of counter-insurgency mantras about protecting locals. All locals.

One diplomat I spoke to posed questions to which some in Canberra might seek answers before the next shooting parties head out from the Australian base in Tarin Kowt: 'Why do we have a situation like an insurgency in Karzai's own backyard? You wouldn't expect a Pashtun president and what essentially is a Pashtun government to have such a problem on their own turf, would you? If we think of Karzai as the great southern tribal elder, Oruzgan under his presidency should be good. It isn't—why?'

The United States no longer hides its loss of faith in the Afghan president. It went along with his bid for re-election only because the opposition was unable to back a single candidate who could give the incumbent a run for his money. And in the event that he is returned, Washington has been manoeuvring, even before Thursday's vote, to appoint to a new Office of the Prime Minister the technocratic Ashraf Ghani—another intellectual who, as a highly respected former World Bank economist, might have done better as a candidate for president if Afghans could have understood his jargon.

Distracted by the security demands of the election, Barack Obama's new military chief in Afghanistan, Stanley McChrystal, has delayed his 60-day review of the American adventure in Afghanistan. But the notion of Oruzgan as a laboratory sits well with the general's intention to shift the effort more to protecting, and thereby winning the hearts and minds of the people, than blasting away at a monolithic Taliban that might not exist. McChrystal has not shared with the world his view of Karzai. But his appointment of the Australian counter-insurgency guru David Kilcullen to his headquarters staff gives us a sense of the advice going to McChrystal.

Kilcullen, a White House adviser when his description of the invasion of Iraq as 'fucking stupid' found its way into print just weeks before last year's presidential election, held nothing back when he spoke this month at the United States Institute of Peace in Washington. He compared Karzai to the South Vietnamese president, Ngo Dinh Diem. The Afghan president, he said, 'has a reasonably clean personal reputation, but he is seen as ineffective. His family are corrupt. He's alienated a very substantial portion of the population. He seems paranoid and delusional—that's the sort of things we were saying about President Diem in 1963.'

That assessment and its echo of Vietnam hung in the air at my earlier late-night garden meeting with the diplomats in Kabul. Assessing Karzai's way forward after the poll, one of them predicted that, far from bowing to international demands—such as those on Thursday from Prime Minister Kevin Rudd and Foreign Minister Stephen Smith—that he change his ways, a re-elected Karzai would use his new mandate to manipulate the United States and its allies to continue fighting his local opponents.

'That's what Oruzgan is about,' the other said. 'We are supporting organised crime and the people don't like it.'

THE ROAD TO PERDITION

Gardez, Afghanistan
26 September 2009

As ominous as the spot thunderstorms electrifying the mountain air at this time of year, Jalaluddin Haqqani's and Pacha Khan Zadran's shared history of victories and defeats rumbles menacingly across the craggy south-east. And just as theirs is no ordinary falling out, the $US100 million bid to link the remote, eastern border city of Khost to the hub-city of Gardez, south of Kabul, is no ordinary road project.

Standing between them, astride a ribbon of bitumen snaking its way towards one of Afghanistan's most treacherous mountain passes, is the unlikely figure of Robert Campbell—a lean, leathery US Army colonel who finds himself slipping between the sliding doors of time. On one side, ancient tribal enmity, big-man chest-thumping and insurgency diktats issued amid feuds, internecine ethnic loyalties and strange codes of honour and conduct; on the other side, a faltering, US-led bid to root democracy in the parched, rocky valleys of the Hindu Kush.

Inevitably, the tale of Haqqani and Pacha Khan entwines with that of a huge effort to build this new road, as a parable on the crisis gripping their homeland. Told in several parts, it is the story of Washington getting one up over Moscow. It's a tale of Afghan powerbrokers milking the international donor community, hedging their bets while playing footsies with the Taliban and other insurgencies, because they remain to be convinced that Washington and its allies will not cut and run.

More than that, it reveals the dual dialogue that is a flaw in the glass of a chaotic effort to haul Afghanistan into the twenty-first century. Local leaders, from the president down, tell the world what it wants to hear, while tribal elders and local warlords kowtow to those above them in the power chain as they carve up the country and its people on their own brutal, near-biblical terms.

Connecting Khost and Gardez, the K–G Road is part of a grand design to break five strategic centres away from economic and social dependency on neighbouring Pakistan. By linking them together and to the national ring-road, they might be hooked back into Kabul's orbit.

In Paktia province, people worry about who will control the road. Will Jalaluddin Haqqani slap a tourniquet on it and hold the city of Khost to ransom—as he did so relentlessly in the past? Will Pacha Khan Zadran throw up checkpoints to extract tolls from all who pass—as he did so voraciously in the past? For Americans stuck between them, the contest is as much about a showdown between two old tribal enemies as it is about the longevity and viability of the Kabul government.

Campbell, the American colonel, knows the stakes are high and that he dare not underestimate either opponent. 'They have very different objectives,' he tells me while patrolling the K–G

Road late last month. 'Pacha Khan wants to control commerce on the road; Haqqani wants to control Khost.'

Haqqani's whereabouts are a mystery. 'The last I heard, he was in Pakistan—in Miram Shah,' says a senior US officer, referring to a small town in the wilds of Waziristan, just over the border. When I previously searched for Pacha Khan, the Pancho Villa lookalike was at home in the woodcutters' village of Wazi Zadran, lolling on a pile of floor cushions, his girth ample and the whiteness of his teeth visible below the black-dyed moustache. A belt of bullets stretched diagonally across his chest as he worked a great length of cotton into a classic Pashtun turban.

This time he is in a private hospital in suburban Kabul. Lifting his hospital-greens, he reveals a flabby stomach and the bandaged wound of his hernia operation. Bare-headed, Pacha Khan is in an armchair. The warlord has not shaved in several days. A briefcase is on the floor and an AK-47 against the wall. Armed men guard the corridor and the street outside. Huddled in a corner beside a small primus stove and its bent teapot is an old woman. Almost cowering, she pulls a veil across her eyes because two male strangers have been ushered into the room.

Pacha Khan has a great sense of entitlement. 'One-third of this country belongs to me,' he says before revealing he views power more through the prism of past factional wars than the permanence of the nascent Afghan state. 'I share equal rights with [President] Hamid Karzai and Abdul Haq [another former mujahideen commander executed by the Taliban as he organised a 2001 uprising]. By rights, I should be Karzai's deputy or defence minister. He refuses me, but I could bring peace to this country in less than a year.'

Pacha Khan has a problem, however. Within the local dynamic, Haqqani's bloody and brutal opposition to the Kabul government and its US-led backers leaves him little room to manoeuvre on the anti-Kabul, anti-US side. Despite him being the first old-guard warlord to violently challenge the Karzai presidency, Pacha Khan is obliged, however reluctantly, to line up with Kabul and the Americans. Haqqani sucks all the oxygen of opposition.

'I don't oppose Karzai,' Pacha Khan says. 'The president is a good national figure. There is no alternative and I ordered our people to vote for him. We don't clash . . . I just demand my rights every now and again.' He finished there, but might have added: 'And Karzai ignores me.'

He is at pains to deny that he and 59-year-old Haqqani were ever close. 'I reject that we were friends,' he insists. 'He always had his own ideas—even in the time of jihad [the 1990s]. Now he works for Al-Qaeda and the ISI [Pakistani intelligence service]. He serves their agenda; I support the Afghan government.'

Pacha Khan and Haqqani come from opposing sub-tribes of the Zadran tribe, which sprawls across a dozen high-mountain districts in three eastern provinces. Pacha Khan is Supeer; Haqqani is Mizai. Haqqani has tried three times to kill Pacha Khan. That pales against US efforts to assassinate Haqqani— usually by dropping bombs on suspected hideouts on either side of the Afghanistan–Pakistan border. Last year, Haqqani's bearded face emerged from a Taliban propaganda video to taunt the Americans: 'Now as you see, I'm still alive.'

In his Kabul hospital room, Pacha Khan's gold fillings flash the indignation. 'Haqqani keeps launching these suicide-bomb attacks on me,' he says. 'Each time God saved me. Some of my men were injured in the attacks, but Haqqani will try again and again and again as long as I am alive. We are enemies.'

Both men were Washington darlings when they fought side-by-side with huge supplies of American arms against the Soviet occupation in the 1980s. Pacha Khan was paid American millions to have his militia join the failed chase for Osama bin Laden after the Taliban fell in 2001.

The Americans see Pacha Khan almost as a cartoonish representation of the Afghan warlord trying to assert authority in the face of a significant Haqqani challenge. 'Cuddly evil,' says one. Others opted for the descriptive 'scumbag'. 'To describe this guy as pragmatic is a massive understatement,' said another of the warlord's wild record of switching sides and lashing out in fury when he does not get his way.

In the aftermath of the US-led invasion of Afghanistan, Pacha Khan was made to cough up 42 truckloads of heavy arms. He refuses to disarm entirely and is presumed capable of fielding 2000 to 3000 fighters.

After the fall of the Taliban, the warlord was so impressed with American firepower he arranged for it to be turned on his enemies. He lied to the Americans that a convoy of elders bound for Kabul to attend Karzai's 2002 inauguration were Talibs. The Americans bombed, killing more than 60. 'He knows how to eliminate his political rivals by whatever means,' says a US military analyst.

The CIA assessed PKZ—its name for Pacha Khan—as 'brutish, mercurial and unstable'. His eldest son was killed in an early 2003 clash with US forces. Last year, Haqqani's youngest son, Omar, died in a clash at the Satukandav Pass, the highest point on the K–G Road. Campbell, the American colonel, is clear about Haqqani: 'His business is killing people and trying to de-legitimise the Afghan government.'

For Afghans, the Haqqani myth is rooted in his fierce fighting against Soviet occupation forces in the 1980s—and his 1991 capture of Khost from the Moscow-backed Kabul government. He allegedly introduced suicide bombs to the Afghan war. Haqqani was Paktia governor under the Taliban; Pacha Khan held the post under Karzai. Both men see Khost as a prize worth fighting for.

When Pacha Khan was sacked from the job, his men took to the streets, guns blazing, as he tried to bomb his way back into office. Angry US Special Forces were caught in the crossfire, but their plans to arrest the warlord were stymied by a decision in Washington that Pacha Khan was untouchable. When Pacha Khan was arrested in Pakistan in 2002, his militia attacked Afghan government installations in the south-east for two years. A year after the Taliban fell, Pacha Khan forces were driven out by rivals who exploited confusion generated by a rumour that Americans had arrested Pacha Khan. On another occasion, Pacha Khan laid siege to Khost because the Americans spurned him. As much as the Americans distrusted Pacha Khan, they worried he would bolster the respectability of the Taliban and Al-Qaeda if he defected to them with his mujahideen warlord credentials.

These days Campbell reckons he has Pacha Khan's measure. 'He has a shady past, but now he is on the side of the government. He wants this road to happen.' Why? Because violently extorting tolls from truck drivers is profitable.

'Haqqani wants to dominate the road so that he can hold Khost to ransom,' says Campbell. 'He wants to own the road to stop traffic getting through by closing it when he likes—and his use of foreign fighters makes him a force to reckon with.'

An analyst on Campbell's staff says Haqqani's opposition to the road is rooted in denying 'people access to the outside world'. 'He wants to keep the people as they are—prisoners of their ignorance and religion. Haqqani figures that if he makes the road as costly as he can, we'll be forced to pull out.'

Of Pacha Khan, Campbell says locals 'will think about trying to shut down the road if they don't get what they want [from Kabul]. They are not fools—they feel left out and they know what's going on. Pacha Khan is a powerful force. He lives in Kabul and comes back here like an evangelist, making speeches and riling up the people. Then he leaves and the elders have to deal with the aftermath.'

Poverty is deep in the Zadran Arc. Villagers eke out an existence, farming crevices or narrow ledges in the mountains. Illiteracy is high and some American officers worry that children's growth is stunted. The only non-farm employment is driving jingle-trucks with their decorative chains dangling from the bodywork. So the Zadran staunchly defend the K–G Road, right?

Well, no. In the mountains, something doesn't add up. Zadran are swathed in warrior heritage. Haqqani and Pacha Khan are legends because, as mujahideen commanders in the 1980s, they sensationally defied all but one short-lived Soviet effort to break the mujahideen grip on the K–G Road.

Today, some locals risk their lives by working on US bases and last year there were loud demands for funding and authority for them to stand an *arbaki* force—a local militia to defend the road. But they shun service in the new Afghan security forces and their warrior instincts don't kick in unless a bag of money is on the table. 'At times we tell the elders that they are an embarrassment to themselves,' says US Sergeant Brent Koegler. 'They got the Soviets out of Afghanistan, but they can't fight twenty Talibs who threaten their village? They're supposed to be awesome fighters.'

This indifference by locals is staggering in the face of excoriating speeches by Pacha Khan and other senior figures at a community meeting last year at Combat Outpost Wilderness, as work began on the road.

Warning people their fence-sitting embarrassed him, Pacha Khan demanded they take sides. 'Don't shame yourself into being stuck in the middle, by not picking a side and not fighting,' he hectored. 'It is shameful to be whining to the government one minute that you can't fight the Taliban and at the next moment telling the Taliban when they come to your door that you are on their side.'

General Said Gul, chief of staff of the Afghan National Army, told the people: 'We let you keep your weapons in the name of your Pashtun culture, [but] things have to change. If my enemy continues to shoot at me from your doorsteps, I'm not going to respect your elders or your tradition. I keep hearing that Paktia is the land of respect, the land of the brave, the land of the proud. What pride? What bravery? What respect? I don't see any of it. I was sent here to protect your sisters, your wives and your kids. And if you are the enemy, how am I going to fight you and protect them?'

At the Kabul hospital, Pacha Khan sets out his solution. It was wrong, he says, to let a major contract for the new road go to an Indian firm. 'I warned them to give the contract to the Turks, not the Indians. The road will not be finished unless the Turks get the construction contract and I get the security contract—the budget should be split between us.' He insists he does not have a particular Turkish contractor in mind, with an eye to a big fat kickback.

Seemingly oblivious to the loathing prompted by his extortionate toll collections on the road just a few years ago, he goes on: 'I would have to set up checkpoints and patrol the road.'

But would Pacha Khan do a better job than the South African firm managing the security cocoon around the roadwork? He feigns ignorance. 'South Africans? I've not seen them on the road. All I hear about is IEDs [improvised explosive devices], kidnappings and terrorists running around. There'd be none of that if it was a proper Afghan security operation. I have an army of 3000 fighters. I would defeat Haqqani—he is a thief who comes in the dark. You should ask the Americans why they can't beat him. They have more than 60,000 troops and forces from 40 other countries and they still can't deal with him. And if he operates from Pakistan, why are the Americans not putting more pressure on Islamabad to shut him down?'

Kabul will not allow Pacha Khan a look-in. It fears the Zadran's fierce independence and seeks to weaken and undermine the tribe, lest there be an uprising in a region traditionally left to manage its own affairs. The Zadran claim as their right the Ministry of Borders and Tribal Affairs but have been denied this influential post for nearly twenty years. No Zadran has been made a foreign ambassador. Efforts last year by elders to iron out differences between Zadran sub-tribes ignited American speculation that the Zadran were bent on resisting Kabul.

Says Pacha Khan, with a wagging finger: 'We should not be forgotten, but we don't get what we deserve in terms of schools, clinics and economic development; we don't get the jobs we need. It concerns me that Paktia is seen as the forgotten province.'

The Haqqani network is the only significant element of the insurgency not based inside Afghanistan. His local training camps and support network are supplemented by lethal long-range hit-and-run missions by mostly foreign fighters based in Pakistan. Influential as he is in Paktia, however, Haqqani must work with the reality that tribes do sit on the fence, play his game but also play America's. 'They want to keep in touch with the Americans and Kabul,' says Thomas Ruttig, a 25-year veteran of the region who is a member of the Afghanistan Analysts Network. 'The Zadran are split, but the tribes are strong.'

The Haqqani network is judged by analysts to be the most irreconcilable of the Afghan insurgency units. Haqqani is believed by the United States to be the Taliban figure most closely linked to Osama bin Laden's Al-Qaeda, to be in receipt of Arab funds and to get help from sympathetic elements of the Pakistani military and intelligence services in cross-border movement and in hiding his operatives in Afghan refugee camps in Pakistan.

American eavesdropping last year reportedly heard the Pakistani military chief of staff, General Ashfaq Parvez Kayani, describe Haqqani as 'a strategic asset'. Colleagues of the general were overheard warning Haqqani of attacks against his forces. In the 1980s war against the Soviets, Haqqani was one of Washington's strategic assets, receiving significant funds and huge arms shipments.

'Today, Haqqani seems to enjoy a "most-favoured" status among some Pakistani and Saudi authorities who repeatedly have suggested including him as a "moderate" in attempts to start negotiations with insurgents,' Ruttig writes in a paper published in July.

After the 1990s civil war, Haqqani threw in his lot with the Taliban and their Saudi Arabian guest: bin Laden. He went from being Washington's well-funded mujahideen darling to sworn enemy. Haqqani, one of the most powerful American-backed mujahideen warlords against the Soviets, was undefeated in the subsequent mujahideen civil war. With the mid-1990s emergence of the Taliban, he signed up with the fundamentalists, reportedly making available his plentiful stocks of US-supplied Stinger missiles. His reward was to be the first non-Talib in the Kabul ministry and later commander of Taliban forces and governor of Paktia. There, he formed a personal and organisational bond with bin Laden, who had his Al-Qaeda training camps near Khost.

Shortly after the Taliban fell, Haqqani was courted by the United States and Kabul. He was reportedly offered the post of Karzai's prime minister. Later his brother Ibrahim and son Ishaq were arrested and used unsuccessfully as bargaining chips to turn Haqqani. Haqqani told reporters in Islamabad late in 2001: 'We will retreat to the mountains and begin a long guerilla war to reclaim our pure land from infidels and free our country like we did against the Soviets . . . We'll deal with [the Americans] in our own way.'

Haqqani is believed to be a member of the Taliban leadership council and to have embraced the fugitive Taliban leader Mullah Omar as his spiritual leader. But Haqqani operates his own command, a semi-independent warlord with autonomy from the Taliban. 'Haqqani's strength is intimidation,' says the analyst Ruttig. 'He is ruthless, so he intimidates people.'

Haqqani has extended his operations into the provinces of Wardak and Logar, on Kabul's doorstep. He has been blamed for last year's assassination attempt on Karzai; last year's bombing of the Serena, Kabul's only five-star hotel; last year's suicide attack on the Indian embassy in Kabul; and a car-bomb attack on NATO military headquarters in Kabul in the lead up to the 20 August 2009 presidential election.

He refused to agree to Mullah Omar's 2006 order to cease attacks on ordinary Afghans. 'Haqqani would be responsible for two-thirds of all the strife there [in the Zadran Arc],' ventured an American analyst. 'Some of the communities are very Taliban, and much of the rest is neutral. No one in the whole area is pro the Kabul government or the NATO forces.'

Haqqani, who has an Arab wife and funding from Dubai and other Arab regions, was excluded from the Bonn process, where the international blueprint for Afghanistan was stamped after the fall of the Taliban in 2001. His nemesis Pacha Khan was at the top table for festivities, hob-nobbing with diplomats. 'His fury at being left out is the reason for his resistance,' says US Captain Gary McDonald at Combat Outpost (COP) Dyesai in the depths of the mountain pass. 'How much of that is in play?

The son has to continue the father's war because the father was so disrespected.'

In the way of the tribes, Pacha Khan's son has been installed as the sub-governor of Wazi Zadran, the seat of Pacha Khan's power. When the Taliban fell, the son was a twenty-something car dealer in Dubai. 'None of the father's presence,' says a senior American officer. 'He watched out for the family interests, but he is not very dynamic.' This arrangement leaves much of the running in Paktia to Haqqani.

The fathers may be handing power to the sons and, in Paktia, the Americans are banking on leadership shortcomings in the younger generation. But already the Americans rank Haqqani's son Serajuddin, 35, as an influential insurgency leader in the east. He is understood to have taken over the day-to-day running of the terrorist network. 'The Haqqanis have had a successful succession,' says a US analyst. 'But I can't say the same for Pacha Khan and his boy.'

Pacha Khan bridles at the suggestion his warlord days are over. As my question to this effect is translated, his entire brow quivers. Stabbing a finger in the air, he says: 'I have not delegated my power or authority to anyone—my son is just the district chief to help secure the area. I'm 58—and still a strong man.'

Colonel Campbell is disarmingly frank about his circumstances. With nineteen years of conventional military service behind him, he is also a model spokesman for Washington as American forces in Afghanistan attempt to switch to the counter-insurgency objective of protecting people and growing communities, instead of relentlessly pursuing the enemy in the gaps between communities. 'What I have changed in the lives of the people will be the indicator of my success,' says Campbell. 'Beating my chest on rounds fired and enemy kills is one thing . . . I can kill 150 fighters, but next year another 150 will come over the mountains. What I have to do is create an environment in which they can't come back.'

While remaining 'on the offensive' and looking for the enemy, 'we look for sources of discontent that can be exploited by the Taliban and we try to fix them. We have to be the anchor that pulls the people towards the Kabul government. If they are afraid, we have to separate them physically and psychologically. The people are the centre of gravity.'

As the Afghanistan crisis enters its ninth year, there is a growing sense that the number of Americans in Central Asia is insufficient, and that the 'more' that Barack Obama might provide won't be sufficient to make a real difference. 'The first eight years have been wasted,' says Thomas Ruttig. 'And it is very difficult to answer, "What do we do now?" We've been talking up a rosy picture for the last five years—and now we have awakened to a nightmare.'

Insurgency leaders are wont to claim time is on their side; that the Americans will be ground down and will leave. But at COP Dyesai, Sergeant Brent Koegler has seized the sentiment as his own. 'We can wait out the Taliban . . . we just have to keep doing what we are doing.'

Koegler seems to embrace the local *inshallah* principle of deferring to a higher authority—God willing, things will happen. His boss, Neal Erickson, doesn't buy it. 'I hope it's not *inshallah*,' he says. '*Inshallah* is nice, but it doesn't get shit done.'

NEW ROAD PAVED WITH PROMISES AND PROJECTS

Gerda Serai, Afghanistan
28 September 2009

All who travel the K–G Road come to Gerda Serai, a hovel in the hills that depends for its existence on the heaving through-traffic. Its spartan, dust-coated bazaar is a hotch-potch of basic travellers' needs: mechanical services, a ramshackle hotel, take-your-life-in-your-hands food stalls. Dogs run in the pot-holed, flooded street. But something is happening here that the Americans must manage expertly. Their lives depend on it.

Gerda Serai sits on a turn in a valley which is too narrow for the $US100 million road, the bazaar and a river that runs wild when the mountain snows melt in the spring. So, to make room for the new blacktop when it comes through next summer, the bazaar must be moved.

As US Colonel Robert Campbell's convoy eases to a halt at the entrance to the bazaar, he sets out the challenge. 'They'll be given new shops. It'll be an enemy victory if we bulldoze this place without providing new ones,' he says, as his nervy troops throw a cordon around the convoy.

Campbell mooches through the bazaar, becoming an actor in a game of bluff—his own terrier-like watchfulness is sheathed in hail-fellow, well-met repartee with locals who, for the most part, respond in kind, but it has to be assumed that some of them are Talibs or friends or relatives of the insurgents who are playing the same game. 'The enemy's not far away,' he says. 'They're watching us now, working out what we are doing so they can intimidate the people.'

Deeper into the bazaar, men who have built a high retaining wall to stop the new road from falling into the river grouse because they have not been paid for their hard work. 'The road won't come this year,' Campbell tells them, before invoking a Muslim term that absolves him of all responsibility by deferring to a higher authority. 'But next year, *inshallah* [God willing].' Campbell is looking for information: had the insurgents bothered them as they built the wall?

'No,' says Ezat Khan, one of the stonemasons.

'But you know the enemy's in the area? You will report any suspicious activity?' Campbell asks him.

'Yes, we will tell the police.'

Campbell crosses the road to engage a thick-set, heavily bearded man who stands chest forward, hands on his hips—this is one of the local strongmen, Haji Keyle. The American sticks to his scripted patter about the road, but as he wraps up, there's a new edge to his voice. 'You stay out of trouble, you hear?' And that, we might have thought, was the last we would hear of Haji Keyle.

The Americans here are spirited, even upbeat. But the more they talk, the more difficult it becomes to understand their confidence. In these parts, in these times, nothing can be taken at face value. The Americans fully understand the push-me, pull-you power of the local warlords: Jalaluddin Haqqani, who, with his son, is the bridge between the Taliban and Osama bin Laden's Al-Qaeda; and Pacha Khan Zadran, who is erratic and brutal but seemingly acceptable to the Americans because, for the time being at least, he says he supports President Hamid Karzai—a position that could change with any coming phase of the moon.

The challenge is in reading which of the locals run with the Taliban, and why—be it out of a loyalty as old as memories of fighting the Soviets together, or from intimidation as fresh as yesterday's threat to behead village elders, which often would be posted on the mosque wall.

Perplexing the Americans is Haji Sangeen, an elder pivotal in their relationship with the people of Gerda Serai, but who they suspect has ties to Haqqani and his terrorism network. 'Haji Sangeen works with us and with Kabul,' says Neal Erickson, a young US Army captain, as he elaborates on the complexities of the local equation and on how the tribal leaders try to stay alive. 'Some of the other elders don't know yet if they want to side with us or with the Taliban. Haqqani still has his old mujahideen links. Everyone here fought the Soviets and those who fought with Haqqani remember him as a good guy who still helps some of them with medical costs. Elders who sided with Haqqani in the past will do what is best for their own; they will go with the development projects. But I'd put money on it that they still have connections to Haqqani; they provide intelligence and shelter, but maybe not as actively as in the past.' And for one of the young captain's military colleagues, that uncertainty extends to Haji Sangeen. 'He sits on the fence—we don't know which way he'll fall,' he says.

As they enter year nine of this conflict, it is remarkable that the Americans still grope to understand the people they are attempting to pacify. An offshoot of the Mogul tribes, the Zadran broke away after a rift eons ago. 'The original tribe lived to the north and what became the Zadran came to this harsh area,' says an American analyst before invoking the film *Deliverance* in an unsettling description of the people and their culture. 'This is the West Virginia of Afghanistan—they moved to the mountains and they did not evolve. They are very clannish, xenophobic.'

When the winter snow closes in, the entire area becomes isolated for up to six months, during which the locals nurse grievances and massage their anger at the world, prompting this observation from an American: 'That's their biggest problem. They feel disconnected and, boy, are they pissed off by what they say are a lot of broken promises.'

Grappling to explain the Zadran people, another US analyst at Gardez powers up a computer and calls up a recently commissioned anthropological study. 'It says they are savages,' he says, incredulous. The analyst refuses to endorse the report's terminology, yet he is taken by some of the sentiment: 'A savage is someone who has no self-restraint and no moral obligations in terms of himself and his own desires. As an assessment of these people, that's possibly unfair, but there is an element of "It's all about me and screw everyone else because I want my share of the pie—and I'm going to get it."'

The American officer reads the critical paragraphs from the computer screen. 'The Zadran have been written up as a small tribe, but they are the biggest in the south-east. Their manners resemble the Waziris [who straddle the nearby border with Pakistan] and the Kharotis [also concentrated in the east], from which we may infer that they are utter savages. They live in small villages . . . they are great robbers and their country was a refuge for bad characters.'

Thomas Ruttig, a member of the Afghanistan Analysts Network, is shocked by the anthropologists' assessment of the locals as savages. 'I take exception to that,' he says. 'I have been working in Afghanistan for 25 years. They might look like savages, but they have a sophisticated political understanding.'

Explaining how he had been able to inoculate German-funded development projects from insurgency attacks by getting the locals to remind the Taliban that the work was a one-off chance that would benefit their communities, Ruttig says: 'One of these "savages" said to me, "We know who the Germans, the Swedes and the Americans are."'

The 'savage's' point, and Ruttig's, is that America's military tactics have created so much local hostility that it has become difficult, if not impossible, for the locals to accept the US presence and Washington's aid. Ruttig says that local people he knows in Khost, at the far end of the K–G Road, who had long supported the presence of foreign troops, turned against the United States earlier this year after a controversial civilian casualty. 'They told me they had no option but to join a tribal uprising. There is great hostility to the Americans, but it is not because the people are savages.'

There are moments in Afghanistan when the locals flick a light switch for a foreign observer, revealing in the simplest exchange all the complexities that make the US-led campaign to rebuild Afghanistan so daunting. Early one morning at COP Wilderness, amid the strewn carpets of the *shura* hut in which the Americans meet and greet local leaders and officials, Colonel Campbell sits on the floor next to the richly bearded and steely blue-eyed Haji Sangeen, the strongman from Gerda Serai.

Campbell, cross-legged on the floor in socks but no shoes, shoots the breeze on a range of local issues: progress on the road, moving the bazaar and income for locals when the road is finished. Haji Sangeen is an imposing figure; his anthracite beard is burnished with henna, his blue eyes—rare among Afghans—are riveting.

Campbell is a Pentagon pin-up boy, seeming to relish a challenge to his nineteen years of military service which he admits, beyond Haji Sangeen's hearing, is confounding. 'I came into the army to kill people, for a sense of adventure—not to sit in meetings like this or to foster development. I want an army formation to manoeuvre on top of—but this is not that kind of war.'

Asked about Haqqani's power and influence in the district, Haji Sangeen plays a straight bat as he speaks through an interpreter. 'The people are tired of him,' he offers. 'Our people do not support Haqqani. They will not follow his orders and those who followed him have fled to Pakistan.'

Likewise, he dispatches Pacha Khan. 'He is from a different sub-tribe and he has alienated our people . . . always siding with his own people.' He reconsiders. 'But Pacha Khan is still important and relations are improving.'

Campbell then makes a plea that can be described only as heartfelt: 'I know you can't physically stop the enemy coming back. But I want to create a place where he is not welcome, where there's no support when he returns in the spring. I ask for your help in finding the enemy and in talking to the people to make sure they don't support them when they come down from the mountains for supplies. Every year we have to make this place stronger, give the people something to be proud of, something that belongs to them that they will want to protect,' the colonel concludes.

But this wily tribal elder ignores Campbell's plea, instead upping the ante with a demand for more projects. 'This is a remote, backward area,' he parries. 'We have rivers that can give us electricity . . .'

Campbell counters, 'I want to be smart about projects. If we try to do too many, we'll not be able to control them to ensure they are properly built and operated.'

Haji Sangeen does not miss a beat. He presses what he believes is his advantage. 'Our main issues are clinics and electricity. In my village we have a problem with snow blocking the roads; in winter we have to transport the sick by wheelbarrow, because we can't use cars and trucks.'

Campbell calls a truce. '*Inshallah*, this will be the last year that you don't have a good road.'

Haji Sangeen seems to agree. 'The US has delivered on all its promises. Our people see the Americans every day and trust them increasingly. This is very good.'

Later, one of Campbell's senior colleagues explains that Haji Sangeen is playing for time, gouging what he can from the Americans and in the full knowledge that the constant rotation of US military officers and aid officials will deliver to his door an American who will think that local hydro-electricity is a great idea. 'Haji Sangeen will get his power plant,' the officer says. 'You watch.'

Watching in intense silence as Haji Sangeen speaks is the rest of his village delegation. Ordinarily someone of his standing would meet the likes of Campbell or a journalist like myself alone—but it is safe to assume there will be local reports back on this encounter and a need for reassurance that Haji Sangeen has not deviated from the local script.

'A couple of years ago, Haji Sangeen would have said "Yes" to the American colonel, but now he is afraid—he knows the Taliban will come later,' Ruttig, an expert on the political dynamic in the south-east, says later. 'My guess is that he would have told the Taliban he was going to see the colonel. To do otherwise would be to risk his life.'

It was only after Colonel Campbell's encounter at the Gerda Serai bazaar with Haji Keyle, the man he warned to stay out of trouble, that the depth of the Americans' suspicion about key local players emerged. Campbell explains Haji Keyle's role in the community. 'That one's influential—a lot of the young people listen to him,' he says. 'He has a questionable past . . . he's been dealing with the enemy. We're watching him,' by which Campbell means every time Haji Keyle uses his mobile phone, an American intelligence officer listens to his every word.

Absent from the bazaar during Campbell's street-walk was another powerbroker under the same microscope. Maiki Khan is a towering figure, but what particularly interests the Americans is his family ties—he reputedly is married to Haqqani's sister. The suspicion is that Maiki Khan is part of what sometimes is described as Haqqani's 'shadow government'. A US military analyst explains: 'They are still loyal to Haqqani and they have people in the Kabul government who still play both sides. They grew up with Haqqani. They are not very effective, but this is a network of people tied to other people who seek to influence the locals.'

One of Campbell's analysts reckons there is an even chance Maiki Khan will be locked up by the Americans. But Campbell says that removing such prominent figures is not an easy decision. 'I have to be careful. People look up to these guys, so if you push them out of the community you have a problem on your hands. But we did lift a member of the Gerda Serai shura—he was bad.'

Campbell stops short of a final call on the allegiances of Haji Sangeen, who is a man on whom the Americans have to rely in Gerda Serai. As though in conversation with himself, the colonel says: 'Haji Sangeen? We don't think he's doing anything crooked . . . *we don't think*, yeah.'

AFGHAN INSURGENCY GIVEN NEW LIFE BY THEIR ENEMIES

An address given at a conference organised by the Centre for
Arab & Islamic Studies at the Australian National University
Canberra, Australia
22 October 2009

In their rush to congratulate President Hamid Karzai on
buckling to a second Afghan presidential election this week,
world leaders heaved a sigh of relief. But none bothered—at least,
not in public—to canvas the part played by the international
community in bringing Afghanistan to the brink. That is what
makes the 60-page assessment of the conflict by US General
Stanley McChrystal a damning document—more because of
who he is than what he actually has to say.

The handling of the crisis by the US-led coalition has its many
critics. But seeing so many of its shortcomings articulated with all
the authority of a top American general makes startling reading.
Since the report was leaked in Washington last month, the debate
has been narrow, focusing on the question of sending more

troops than on what amounts to McChrystal's condemnation of the conduct of the venture.

The detail is excruciating. Consider that the general's judgement calls come as we embark on Year Nine of this conflict. The recklessness with which Afghanistan was minimised as needing serious attention and denied resources until now is beyond belief.

After eight years, Washington finds itself in the same position as the Soviet Union was in Year Eight of its occupation of Afghanistan, seemingly having learnt nothing from history—until McChrystal's bombshell assessment.

I want to read from a defence official's letter dated 17 August. He calls for an honest admission of failure after eight years, citing the squandering of huge material resources and considerable casualties and a failure to stabilise the country—militarily or politically. Most of the population has lost trust, because the campaign is bogged down and a strategic breakthrough is unlikely.

'The experience of the past years,' he continues sombrely, 'clearly shows that the Afghan problem cannot be solved by military means only. We should decisively reject our illusions and undertake principally new steps, taking into account the lessons of the past, and the real situation in the country . . .'

That might have been a note to General McChrystal as he prepared his report—but the date was 17 August 1987. And the author, Colonel K. Tsagalov, was addressing the then newly appointed Soviet defence minister, Dmitry Yazov.

Same ole, same ole . . . The two wars are replete with dispiriting similarities. Perhaps the most striking for my purposes is the near identical position on the timelines, in which Moscow then, and Washington now, are placed. Timed from the date of their respective invasions, only three months separate the letter by Tsagalov and the report by McChrystal. And just eighteen months after the Tasgalov letter, General Boris V. Gromov walked over a bridge on the Amu Dari and into Uzbekistan; he was the last of the Soviet occupation forces to quit Afghanistan.

McChrystal, I fear, has arrived too late—for Afghanistan and for Washington. He is asking for a huge act of faith on two fronts: first by the international community, and second by the Afghan people. But after almost a decade of these constituencies having their trust abused, the miracle promised by McChrystal is a mirage, an ephemeral outcome that even with inevitable, subsequent requests for thousands more troops and billions more in reconstruction dollars likely will not eventuate. The general wants a blank cheque for a jalopy on which he offers no warranty.

I have been asked to address the 'strength of the insurgency'. But quite apart from the usual considerations of its fighting numbers, weapons and funding, the Afghanistan insurgency's greatest strength is the combined and, for a long time quite deliberate, weakness of the coalition and its treacherous allies in the Kabul government. The McChrystal blueprint might have worked in Year Two or even in Year Five of the conflict—and I stress *might have*—but at this stage it's too little and it's too late.

The greatest strength the Taliban has had—and still has—is time. I'm indebted to US Ambassador Eikenberry for first drawing to my attention a quote that already is a *leitmotiv* of this conflict. As he told it, either he or one of his officers was quizzing a Taliban captive on the insurgency's view of how the crisis would unfold. 'The trouble with you Americans,' the prisoner said, 'is you have watches—we have time.' And it was the coalition that gave the Taliban time—in spades.

Put to one side, for a moment, the sobering lessons to be learnt from other counter-insurgencies and the viability of regimes once their foreign occupation props are pulled away. Had the Bush administration decided against its urge to abandon Afghanistan because it wanted to invade Iraq in 2003; had it made available for Afghanistan just half of the billions that went into the Baghdad black hole; and had we been asked, at the same time, to entertain McChrystal's blueprint before the Taliban ran amok and before jaundice seized public and political will in coalition capitals, McChrystal's plan might have been embraced—even in the knowledge that what he proposes is just a down payment. He'll be back, wanting more troops and more cash in years to come.

The cornerstone of McChrystal's plan is sending up to as many as 65,000 new troops and a switch from the coalition tactic of chasing the enemy in the spaces between population centres to protecting the population centres. It is not as though this is not happening now. Last month I reported on a bold initiative to build a US$100-million road between Khost and Gardez, hence its name, the K–G Road. It is in Haqqani country in the south-east. American officers I travelled with enthusiastically follow the letter and spirit of McChrystal's plan. They provide over-arching security while a local militia has been retained to guard the construction gangs which, absurdly, given the regional dynamic, work for a key foreign contractor from India. I mean, talk about baiting the Taliban!

But despite the constant American presence on the ground and in the air, and the gift of a fabulous road taking shape before their eyes, the locals are reticent. Sullen. In the village of Gerda Serai, the main centre of commerce on the road, the Americans have already lifted one of the elders and they suspect that two other key local powerbrokers with whom they interact are two-timing with the Haqqani network, gouging American aid for what they can—but not actively bringing the local population on side.

McChrystal contradicts himself and dozens of analysts who have offered their tuppence worth on timing. He writes: 'Failure to gain the initiative and reverse insurgent momentum in the near-term . . .' and here, lest there be any doubt, he inserts a bracketed reference to make clear he is talking about the next twelve months, '. . . while Afghan security capacity matures, risks an outcome where defeating the insurgency is no longer possible.'

It does not add up. One of his more high-profile advisers, David Kilcullen, is on the record anticipating two more years of what he called 'significant combat'. At least three of McChrystal's twelve months will have elapsed before Obama makes a decision. And moving thousands of troops and equipment seems to take forever. It will be the end of this year before all of the mere twenty-odd thousand troops that Obama signed-off on back in March will be on the ground in Afghanistan. And the same goes for the few-hundred-strong surge of civilian personnel authorised by the president at the same time—they'll still be straggling into Kabul early next year.

It's too late for McChrystal to make protecting the most threatened sections of the Afghan population the key objective, because both the Kabul government and the coalition lack credibility in the eyes of the people. In the absence of any significant Afghan government presence much beyond Kabul, it is the American military and aid workers—and those from several other coalition countries—that are seen as the face of government and as keepers of the cash, of which there is not enough and which takes forever to translate into meaningful development.

McChrystal rightly points to the coalition's preoccupation with force protection, which undoubtedly is one of the greatest drains on coalition, UN and NGO efforts and resources in Afghanistan. 'We operate in a manner that distances us—physically and psychologically—from the people we seek to protect,' he says.

Not unreasonably so, given conditions on the ground. The United Nations rates more than 60 per cent of the country as unworkable for its expatriate staff because of violence. The

International Council on Security and Development reckons the Taliban now has a permanent presence in 80 per cent of the country. And just ahead of a redaction in his report, McChrystal coyly states: 'The insurgents control or contest a significant portion of the country . . .'

McChrystal urges his men to peel off their bullet-proof vests and helmets; he does it himself on some of his village walkabouts. But such is the violence on the route of the K–G Road that US personnel are allowed to travel only in the super-protective MRAP vehicles. Late last year when I embedded at Forward Operating Base Tilman, on the Pakistan border, US Captain Dave Connor impressed me greatly with his soldiering skills, but in almost two weeks his men got beyond the wire just three times—every time hunkering in the MRAPs. On a single patrol he had three IEDs in the space of just a few hundred metres; he had a barrage of rockets into the base. And when he did venture out on a foot patrol, Taliban fighters were on the near ridgelines, as his men were the first foreigners to visit some of the villages in two years. Out there, the Kabul government simply did not exist—the locals saw themselves as part of Pakistan, socially and economically.

McChrystal wants to change coalition operational culture to interact more closely with the population. But from a soldier's point of view a good portion of the population is not to be trusted. In the Zadran country, straddling the K–G Road, an American officer told me: 'The only difference between a Zadran woodcutter and a Talib is that one carries an axe and the other a gun—and when the Talib drops his gun, he becomes the woodcutter's mate.'

McChrystal quotes Afghanistan's defence minister, Abdul Rahim Wardak, whom he finds 'insightful', with his 'victory is within our grasp' spiel. Why would he believe him? This is Karzai-speak, part of a parallel discourse in which seemingly sincere words are uttered for the benefit of the international community while Afghan powerbrokers, corrupt and greedy, go about syphoning off international funding and chopping up the country as they see fit. If just half of the Kabul cabinet genuinely believed as Wardak professes, and if they acted accordingly, this war might be over by now. Instead, the Kabul kleptocracy is in a fine position. Given that Obama's last option is to cut and run entirely, they know the billions will continue to pour in and, one way or another, they'll be able to keep skimming.

McChrystal believes that all will be well when, as he puts it, a new coalition operational culture connects with the powerful will of the Afghan people. But it wasn't the Taliban that showed such contempt for the will of the Afghan people during the recent election campaign—it was their president and Washington's ally, Hamid Karzai. Having said that, McChrystal is refreshing in his unvarnished acknowledgement of the Kabul government's lack of credibility in the eyes of the population: weak state institutions, malign action of powerbrokers (they're the ones that Karzai keeps inviting back into his circle), widespread corruption and abuse of power by various officials (again, friends or friends-of-friends of Karzai).

Especially galling is McChrystal's charge that the coalition had not sufficiently studied the people and their varied needs, identities and grievances. Again, put to one side Washington's empowerment of warlords and militias at the time of the invasion and its arm-twisting to force the result it wanted at the Bonn conference. There has been no shortage of reports on the human rights expectations of Afghans upon being liberated from the Taliban by various arms of the United Nations, by Human Rights Watch and, most courageously of all, by the diminutive Nadir Nadery and his team at the Afghanistan Independent Human Rights Commission; they polled literally thousands of Afghans on their yearning for a break from the violent and corrupt predators who effected their decades of misery, a good number of whom again have their snouts in the trough . . . all at Karzai's invitation.

In his shameless effort to steal the election, Hamid Karzai proved the resilience of traditional Afghanistan horse-trading as politics—and it leaves little room for the aspirations of ordinary Afghans, democracy as we know it, and the institutional checks and balances that we take for granted in Western democracies. You need go no further than Karzai's refusal to acknowledge the rigging of the election when he buckled on Tuesday.

But many Afghans will be offended—rightly—by McChrystal's limited recipe for holding the Karzai gang to account. 'Success does not require perfection,' he writes. 'An improvement in governance that addresses the worst of today's high-level abuse of power, low-level corruption and bureaucratic incapacity will suffice.'

Eight years in, it is incredible that McChrystal could write of the coalition operation: 'Afghan social, political, economic and cultural affairs are complex and poorly understood. [The coalition] does not sufficiently appreciate the dynamics in local communities, or how the insurgency, corruption, incompetent officials, powerbrokers and criminality combine to affect the Afghan population.'

I have to say, it makes you wonder what newspapers they read at the Pentagon and the State Department, because all this has been the stuff of wall-to-wall media reporting from Afghanistan since the fall of the Taliban.

McChrystal rightly challenges as popular myth the notion that Afghans do not want governance. I was taken aback on a recent visit to Gardez, in Paktia province, when a US military intelligence officer invoked the film *Deliverance* in describing the people and their culture. 'This is the West Virginia of Afghanistan,' he told me. 'They moved to the mountains and they did not evolve.'

And I was shocked when one of his colleagues shared sections of a classified study, commissioned from three anthropologists, which likened the local Zadran tribe to others in the border region before stating, and I quote, '. . . from which we may infer that they are utter savages'.

Afghans do want governance—they want good governance. But they have been ripped off every time it's been within their grasp. And the worst rip-off has been in the last eight years, because democracy and good governance were the gifts offered by the West—by governments that supposedly knew about these things.

McChrystal is advising President Obama that the severity of the insurgency threat now surpasses the capabilities of current coalition strategy and that he defines 'defeating the insurgency' as reducing it to a point at which it no longer threatens the viability of the state. Laying out the insurgency's designs on Kandahar and Khost, McChrystal warns: 'Despite the best efforts of the [Kabul government and the coalition], the insurgents currently have the initiative.'

In addressing insurgency funding, he acknowledges the usual sources: drugs, smuggling and donor networks in Pakistan and in the Gulf. He fails to mention the substantive petty cash they derive as a share of the cost of most internationally funded supply and construction projects in the country—extracted at the level of local haulage and construction contractors, sometimes to the tune of 30 per cent of the value of their contract or, as expressed recently by a Kabul transport operator, $A5000 to $A6000 for each fuel tanker travelling the Kabul-to-Kandahar road.

Endless reports of anywhere between a dozen and 100 Taliban dead in constant skirmishes have done nothing to dent the insurgency's fighting power. On the contrary, McChrystal points out, a coalition fixation with violence has masked the insurgency's infiltration into the daily life of ordinary Afghans: setting up local shadow governments, arranging courts and levying taxes. They appoint their own officials and manipulate local grievances. Locals who stand in their way are gunned down or beheaded . . . that doesn't happen too often because, unlike coalition or Kabul threats, a Taliban threat is taken seriously.

In stating that popular enthusiasm for the insurgents 'appears limited'—again, they are McChrystal's words—the general misses the point. In their refusal to back Kabul or the coalition, Afghans are not saying yea or nay on the Taliban in isolation; the call they make as they go about their daily existence is on the credibility of the Taliban compared with that of the Karzai government and the coalition. Eighty per cent of the population is rurally based and they well understand the basics of survival in the simple confines of their personal space and expectation: they want to work their fields in peace, get to the bazaar and back safely; they are not overly fussed about their children getting to school.

In assessing the insurgency, McChrystal declares it, or them, to be sophisticated, organised, adaptive, determined and nuanced across all lines of operations . . . with, he goes on, 'the capacity to exhaust the coalition and to prevent Kabul from governing the country'. Much of his report leads to a conclusion that the very opposite applies to Karzai and the coalition's operations. Especially disturbing is his conclusion: 'There are no clear lines separating insurgent groups, criminal networks (including narcotics networks) and corrupt government officials.' He says, 'Malign actors within the government support insurgent groups directly, support criminal networks that are linked to insurgents, and support corruption that helps feed the insurgency.'

All this didn't come into being with a puff of smoke—it was mismanaged into place by the West. Right now, I'm frightened for Afghanistan. I read McChrystal and I look back over twenty or more assignments in the country since just before September 11 and my fear is that he has missed the boat.

The Taliban is stronger, more violent and more in control than at any time since it was dislodged from Kabul in 2001. Foreign forces, mostly American, are dying at a greater rate and hundreds of billions of dollars are being squandered for no apparent return. Public and political support for the war has peaked and is now declining in the United States and in other coalition countries. As Hamid Karzai continues to demonstrate with his election fraud and his response to its exposure, the Kabul government is rotten from the top.

As Obama considered additional troops early this year, I spoke with one of his generals at the Baghram air base, north of Kabul, on the numbers that might be needed. The general drew on American counter-insurgency doctrine for his back-of-an-envelope calculation.

Totalling the nascent Afghan security forces and adding in the 65,000 foreign forces then in the country, he arrived at a current security establishment of 215,000. But based on the US doctrinal requirement of one security member for every 50 in the population, he came up with a theoretical need for a 600,000-strong combined security force. 'Apply good judgement, technology and other factors and you have to come in at an estimate, I'd say, of about 400,000.'

He lists the non-military negatives: a parasitic government, a feeble economy, rampant corruption, widespread illiteracy, impossible terrain and 1000 years of cultural and tribal complexity. He concludes, 'You're damned right it's complicated.' Reminded that Obama then was looking at a fraction of the nearly 200,000 extras required, the general snapped, 'That's right—go figure.'

Even if Obama gives McChrystal the 40,000 or 65,000 he is requesting, he still doesn't get halfway to filling the gap. Given the fraught politicking around the McChrystal report, I don't see the general getting all that he asks for. I figure there will be a compromise, perhaps some extra troops as the international community changes tack in its regional strategising—perhaps a shift to the option favoured by Vice President Joe Biden, who favours less troops on the ground but greater use of drones and other attack aircraft on the Pakistan–Afghanistan border.

And where might that leave ordinary Afghans, in terms of their well-founded expectations for a decent new life back in 2001? Ironically, one of the successes of the new Afghanistan has been education. The kids that got into school after the flight of the Taliban have had eight years of education—but for what, apart from frustration and anger at the failure of this Western adventure?

Afghanistan has already been dubbed Obama's Vietnam. Now McChrystal has dropped what most likely will be the weightiest foreign-policy decision on the president's desk: escalate or fail, as my colleague Dexter Filkins put it in the *New York Times* recently.

A recent American intelligence estimate put the insurgency's full-time fighting strength at no less than 25,000, up 25 per cent on the previous year. There should never have been a debate about how strong the insurgency is. They were on the run in 2001 and they came back, only because they were allowed to.

IRAQ

THE DEVILS THEY KNEW

Baghdad, Iraq
26 July 2003

They seem ungrateful. The world's media are filled with gruesome pictures of the dead Uday and Qusay Hussein, a gift from Washington, and all the Iraqis do is complain about the terrible reversal in their day-to-day lives.

Sacked government industrial workers protest at one Baghdad intersection, demanding to be returned to the public payroll so they can feed their families. Two blocks up, hundreds of prisoners recently released from Saddam's cruel jails demand to know why the soldiers who sustained Saddam are being paid by Washington while they, the victims of the regime, are not.

Washington just doesn't get it. Even the prospect of the early capture or death of Saddam will not reduce the intolerable summer heat that Iraqis suffer with little air-conditioning or refrigeration because the United States' war against Saddam wrecked the electricity grid.

The promise of a new Iraqi democracy is a blurred bauble when the Americans threaten to confiscate the machine-gun

Mohammed al-Ezedeen has taken to carrying since three of his friends were executed by different gangs of car thieves, and when a businessman, Faras al-Hadi, can count off half-a-dozen friends and neighbours who have been victims of Baghdad's new wave of car thefts and home robberies. Mustafa Abdul Hamid says, 'I can't leave my home after sunset, but . . .' and the 68-year-old pauses to mimic a drum roll, 'they tell me I have freedom of speech.'

It's 10 a.m. and already it's so hot at a road-stop on the drive in from Jordan that dogs lying in the shade quiver like jelly. A little further on, you know that this corner of Iraq remains in total darkness because the pylons that used to deliver electricity are bent and buckled, staggering like drunks.

Highway robbery is so prevalent that travellers sit bolt upright, scanning the horizon because every vehicle may be an attacker. United Nations drivers have been warned not to drive over even a Coke can because it might contain an explosive.

When you arrive in Baghdad, the city is a military-run pigsty. The charred hulks of looted government buildings, some stripped to shells, are a memorial to the lack of US planning for after the attack. Rubbish burns in the streets and by 6 p.m. the exotic old heart of the city around Rashid Street, where crowds would flock to some of Baghdad's most colourful teahouses, is surrendered to the gangs. Drive through and you can smell the danger.

There were some postwar improvements in water and power supplies. But, according to a United Nations background briefing, they have been set back by sabotage attacks from the anti-American resistance. Hospitals are functioning 'more or less', but are hampered in their efforts to get supplies because there are no communications.

Now there is a new health crisis. It is estimated that there has been a doubling in the number of children dying from diarrhoea-related diseases. In Basra, in the south, last year's

29 cases of cholera is already 100, reflecting an estimated doubling in the amount of sewage flowing into the country's waterways.

Baghdad has become a city of queues: former Iraqi soldiers queuing in the broiling sun to get paid; others in a separate line, hoping to sign up for the new American-run army; people wanting jobs; housewives wanting cooking gas; motorists needing petrol or waiting to snake through another US checkpoint; and the US military on patrol because it's too dangerous for lone vehicles.

Communications and media are so bad that the Americans have great difficulty getting their story across or putting down rumours, such as the US troops use their wraparound sunglasses to look through the clothing of Iraqi women to see their naked bodies.

The American bombs so pulverised the local telephone system that the best way to contact someone ten blocks away is to make a satellite phone call to London to be automatically patched back to Baghdad through another sat-phone line. You could drive uptown, but traffic becomes so gridlocked that it can take 75 minutes to crawl 100 metres.

The Al-Rasheed Hotel, once the home of visiting journalists and diplomats, and all the other government buildings commandeered by the Americans hunker behind a maze of earthen barriers and tangles of razor wire.

Abdul Jabbouri, a 36-year-old teacher, said: 'The Americans have robbed us of our nights. I love the freedom of the day walking down the street and not being pestered by a government stooge demanding to know my name and whether I'm up to date on my national service. But the security crisis forces all business to close at 3 p.m. and after 6 p.m. it's just too dangerous to be out.'

When Faras al-Hadi criticised Saddam obliquely in an interview with me late last year, he was rebuked by the regime. And when I went looking for him this week a banner stretched across the front of his consumer-goods business, in the teeming Bab al-Sharqi district, apologising because the looters had cleaned him out and now he was operating from temporary premises on a quieter stretch of Sadoun Street.

Dressed immaculately in Western attire—neat buttoned-down collar, smart dark tie and a silk jacket—he perched on the edge of a sofa in his makeshift office, saying: 'We were living a tragedy before the war and now we are living a different tragedy. In a way we were happy before. But now we are unhappy and it's going to get worse. Communications are improving but power and security will take a long time.

'But it's the political situation. There are so many parties and some of them are getting violent. The fundamentalists use violence and it's frightening. They threaten cinemas, CD shops and alcohol outlets that they will be attacked if they do not close down.

'There is no sense that the United States is in control of the political process or anything else. Most people—I would say about 90 per cent—are against them being here. But now we don't want them to leave, because we do not have a police or military force. So people are saying that life under Saddam was better. We didn't expect this.

'What we have gained is a lot of newspapers and political parties and satellite receivers, but it's not really freedom—it's chaos. I know I can say what I like to whomever I like now, but what does that mean if I can't earn the minimum I need?'

Wamidh Nadhmi, a political scientist who was game to criticise Saddam before the war, also believes that the Iraqi Governing Council is doomed to failure. Claiming that he declined to become a member, he said: 'In the Saddam years we had no public opinion. We learnt nothing about the operation of government ministries. Now there are more than 100 newspapers from which we still learn nothing. There is no public discussion of the American plans.'

Ali Abdullah, who helped set up the Freed Prisoners' Association, echoed a general wariness about those who have gone feet-first into this US experiment in democracy: 'The parties think only of their own interests—each thinks of its own gangs, its fortunes and a lunge at authority. The Americans are forgetting about most of the people. Most of us have been here all our lives and we are poor, and hungry. But they deal only with the rich, the powerful and the exiles who have returned.'

Much of the local criticism is echoed in a Center for Strategic and International Studies report commissioned by the US defence secretary, Donald Rumsfeld, which was released last week. Warning that the next year would be decisive and that the next three months were crucial in the battle to win the support of the Iraqi people, it called for a huge boost in resources so that a civilian-led, rather than a military-led, rebuilding might be executed while big US-troop numbers remained in Iraq.

Mustafa Abdul Hamid, the technician who laments that he can't go out at night, was not consulted by the CSIS team that visited Iraq, but he thought for a while about what a senior US military officer described to me as its carrot-and-stick approach to stabilising Iraq. Then he asked this question: 'Do you accept a coffee from the hand of a man who has a gun in his other hand? We are beholden to the United States for ridding us of Saddam, but they just don't understand us.'

BAGHDAD WITHOUT
A MAP

Baghdad, Iraq
23 August 2003

The United Nations is packing up. In the wake of Tuesday's suicide-bomb attack on its Baghdad headquarters, almost half of its distraught staff are expected by this weekend to have opted to leave or to have been ordered out of the country for their safety.

The attack, which killed at least 23 and injured more than 100, has ratcheted up a pervasive sense of insecurity in Baghdad. Officials, from the United Nations Secretary-General Kofi Annan down, have been insisting it is business as usual, but United Nations teams have been seen heading away from hotels with their bags packed. On Thursday a senior United Nations official, Ramiro Lopes da Silva, confirmed in Baghdad that the numbers were likely to fall from 350 to about 200 by this weekend.

The United States has stepped up its patrols across the country and by Wednesday night American teams had materialised at city hotels used by the United Nations, unwinding long, loose springs of razor wire and moving tanks into place.

A shiny-faced young soldier manning a barricade near a clutch of small hotels in the south-east of the city told me: 'We just don't know who'll get bombed next.' Nobody does. But chances are the next bomb will be even more spectacular and it is likely the target will be another significant symbol of Western power in a city that wears its occupation badly.

The escalating selection of targets by the resistance is as menacing as it is studious. Initially, the hits were small-time and almost exclusively on US troops. Then came low-key sabotage of infrastructure. There followed the killings of a few foreign contract workers and a couple of journalists. After that the Jordanian embassy was bombed, representing one of the weakest governments the United States might attempt to bully into providing troops to put an Arab face on the occupation. Then more daring strikes on infrastructure—oil and water—and now the United Nations itself, the big daddy of the army of humanitarian organisations that flock to people and places in crisis.

Speculation on the next target is endless. Will it be the exposed and unprotected Al-Hamra Hotel, where one of the biggest contingents of foreign press gather around the swimming pool in the cool of the evening, or one of the foreign businesses lured here by the whiff of the reconstruction dollar? And speculation about the perpetrators, particularly by key members of the US administration, is veering dangerously towards a fundamental error in understanding the challenge that confronts the United States in postwar Iraq.

It suits the White House to brand what is happening in Iraq as terrorism. It sits neatly with the now-discredited case that it used to justify war against Iraq. And US credibility has been so devalued by lies and half-truths on the road to war that it is difficult to assess what it does reveal about the security situation, especially after it has passed through the Washington filters.

The smoke had not even cleared from the United Nations and Jordanian embassy bombings when the US-appointed adminis-trator of Iraq, Paul Bremer, blamed the attacks on Ansar al-Islam, a group connected to Al-Qaeda and to the former regime; and Paul Wolfowitz blamed Al-Qaeda and Baathist 'tail-enders'. Only Bernie Kerik, the former New York police commissioner charged with rebuilding the Iraqi police force, said it was too early to tell.

The Iraqi fightback against the US occupation bears many of the hallmarks of other national resistance movements: wounded national pride (think France), decades of tutoring in hatred of the eventual occupying force (think Palestine) and foreign assistance (think IRA; think US funding for the anti-Soviet resistance in Afghanistan). Members of the resistance I have interviewed made no pretence about the thousands of foreigners, all of them Arab, who have joined the fight. But they denied any active participation by Al-Qaeda, Ansar al-Islam or Saddam Hussein. They were Sunnis and they argued that they had thousands of their own people fighting and willing to fight for a nationally controlled resistance that had banned former Baathists from any leadership position.

Bremer has taken the recovery of foreign passports from dead resistance fighters as proof of Al-Qaeda's intervention in Iraq, but what is far from clear about the foreigners is who sent them and for whom they are fighting. Their kind flocked to Afghanistan from across the Arab homeland to join Al-Qaeda, but no one knows if they have come to Iraq to help the indigenous resistance or as express agents of Al-Qaeda. Saudi authorities this week reportedly claimed that as many as 3000 young men had 'disappeared' from the kingdom in the space of two months and that presumably they were in Iraq.

Much is being made of the sophistication of the bombs now being used. But they are standard guerilla fare; Al-Qaeda does not have the sole patent and the resistance fighters I interviewed volunteered that they were using bomb-making manuals from the disbanded Iraqi military.

Much of the anger and emotion in Iraq today is directed at the Americans. There has been no public outcry at the death of Iraqi civilians in resistance attacks and ordinary Iraqis cite the same reasons for the resistance as the fighters themselves: nationalism, Islam and payback. Saddam does not get a look-in.

A poll by the Iraq Centre for Research and Strategic Studies a couple of weeks ago found that more than half of those polled blamed the violence on American provocation. In key towns in the so-called Sunni triangle, Ramadi and Falluja, the blame rate was as high as 90 per cent.

Writing in the *New York Times* this week, the Harvard terrorism expert Jessica Stern said: 'While there is no single root cause of terrorism, perceived humiliation and a lack of political and economic opportunities make young men susceptible to extremism. It can evolve easily into violence when government institutions are weak and there is money available to pay for a holy war.'

The United States does have access to a textbook example of how Iraqis see and live their lives. If it looked closely at Saddam's years in power, it would see that the dictator's horrible big picture did not intrude on the day-to-day, little-picture existence of most Iraqis.

Like Saddam, the US administration here is preoccupied with the big picture: a new constitution, elections and a study on the feasibility of re-flooding the southern marshlands. But all of this does little to assuage the anger in millions of households that were robbed, by the war, of services they usually took for granted under Saddam: civil security, power, water, telephones, cooking gas, petrol and diesel, an economy and jobs, and more.

Iraqis got around Saddam by hunkering and turning a blind eye to his big-picture emasculation of the nation. The American big picture is just as remote for them, but they bear the brunt of the little-picture emasculation every day under the gaze of an ineffectual puppet administration installed by the United States.

In time we'll know more about the resistance and the extent to which neighbouring countries are manipulating events, and which non-Iraqi terrorist groups are hitching a ride. But amid all the hue and cry about Al-Qaeda and Ansar al-Islam this week, hardly anyone noticed the sage quote from an anonymous administration official in Washington: 'Now we're dealing with a guerilla war, not terrorism.'

THE MEN WHO RULE IRAQ

Samawa Desert, Iraq
8 November 2003

A s silver stars sneak into the night, the date palms become
etched against a blackening sky. In the east, a brilliant orange
light hangs like a sun that just won't set—it's the flare at an oil
refinery deep in the south of Iraq.

We're on the edge of the Samawa Desert, in a huge, open-sided
Bedouin tent that is the centre of Sheikh Ali bin Mohammed
al-Menshed's existence. The refinery is a good kilometre off,
but such is the ferocity of the flare that it casts an eerie glow in
the domain of the sheikh, who is trying to wind down after a
long day.

He whips the black-and-white checked *keffiyeh* from his head
and plonks it next to the ball he has made of his *abaya*, a stylish,
gold-trimmed woollen cloak which he wears over his snow-white
dishdasha, even in the searing half-century heat of summer.

His AK-47, the barrel and butt shiny from regular handling,
lies on the mat before him. A packet of Pine cigarettes rests on

the flat of the gun's butt; his Thuraya satellite phone, with its antenna nimbly pointing into the night, stands in the crook where the AK-47's banana-shaped magazine fits into the gun.

The sheikh is hungry; he orders the slaughter of a sheep to feed himself and about twenty others. He is tired; he yawns frequently, each time throwing his head back to make a noise like the gravelly gargle of one of his prized camels. It's been a long day for the head of the Rizi tribe. It's 9 p.m. and he has just returned from his last engagement—adding the considerable weight of his office to an inter-tribal marriage proposal by accompanying the prospective groom to one of the formal meetings at which, peacock-like, families that might be joined in marriage preen before each other in a show of breeding and wealth.

But in his absence, problems have piled up: a Syrian driver stumbles in, pleading that his truck and its cargo have been stolen by members of Sheikh Ali's tribe; a wizened old Bedouin is distressed because a moneylender is demanding settlement of a debt incurred by the Bedouin's recently deceased son; there are several angry complaints about a get-rich-quick scheme adopted by one of Sheikh Ali's sub-tribes—they have taken to demanding the payment of tribal compensation for crimes they know full well have not been committed by those they accuse.

Dogs go berserk out in the shadows, among the eucalyptus and tamarisk trees. 'That's our classical music,' says the sheikh, laughing off their incessant noise. He has not eaten all day, but tiredness triumphs over hunger and Sheikh Ali bin Mohammed al-Menshed disappears off to bed.

It's close to midnight when the mutton, with rice and a rich broth, finally is brought to where we have whiled away the evening, sitting on colourful oriental mats. The women who cook it are unseen, and small boys bring pitchers of water and blocks of soap for the ritualistic hand-washing before the men-only crowd gathers around the huge platter of food.

While we'd been waiting for dinner, there had been a whispered discussion about the power of the jowly-faced man who had just wandered off into the night, his gun slung over his shoulder. 'Sheikh Ali can fix all of these problems,' intoned a man in a black turban. 'But only with the help of Allah,' said another, as the smoke from his handmade cigarette curled up in the night.

The Western examination of Iraqi society in the wake of the overthrow of Saddam Hussein has been intense, but way too narrow. What seems to be an almost desperate American drive to balance the competing interests of Sunnis, Shiites and Kurds is smothering even the most cursory investigation of the inordinate and more deeply rooted power of the country's tribal sheikhs— men like the enigmatic Ali bin Mohammed al-Menshed.

To better understand tribal Iraq, think about this. If it had not been for a decision by the sheikhs that Saddam Hussein was finished and that their tribesmen would not fight for him, in March of this year the United States might have met an Iraqi military machine that stood and fought, with far bloodier and more protracted consequences than the skirmishes that we now call the Iraq War.

There is a significant body of opinion in Iraq and the Middle East that the sheikhs have the power to scale back, if not to end, the violent resistance against the US occupation; that the continuing attacks on US forces and the provision of shelter for Saddam are a calculated opening bid by the sheikhs in a negotiation process in which they want the United States to recognise their traditional role as keepers of the peace in Iraq.

During my extensive examination of the power of Iraq's sheikhs and their tribal culture in July and August, the same experts argued that it was the sheikhs, not American forces, who would create a secure environment in which the rebuilding of Iraq might develop the momentum necessary to sustain itself; and that unless a significant number of the sheikhs were happy in their 'me-and-my-tribe' view of the world, they could wreck anything Washington might seek to rebuild. And finally, Saddam Hussein cannot stay on the run without the knowledge of at least some of the sheikhs or of people known to them. If the sheikhs were handled properly by the Americans, they might even deliver to Washington a much-needed trophy.

Use your mind's eye to erase the existing national boundaries in the region—these are lines drawn in the sand in earlier Western efforts to protect vested interests, notably oil. In the centuries before they were drawn, this area was carved into warring tribal fiefdoms. Today, the power of the sheikhs and their territorial grip is diminished, but they still have a firm grasp on the life of their people.

The sheikhs were born to rule according to ancient desert customs. Through history, they have been the brokers deciding who would rule between the great rivers: the Tigris and Euphrates. For centuries they have been the swing voters in a land that has stubbornly resisted all attempts at democracy. Even Saddam Hussein discovered—far too late—that he needed the extraordinary ability of the sheikhs to impose law and order over huge swaths of territory, but only if there was something in it for them.

There are about 150 tribes in today's Iraq, perhaps 30 to 40 of whose sheikhs form a heavyweight division that presides over the affairs of about 2000 clans and sub-tribes. In all, they speak for almost three-quarters of the country's 25 million people.

The code by which the tribes live is as enduring as it is romantic and brutal. Pride and honour rule the sheikhs' hearts; survival and revenge rule their heads. The sheikhs have an uncanny knack of picking winners—often switching their loyalty halfway through a dispute or battle. But they will think of their tribe before the nation and, unashamedly, they are greedy.

And, over time, the tribes have been one of the great constants in the life of an entire region which has been racked by conflict; a global region in which, according to an American Arabist who requested anonymity because he is employed by the United States in Baghdad, governments have made it their business to use and control the centrifugal impulses of tribal society. 'Saddam did this pretty well,' he tells me.

The tribes pre-date Islam. The forefathers of those who live in today's Iraq migrated north-east from the arid Arabian Peninsula, seeking the bountiful waters of the Tigris and Euphrates. The prophet Mohammed railed against their 'rotten ways'. The British thought they could be co-opted against the Ottoman empire. They could—but only briefly and, in 1920, they revolted against London, too, and so began a cruel 38-year war of attrition to rid old Mesopotamia of the British.

Today's sheikhs talk about legendary figures as though they knew them: St John Philby, the father of the spy Kim, a British diplomat who careered about the deserts on a motorcycle and drew the lines in the sand that became today's disputed national borders; Gertrude Bell, the Arabist, diplomat and cartographer who was dubbed the uncrowned queen of Iraq; and the man in whose shadow they all walked, Lawrence of Arabia.

Lawrence's 1920 criticism of Britain's lunge at Iraq as 'not far from a disaster' proved correct. Now, more than 80 years later, and five months after Washington's lunge at Saddam Hussein, there's a curious indifference in the American bunkers in Baghdad to the ideas in a caustic explanation for that disaster by the reed-like Bell, when she wrote in a letter at the time: 'I suppose we have underestimated the fact that this country is really an inchoate mass of tribes which can't as yet be reduced to any system. The Turks didn't govern, and we have tried to govern—and failed.'

Arguably, Saddam Hussein failed, too. Those of us who were in Baghdad for the war earlier this year listened in puzzlement to his last speeches, which invariably opened with a litany of flowery greetings to individual tribes. But he left his run too late. Tribe loyalty was always a pragmatic or commercial proposition and by then it had become wafer-thin.

The sheikhs were in no mood to respond to Saddam's last empty entreaties. The reality for them was that there was little left to be squeezed out of Saddam, so why line up their brothers and sons to fight for him? Why protect him? Saddam Hussein might be going down, but the tribes of Iraq would not go down with him, not when the forces of the world's richest and most powerful nation were marching on Baghdad.

It's 8 a.m. and Sheikh Ali seems rested and replete after a breakfast of bread, fried liver and thick buffalo cream. He sits cross-legged in his *mudhif*—the black, 50-metre-long tent in which we spent the previous evening. This is where he hears petitions, dispenses justice and deals with the issues of the day.

Sheikh Ali goes to and from each problem. The ritual is rigid, the manners ornate. All must rise to greet each new arrival with a handshake, or a kiss, and a personal greeting. All remain standing until the last such greeting, and when all have resumed their seats, there is a greeting for the new arrival, which translates loosely as 'Bless your day'. Barefoot retainers offer bitter-flavoured coffee, served in tiny quantities from blackened pots.

Those who come armed lay their weapons on the edge of the mats on which they sat. And in a running commentary—for my benefit—on the morning's debate, there is a great class-consciousness and the attachment of much weight to the words of those who are described as 'respectable' or 'of noble blood'.

The old Bedouin shuffles off, with a promise that a mediator will come to talk to him and the moneylender. The Syrian truckie is anxious—he produces a letter from his employer warning that his home will be confiscated to cover the cost of the lost truck. But the truck has been found, located in an overnight search of the nearby villages by Sheikh Ali's guards.

The head of the tribal clan to which the thieves belong has been summoned. He sits two places to the right of Sheikh Ali, complaining that he does not command sufficient respect to be able to retrieve the Syrian truck. He is met with unbridled anger. Sheikh Ali explodes: 'What am I to do—dismiss you and your family from our territory? I have a punishment worse than death for these thieves of yours! I know their names and, if the truck is not delivered back here within 48 hours, I will have the men arrested in front of their women and we will make those women come and watch as we hand them over to the Americans!'

I'm informed repeatedly that shame in the eyes of women is a greater punishment to an Iraqi tribesman than death. An old man sitting beside me jolts upright when he hears the sheikh's threat, muttering in Arabic, 'Shameful; so dishonourable!'

The sheikhs give and they take, so the art of the tribal leader is about striking a balance. Iraqis who joined me—either as interpreters or drivers—on a tour of *mudhifs* around the country claim to be able to discern the sincere from the hypocritical; and they grade each sheikh in what they insist are six critical tests: hospitality, generosity, reputation, self-respect, bravery and helping the poor.

The result is a disturbing twist of values. Sheikh Hamid Shwash al-Jabouri, whose tribal lands are just north of Baghdad, is criticised more for the quality of the lunch he serves than for the fact that he has recently ordered a father to execute his own son. The sheikhs of Saddam's own Albu Nasar tribe earn more condemnation for the apparent insincerity in their offer of a meal and a bed for the night than for freeloading on the old regime or for their taste for foreign women and whisky. And the only shock as my Iraqi companions observe Sheikh Ali is when he gives money to the poor—the notes he peels from a wad in his breast pocket are Kuwaiti dinars. They believe his alms-giving should be in Iraqi dinars.

Maybe it's too early for some Iraqis to engage in the sort of self-examination that might question the extent to which they acknowledged or even cooperated with Saddam Hussein in the running of his regime. But there's a disturbing and convenient sense of denial among the sheikhs about the horror that often was perpetrated in Saddam's name—and often by members of their own tribes.

Just as Saddam's two daughters (now exiled in Jordan) seemed to forget that their father had both their husbands murdered as they sent him televised expressions of love in early August, the mayor of Abu Ghraib forgot all about his town's most appalling fixture—Saddam's jail and execution centre for political prisoners—when he listed its key features for me. A senior sheikh defends all but a handful at the top of the regime on the grounds that the rest were merely following orders.

But Saddam could see in the sheikhs what Washington apparently does not want to see. In the words of the former dictator's biographer, Said Arburish: 'Iraqi family and tribal connections are supreme. They come ahead of ideology. They come ahead of commitment to the nation-state; they come ahead of all commitments.' Coming from the tribes, Saddam was acutely aware of the potency of their power. So much so that he set out to destroy them in the early years of his regime: he executed and jailed key figures; he outlawed key elements of their culture; and he ordered big internal migrations in the hope of diluting the power of individual sheikhs.

But he turned to the sheikhs when he was confronted with the collapse of the state around him and a crisis of domestic security after the war against Iran and his 1991 defeat in Kuwait. The result was a power-sharing deal that stirred tribal memories of a more glorious and powerful past. Saddam's crippled forces were unable to secure the country, so he paid the sheikhs to organise their tribesmen to do what they saw as their traditional law-and-order duty.

A prominent sheikh tells me: 'Saddam lavished gifts on the trusted sheikhs—three and four cars and a house for a general or for high-ranking party members who were in the tribes. He'd give them farms and write off their bad debts. After a meeting, he'd send them a gift of maybe 5 million dinars [$A3600]; suddenly, schools and hospitals were being built in their towns and villages.'

THE BLOOD KORAN

Baghdad, Iraq
18 December 2003

This book is causing ructions in postwar Baghdad. Its classic Arabic decoration is spellbinding. But there is something grotesque about the burnished brown ink in the calligrapher's exquisite text: it is the blood of Saddam Hussein.

The former dictator's brutality was matched only by an obsession with his proximity to the greats of Arab history: Saladin, the legendary twelfth-century Muslim warrior who, like Saddam, hailed from the sandy wastes of Tikrit; the great kings of Babylon, Hammurabi and Nebuchadnezzar; and Alexander the Great. And, it seems, even Mohammed; for this is no ordinary publication—it is the holy Koran, the teachings of the Prophet.

Until the fall of Baghdad in April, all 640 pages were displayed in individual, gilt-edged frames in a pavilion on an island that sits on a man-made lake at the Mother of All Battles mosque. Its great metal doors were double-locked and viewing by a select few was by appointment only. But as looters rampaged across the city, the mosque's frightened clerics packed up the blood Koran and rushed it into hiding.

Ironically, much of Iraq's treasured literary and spiritual manuscripts and the archives of a turbulent 7000-year history were reduced to smouldering ash when the National Library was torched in April. Scholars weep at the loss, but now a committee of 25 Muslim thinkers has been appointed to decide if this lonely survivor should also have gone on the bonfire. Their task is not easy because of an appalling contradiction: for Muslims, it is heretical to render the Koran in blood, an impurity that should be washed away. On the other hand, the Koran defines absolutely their religious beliefs and culture—it cannot be destroyed.

The blue and white glaze of the imposing Mother of All Battles mosque lures me on every visit to Baghdad. It is here that the Koran for which, over a period of months, the former president donated 24 litres of 'ink' is stored. It was hot when I returned after the fall of Baghdad to find the gates locked. Just across the road from the gates, a man invited me into the welcome shade of a tree. As he gave me a glass of water he alerted me to today's scholarly difficulty, saying: 'It is forbidden to write the Koran in blood, but how could we destroy the holy book from God?'

When I went back again last week, Ala Saleh, the imam, who I was meeting for the first time, stonewalled, insisting bluntly that the Koran was 'gone'. But purely by chance my entry into the mosque courtyard coincided with the arrival of a shaky old man, who alighted from his car under the gaze of a bodyguard. He introduced himself as Abdul Kahar al-Any, a professor of Islamic thought at the University of Baghdad.

The professor intervened on my behalf. After his heated exchange with the imam, it was agreed that if I returned the following day one page of the Koran would be brought from its hiding place—the whereabouts of which Mr Saleh insisted was a secret even from him. The page he produced was the opening of the second book of the Koran, the Surat al-Bakara.

It was wrapped in a towel and had been removed from its frame but the page loses none of its curious intensity by being sealed between two sheets of perspex. The blood lettering is about 2 centimetres tall and the broad decorative borders are dazzling: blues, light and dark; spots of red and pink; and swirling highlights in black.

I was allowed to hold it. And until yesterday it seemed that we might even be allowed to photograph the work. But in the afternoon a message came from the committee of Islamic thinkers: 'too divisive'.

In his office at the University of Baghdad, Professor Al-Any set out his argument against the book. 'Saddam is not a holy man, so his blood is dirty. But some of the scholars say it is okay because in one of his battles, Mohammed's warriors gave thanks for victory with the blood of the enemy on their clothes. I don't accept this. Such a book has never been written in the time since the Prophet, so why should Saddam do it? But there are no guidelines—who among the scholars since would have thought it necessary to write rules for such a thing?'

Some Iraqis say that the Koran emerged from a contract Saddam made with God: he prayed that if he and Iraq survived the 1991 Gulf War, he would write the Koran in his own blood. Back at the Mother of All Battles mosque, Mr Saleh was as perplexed as he was cautious. He asked, 'Why would Saddam do such a thing? I can't understand it.' But asked what should become of the book, which he estimated might fetch $US1 million ($A1.34 million) a page among collectors of personal effects from great names in history, he deferred to the committee of scholars.

Said Ali Alwaah is a revered Shiite cleric. In the 1980s he was imprisoned by Saddam and for 23 years the regime kept him under tight house arrest. Now free to speak, he is in no doubt about the sin of the blood Koran. Falling back on a literal reading of Koranic advice on what to do with that which is *haram* (sinful), he declared: 'This is Saddam's black magic. The Koran is about gold and silver—not something as impure as blood.'

THE BUSH DOCTRINE TURNED ON ITS HEAD

Baghdad, Iraq
22 March 2004

It is late at night and there is some gunfire out in the city, but by its own noisy yardstick Baghdad is eerily quiet for the first anniversary of the start of the war. The loudest noise came from Washington: George Bush's troubled plea for unity in the face of world terrorism. Disagreements 'among old and valued friends', he said disingenuously, 'belong to the past'.

Bush is working to corral his postwar coalition in Iraq. But as it frays at the edges, British diplomats are working up a new attempt to legitimise the Iraq campaign with a proper United Nations mandate. Consider: The Spanish are pulling out unless the United Nations takes over, and President Aleksander Kwasniewski of Poland says he was 'taken for a ride' by the United States on Saddam Hussein's supposed weapons of mass destruction. The Koreans have baulked at moving 3000 troops to Kirkuk in the north of Iraq because they fear for their security; and when the Japanese arrived in the south to protect the Iraqi people they promptly wrote a cheque for $US95 million for the local tribes to protect them from the Iraqi people. Honduras is sticking with its plan to withdraw 300 soldiers in July, and when Bush recently met the Dutch prime minister, Jan Peter Balkenende pointedly refused to say how long he would leave his 1300 troops in Iraq.

Small beer, perhaps. But it is all symptomatic of rising anger and tension among the old and valued friends at the insistence of Bush—who may well be judged by history to have been the ventriloquist's doll for the ideologues around him—and a sense that his very necessary war on terrorism did not need to be swamped by war and its uncertain aftermath in Iraq.

And the old friends just get bolshier. The French foreign minister, Dominique de Villepin, was straight-up in his assessment of the first year. 'The war in Iraq was a mistake, I would even say, a blunder. We cannot fail to see that there are two centres that feed terrorism today: the first is the Middle East crisis, the second is Iraq.' Right behind him was the European Commission president, Romano Prodi. 'It happens in Iraq as elsewhere—Istanbul, Moscow, Madrid. The terrorism that the war in Iraq was supposed to stop is infinitely more powerful today than it was a year ago.'

There have been at least as many terrorist operations in the past year as there were in the previous twelve months, and that is with an estimated two-thirds of Al-Qaeda's known leadership dead or behind bars. The arch villain Osama bin Laden remains free and his terrorist organisation has morphed into something even more dangerous than what existed before the September 11 attacks in New York and Washington. Previously, bin Laden's lieutenants went out into the world, buying into terrorist plots they thought to be worthwhile investments. Subsequently, the Bush administration, with echoes from Tony Blair and John

Howard, has enhanced the myth that it is all and only bin Laden's work.

What seems to have happened is more insidious. The bin Laden chain of command has been superseded by a sort of McDonald's of terrorism, franchise cells and groups that want to be like Al-Qaeda, carrying a torch for the man in the cave without ever receiving direct orders. The word simply goes out in the Arab media and is acted upon without a specific order for action. And when they strike, they pack the punch by claiming that it was done in the name of Al-Qaeda.

The CIA director, George Tenet, told the US Senate as much this month when he said: 'A serious threat will remain for the foreseeable future, with or without Al-Qaeda in the picture.' And Blair's special representative for Iraq, Jeremy Greenstock, almost as though he was surprised by the outcome, applied the Tenet dictum to Iraq when he warned of the damage to the country and its people from terrorism. 'Something new has grown in this area. It has happened in Afghanistan, in Pakistan, in Colombia, in the Middle East peace process and now it's threatening Western Europe—it's already happened in Madrid. Iraq is a now a theatre where they're trying to maximise this damage.' Together, they are admitting that the war in Iraq has helped Al-Qaeda and its followers.

The hotel from which I write, The Palestine, was crowded with the first of the foreign fighters to arrive in Iraq in the first week of war last year. They have long since fanned out around the country and they are thought to number several hundred, working with the desperate and the nationalist in Iraq to capitalise on Arab anger as they challenge the Western invasion of a Muslim country and, at the same time, attempt to split the Bush coalition.

In Iraq and elsewhere, they have turned the Bush doctrine on its head. Just as Bush went after the terrorists and those who harboured them, and threatened those who would not support him, the terrorist attacks in Iraq and beyond have been against those who have helped Bush.

The protest marches around the world this weekend and the fraying at the edges of the Iraq coalition, especially the outcome of the Spanish election, raise a dire question: is terrorism winning over democracy? Superficially, maybe.

But something more fundamental is happening, something very democratic: leaders are being held to account, because the Bush case for war in Iraq has been proved to be a lie that was supported by Blair and Howard. We were told the war was to get rid of Saddam's weapons of mass destruction—they did not exist. It was to save us from the link between Saddam and Al-Qaeda—there was none. This was to be a quick war; the American-led invasion forces were to be welcomed with songs and flowers—but they will be stuck here for years to come and it might be a civil war that gives birth to the new Iraq, not Bush's liberation.

Some good has come of it all. Saddam is gone and Libya has come into line. Syria is nervous. But North Korea and Iran still play nuclear hardball, and the Palestine–Israel stalemate continues to complicate daily life right across the Middle East. And US military resources and world attention have been distracted almost totally from the fight against terrorism.

The goal of freedom for all is fine, even if Bush came to it for the Iraqis thirteen years too late and only after the rest of his spurious case for war fell apart. And it is not enough to drape the country in the flag, to insist that 'we must support the troops' by not debating why they are here, and to have the aimless rah-rah of the State of the Union address. That is the sort of theatre Saddam engaged in.

Enough has leaked from the White House to confirm that the war was a decision made before it was justified. This weekend there was more evidence: Richard Clarke, Bush's counter-terrorism coordinator in September 2001, told American *60 Minutes* that within 24 hours of the September 11 attacks the administration was convinced that Al-Qaeda was responsible, but the defence secretary, Donald Rumsfeld, had complained that 'there aren't any good targets in Afghanistan and there are lots of good targets in Iraq'.

Rumsfeld obsesses about uncertainty. As explained to the *Atlantic Monthly* by one of his deputies, Douglas Feith: 'The need to deal strategically with uncertainty; the inability to predict the future; the limits on our knowledge and the limits on our intelligence.' That's a windy way of saying that the end justifies the means.

But people are not as stupid as the White House would like. Just as Spanish voters saw what their government was doing—using the Madrid bombing for an election-eve smash at ETA, the Basque separatists, when everything pointed to Al-Qaeda—the brutalised people of Iraq are the same. They are indeed grateful to be rid of Saddam, but they loathe this occupation; they deeply resent the security crisis it has visited on them; they feel humiliated by it. And they openly mock the superpower that said: 'It'll all come right.'

The United States in Iraq is still demonstrating what it cannot do, not what it can do. Already it is retreating to the safety of its 'hard' bases and talking up the competence of Iraq's incompetent new security and emergency services, which have had less training than the security staff at your local Target store, so that it can foist the mess on them when sovereignty is handed over on 30 June.

But the United States is so entrenched in Iraq that it is hard to see it being able to devote its full resources to fighting terrorism any time soon.

THE MAKING OF
A MONSTER

Al-Zarqa, Jordan
16 October 2004

We're still in the chalky hills of Amman. But driving north, the desert chic of the Jordanian capital quickly fades to become the cinder-block grime of a sprawling industrial quarter. Here, helpful locals urge us to keep the car doors locked—even as we drive around. There are only a few roadside hawkers, their grapes, watermelons and luscious figs stewing in the midday sun. And a couple of katip men are idle—they sit under faded calico umbrellas with battered typewriters on rickety card tables, waiting for illiterates who'll pay them to write a letter or fill out a form.

Any doubt we've crossed into a different place and space is expunged when Bilat, the driver, slows his clapped-out Kia minibus to negotiate a ruptured and flooding sewer line. As a foul odour fills the bus, he jokes: 'Ah, French perfume . . .' A few hundred metres down the hill, after a threadbare mosque that has none of the customary glitter of the well-heeled end of town, and beyond idle factories and fences festooned with litter that couldn't get away, he formally declares: 'This Al-Zarqa . . . the home of Abu Musab al-Zarqawi.'

The United States has a $25 million bounty on Zarqawi's head. And Washington now bills him as the spearhead of the bloody insurgency that is wrecking virtually all efforts by the US military and the Washington-backed interim regime in Baghdad to assert authority and to impose security in 'liberated' Iraq. He has strewn fear throughout a war-numbed nation, and a nervy and restless foreign community in Baghdad, as grainy videos reveal him personally hacking off the heads of terrified hostages—reading aloud religious tracts and threatening more death.

Zarqawi and the small army he calls Tawhid wa'al-Jihad have expanded their area of operations, taking control of vital thoroughfares in the capital and forcing swathes of country to be declared no-go zones for US forces. At the same time, Zarqawi wrestles with nationalist Iraqi fighters for control of the insurgency's post-Saddam agenda. American crackdowns have little success in curbing the crisis.

Since Zarqawi bounced out of relative obscurity last year, he has been linked to an appalling litany of violence. The attacks range from the horribly grotesque, like the beheading of the Jewish-American businessman Nick Berg, in May 2004, which he celebrated by releasing a video titled 'Sheikh Abu Musab Zarqawi Slaughters an American Infidel', to a barrage of audacious car- and truck-borne suicide bombings that have killed a high-profile United Nations envoy, dozens of prominent religious and political figures, and hundreds of ordinary Iraqis.

Zarqawi has masterminded or inspired the capture of more than 130 foreign hostages in Iraq. Last month the world was forced to hold its breath as two Americans and a British hostage pleaded for their lives, before Zarqawi himself, according to

CIA analysis of the web footage, callously cut the throats of the struggling Americans. Then he roughly decapitated them, holding the heads up for the cameras—and, with a nonchalant twist of the knife, gouged out one of the victim's eyes.

While a separate insurgency group dangled the lives of two young women hostages from Italy—they were subsequently released—Zarqawi imposed a calculated silence on the fate of the Briton who had been snatched with the Americans—62-year-old Kenneth Bigley. It was broken a week later only by the release of another harrowing video of a distraught Bigley, shackled and kneeling in a cage as he pleaded with Prime Minister Tony Blair to spare his life.

Zarqawi knew that he was filling the media space in Britain and around the world with bestial but cost-effective propaganda that would work for him on two levels. He has his own sophisticated PR machine, which talks him up as the single cause of all that is violent in the new Iraq—just as much as the Washington spin doctors do. The Zarqawi profile is so great now that it ceases to matter how many of the charges against him are true; what does matter is that he has become an inspirational figurehead for an insurgency army of as many as 20,000 fighters, which has been able to dig in and establish operational practices and lines of funding and communication for what many observers fear will be Iraq's descent into a bloody civil war. Indeed, the most troubling aspect of Zarqawi's arrival on the battlefield is that he has the determination and ideological baggage needed to manipulate all sides to start an all-out war.

Any quest to discover Zarqawi's past is not the story of just one person. It is also a journey into a fearsome philosophy that is being used to breach the Islamic convention that Muslims should not act violently towards each other.

It is called the Salafi movement, the credo of the fundamentalist Islamic warmongers that provides the religious sanction without which violence could not be perpetrated in the name of Islam. Salafi thought might have languished ineffectually on the fringes of world affairs had not the United States decided to pour billions of dollars in arms and support into an earlier but very different 'coalition of the willing': an informal, pan-Arabist army of volunteers that fought to end the Soviet occupation of Afghanistan in the 1980s.

That ten-year-long struggle was justified religiously on the grounds that all Muslims had a duty to repel the infidel Soviet invasion of Muslim Afghanistan. But it was a further refinement by Zarqawi's prison-cell mentor, the 44-year-old Abu Mohammed al-Maqdisi, that made it possible to encourage the veteran Arab warriors from Afghanistan to gird themselves for other battles; and it was in Afghanistan that Osama bin Laden and Zarqawi learned the undeniable truth of asymmetric warfare—that a bunch of uneducated youths armed only with credit cards and box-cutters could take the modern US empire by the throat; that a few cars loaded with fertiliser could stop that empire's technologically sophisticated army in its tracks.

Hardly anyone knows what Zarqawi really looks like. The American 'Wanted' posters list his height and weight as unknown. The same old passport-like pictures are pasted up: round face, furtive eyes, stubbled chin and beanie-like cap. By many accounts he is not especially bright, but he wears his emotions close to the surface. Accounts of his early days suggest he is prone to tears, sometimes in discussions about God.

Much of what is known about him comes from the prisoners who shared a Jordanian cell block with him for five years after he was convicted in 1994 of plotting to overthrow the regime of King Hussein. A former inmate from Swaqa prison told me

Zarqawi burst into sobs when he rebuked him for beating up another inmate. Yousef Rababa, a teacher of Islamic religious studies who served time for plotting a bombing mission in Israel, said the only softness he saw in Zarqawi was towards his mother.

In a reception room in his comfortable middle-class home, high on one of the rolling hills over which the Jordanian capital is draped, Rababa said that when Zarqawi's mother visited, he would shower, dress in his cleanest clothes and wear cologne. Sitting in an adjacent cubicle, the teacher eavesdropped on some of the mother–son meetings: 'He was always seeking her forgiveness and blessings; he'd wish her happiness, too.'

Zarqawi's acts of violence in the past six months have taken him into the lounge rooms of the world. But nobody, least of all the Americans, is sure of where he hides in Iraq. It seems implausible that he would base himself in Falluja, the Sunni city that has refused to surrender to US force. But late last month the London-based daily *Al-Hayat* published an interview with an unnamed Zarqawi associate who claimed to have met Zarqawi there 'recently'. The United States insists he is there too, but there have been no confirmed sightings, and constant and powerful bombing of what it describes as Zarqawi safe houses has so far failed to curb the rate of insurgency attacks, to turn up a body, or to prompt a claim for Washington's ransom from anyone who might have tipped them off to Zarqawi's whereabouts.

It is noon and the backstreets are virtually deserted. Zarqawi's family still lives in an area called Al-Kasara, where the dusty, mottled sprawl of Al-Zarqa runs abruptly into the wall of an abandoned quarry on one side and an old cemetery on another. In the street where the young Zarqawi kicked a ball, a child labours to get a kite aloft. But there is no response to my banging on a heavy metal gate set in a wall that surrounds the family's drab two-storey house. There's a satellite-TV dish and a lonely olive tree. Across the way, rubbish spills from a dumpster.

A few of the neighbours straggle towards the Al-Falah mosque for prayers—this was where Zarqawi spent much of his time. 'They don't talk,' a passer-by volunteers about the family, and others explain why. Zarqawi's brother-in-law, Salih al-Hami, had spoken publicly a few weeks earlier and still has the bruises from a doing-over by Jordanian security-service officers.

A circumspect shopkeeper, who gave his name as Abu Mouad S'waha, says the *mukhabarat*—the collective name by which Arabs refer to all security agents—had been making more visits to the area as Zarqawi's activities in Iraq drew more attention, and were warning people not to talk to outsiders about Zarqawi. 'They think they can shut down the story,' the shopkeeper says.

The locals are cautious—the shopkeeper the only one to give his name—but they all talk; some worry that the character beaming back from Iraq by news satellite is so big that he must be a creation of US propaganda. But they all, it seems, want visitors to acknowledge their pride in Zarqawi. 'How did such a normal guy become so big?' asks a man outside the mosque. 'We pray for him, because he is one of us,' another with a bushy white beard tells me.

And despite the pervasive reticence, they offer up the essentials of the Zarqawi story, which varies from 'local boy makes good' to 'who'd have thought he had it in him?' Some of them see great symbolism in the proximity of the local cemetery to Zarqawi's home.

As a restless teenager he emerged as a hard-drinking, knife-wielding tough who was not greatly interested in school or religion. His father was the local *mukhtar*, an unofficial community counsellor from whom people sought advice. But his father's early death thrust added responsibility on the young Zarqawi.

One of the locals explained to me: 'The only way to survive in Al-Zarqa was to be tough [and] he had a duty to protect his family, especially his sisters.' Another says that one night in his teens, Zarqawi drank so much that he fainted—and that when he came to, he vowed: 'Never again.'

The young Zarqawi worked for a time in the municipal electrical service. He soon drifted out of that job, but mystery surrounds just how he ended up in Afghanistan in 1989. For years, the Saudi government had been paying young Arabs to fight in Afghanistan, but by then the Soviets were in retreat from a conflict that had become their Vietnam. There are reports that Zarqawi fought to drive the Russians out of the eastern city of Khost, near where bin Laden would later locate some of his training camps. But others refer to him only as an aspiring writer for a magazine called *Al-Bonian al-Marsous*, 'The Strong Wall'. They say he listened closely, but kept to himself.

Before he was silenced by the Jordanian authorities, Salih al-Hami, Zarqawi's brother-in-law, told the Arabic television channel Al-Jazeera that Zarqawi had been a sponge for Salafi literature in Afghanistan but had been reluctant to join any of the battlefront groups—particularly Osama bin Laden's Al-Qaeda.

Zarqawi returned to Jordan in 1992, confused by emerging signs of a protracted civil war in Afghanistan in the wake of the Arab triumph that Salafi philosophers had promised would deliver an Islamic nirvana. Some who observed him at the time thought he was ripe for the hardline speeches of Al-Maqdisi, the Salafi scholar who also was from Jordan.

These two had met in Pakistan and together they set up Beit al-Imam, a help group for fighters returning to Jordan from Afghanistan. It was hardly surprising that many of the fighters were looking for a new cause: bin Laden found his in Saudi Arabia, in Riyadh's deepening military reliance on the United

States; and for Al-Maqdisi and Zarqawi, it was the social and economic malaise threatening to sink Jordan in the wake of the 1990–91 Gulf crisis.

The journalist Abdullah Abu Rumman soon detected a strident new message in Jordanian discourse: 'Al-Maqdisi's speeches were full of fire. He condemned the government and he branded the Sunni clerics as instruments of the regime; he called them *taghout*. This was the first time we'd heard this old word used to describe Muslims as infidels.'

A Kuwait-born Palestinian, Al-Maqdisi's real name is Isam al-Barqawi. He studied physics and chemistry in Baghdad as a young man, but abandoned his course to go to Medina, in Saudi Arabia, to take up the religious studies that would shape his Taliban brain.

His two wives still live at Rusaifeh, in the urban corridor between Al-Zarqa and Amman. In his absence, his house is said to run much as Zarqawi's does—the children are barred from attending school and are made to study only religious texts at home. Television is forbidden. And when Al-Maqdisi was hauled before Jordan's State Security Court recently, there were audible gasps when, brimming with pride and emotion, he announced that his fourteen-year-old son had died fighting with the insurgents in Iraq.

In 1994, Al-Maqdisi was jailed amid rising fears among officials in Amman over the growing band of followers inspired by his rants against the regime. On being convicted of plotting the overthrow of the Jordanian government, Al-Maqdisi was sent down for fifteen years. His jailing would be the making of Abu Musab al-Zarqawi, who went into the slammer with him—on the same charges.

Swaqa prison sits alone, on the edge of a highway that cuts like a ribbon of steel through the Jordanian desert, running south from Amman to the Red Sea port of Aqaba. It was a menacing place where prisoners were forced to cluster according to their beliefs—political and religious, or around leaders they thought would protect them from violence. Inmates say Al-Maqdisi and Zarqawi gathered their supporters in a tight knot under Al-Maqdisi's leadership.

The section of Swaqa that housed political prisoners had four dormitories with bunk bedding for about 30 prisoners in each. Al-Maqdisi took over a whole dormitory, which became his tiny, Taliban-like lair. As his lieutenant, Zarqawi was the enforcer of a strict code of conduct: group members had to seek permission to talk to other prisoners; their book reading was censored (Zarqawi punished a prisoner for reading *Crime and Punishment*) and the only press reports they had were clippings on events in Afghanistan; they could listen to the TV news, but the screen was permanently covered lest they see a woman newsreader. In the middle of all this was Zarqawi's 'tent'—he had draped the sides of his lower bunk bed with blankets, screening out the world as he laboured over the Koran.

The group was barred from organised sport with other prisoners and was made to exercise in a makeshift gym in which Zarqawi had fashioned weights from tin buckets of rocks strung on lengths of timber. To leave the group was to be sentenced to solitude for the rest of a prisoner's sentence; to join others was an act of betrayal that met a violent response. Several former inmates claimed Swaqa was the sort of place where, for sport, the warders would cuff prisoners to a hook high on a corridor wall so that passing officers could take out their frustration by beating them. Inmates said that in such cases, Zarqawi would attack an approaching officer to draw his attention away from the cuffed prisoner. 'He was very brave—when I arrived at Swaqa he was already in solitary,' one of them told me.

Members of the Al-Maqdisi–Zarqawi group were required to dress in the same Wahabbi style: the scraggy beard, short hair on their heads, *dishdashas* that came to just below their knees and, always, the black head-cloth that was the uniform of the Taliban in Afghanistan. Rababa the teacher said it was a hard group to penetrate, but he had bargaining power in the form of money from outside donations. Zarqawi took to giving passionate sermons on Fridays, usually on the failings of the Jordanian regime. He had none of Al-Maqdisi's charisma, but commanded the respect of his followers.

The majority view among the prisoners was that in those early days, Zarqawi was a deputy to Al-Maqdisi. A former inmate warned by the Jordanian authorities not to be interviewed nevertheless told me: 'We just didn't believe that he was, or would become, important. For our group, Al-Maqdisi was the important figure and we used to spend time trying to understand his ideology because it was extreme stuff; he was saying that the king and the Jordanian army and other security services were infidels and therefore it was right to use force against the regime. But Zarqawi had no ideas of his own, just whatever Al-Maqdisi fed to him. So if we had the main guy there to talk to, why would we waste time with Zarqawi?'

But Zarqawi was not going to be anyone's number two for long. Several former inmates recounted a power struggle in which Al-Maqdisi's sullen and serious pupil challenged his control of the group.

In Jordanian parlance, Zarqawi was the only 'East-banker' in the group. This was a critical advantage in his struggle with Al-Maqdisi. To come from the east bank of the Jordan River meant Zarqawi was of the powerful tribes that are the bedrock of the Jordanian establishment—he was of the legendary Beni Hassan tribe that watched over Jordan's border with Iraq and had delivered national leaders and many who served in the military and the intelligence services. Unlike the dislocated Palestinian Al-Maqdisi, Zarqawi's life was not governed by an instinctive fear of state officials—particularly the police and intelligence services.

But Zarqawi had another advantage. Both he and Al-Maqdisi were treated as heroes of the war in Afghanistan. However, Al-Maqdisi had done his religious philosophising from Peshawar, certainly a gateway to the Afghan theatre of war, but located well inside the borders of neighbouring Pakistan. So as the only true Afghan veteran in Swaqa, Zarqawi's pedestal was that little bit higher.

A fellow inmate recollects the differences between the two, noting Zarqawi's blunt ideological persistence: 'Al-Maqdisi could discuss literature, poetry and politics with all the confidence of his education, but Zarqawi knew none of this . . . just the Koran, which he memorised in prison—all 6000-plus verses.' In contrast to Al-Maqdisi, Zarqawi subjected newcomers to a sudden-death assessment: 'He'd talk to new prisoners, check their views on the regime and the police and decide very quickly if they were good Muslims or infidels, and whether or not they could join his group.'

As the leader of another inmate group, the teacher Rababa met for frequent discussions on prison issues with both Al-Maqdisi and Zarqawi. He observed the widening personal rift between them. 'Zarqawi told me that Al-Maqdisi had a behavioural problem,' he recalls. 'He accused him of selfishness and of negligence in his religious observances. Zarqawi saw Al-Maqdisi as two-faced because he was a religious scholar who also had a love of life.'

As Rababa saw it, Zarqawi was the opposite: 'He loved his growing authority; everything had to be so serious, and his instinctive response if he felt threatened or cornered was to lash out. He had a strong personality, but Zarqawi didn't seem to have a vision for the future. His ideology was limited and his arguments in defence of it were even more limited—he had no interest in a dialogue. At the end of the day he was just like Bush, telling us, "You are with me or against me."'

The other prisoners were struck by the number of disciple-like visitors who came to see both men, and the weight of the business they discussed and what it revealed of Al-Maqdisi's power and influence. One told me a group of Saudi Arabians had come to receive Al-Maqdisi's religious blessing before the explosion of a 1500-kilogram-plus truck bomb at the Khobar Towers residential complex in Riyadh in 1996, where nineteen US servicemen died and almost 400 others were injured. The Khobar attack has come to be seen as the opening strike in a campaign that has effectively driven the US military out of Saudi Arabia.

Another cell-block colleague saw the difference in the two men's propensity for violence: 'Al-Maqdisi was a coward . . . afraid of the warders. It was always Zarqawi, who was physically stronger, who went on the front foot confronting the guards.'

All the time Al-Maqdisi was watching Zarqawi, seemingly aware that he was being undermined but unable to do anything about it. It was about four years after their arrival at Swaqa that prisoners outside the Beit al-Imam group realised Zarqawi had slid into the leadership. Rababa the teacher observed that by the time of their release, Al-Maqdisi and Zarqawi no longer spoke to each other.

After his release, Zarqawi was back on the streets and in the mosques of Al-Zarqa. Unhappily, according to his brother-in-law: 'I felt he was bored; I felt he was bitter. I felt the spirit of jihad inside him. He was dying to get out of this country.'

Jordanian intelligence had a special unit to monitor the activities of Jordanians, like Al-Maqdisi and Zarqawi, who had become Afghan Arabs. According to a well-placed observer in the Jordanian capital, the unit had a clear task: 'Harass these guys to make it difficult for them to get jobs and, hopefully, to drive them out of the country. They blocked whatever Zarqawi wanted to do—at one stage he tried to buy a pick-up from which to sell fruit and vegetables, but they would not give him the paperwork. They were always harassing him, pulling him in for interrogation.'

The Amman lawyer who had represented Zarqawi at his trial, Mohammed al-Dweik, saw what was happening: 'He came to see me. He wanted to live here and work here and to have a family—but the Interior Ministry would not give him the paperwork. Here in Jordan we beat and torture people like Zarqawi and make them want to leave the country—so he went back to Afghanistan.'

But here there was something that didn't quite add up in Zarqawi's story—a period in which he cooled his heels, perhaps deciding on what course his life should take. The thug and firebrand of Swaqa left prison brim-full of Al-Maqdisi's war cries and then stormed off to Peshawar which, early in 2000, was still the gateway to what by then had become Taliban-controlled Afghanistan. Crossing the border should have been a doddle, but he seemed to hesitate, instead bringing his sick mother to Pakistan, hoping the air would be better for her. And when he finally headed west through the Khyber Pass, it was because he was forced to, after Pakistani authorities arrested him for over-staying his six-month visa.

He was jailed briefly and ordered to leave the country. Jordan was no longer an option as he had been named there as a suspected terrorist, so Zarqawi packed his mother back to Amman, where she died early this year as she prayed that her son would die in battle, according to the *New York Times*. Zarqawi headed for Kabul.

It seems to have been a turning point and he chose the moment to abandon his old identity, so well-known to authorities in Jordan, as he entered a new theatre of war. Having previously lived and travelled under his birth name, Ahmad Fadil al-Khalayilah, Zarqawi decided to honour his home town, Al-Zarqa, by taking 'Zarqawi' as his *nom de guerre*. He arrived in Afghanistan a year or more before September 11 and the US 'war on terror'.

The question the Americans would like answered is whether Zarqawi has struck any sort of deal with Osama bin Laden. What happened on his return to Afghanistan and his movements since then are murky. Al-Jazeera television reported that Zarqawi fought with Al-Qaeda in the last big battles in Afghanistan, including the US assault on Tora Bora. But in June, US Secretary of Defence Donald Rumsfeld undercut much of Washington's argument of a link when he said of Zarqawi: '[He] may very well not have sworn allegiance to [bin Laden]. Maybe he disagrees with him on something; maybe because he wants to be "The Man" himself.' And in the *Al-Hayat* interview published in September, Zarqawi's unnamed associate was quoted as saying: 'I wish he was Al-Qaeda's representative in Iraq. But the truth is he has his own organisation, he is not an Al-Qaeda member and he has no connection with Osama bin Laden.'

Clearly, Zarqawi would have needed the blessing of the Taliban's leadership to operate in Afghanistan before September 11. But he did seem to be in pursuit of an agenda different from that of bin Laden. He set up a jihadist training camp at Herat in the west of Afghanistan, far away from bin Laden's camps on the eastern frontier with Pakistan. He complained to family friends that senior Al-Qaeda types worried that he was too strict on his followers; he objected to their acceptance of Saudi donations; and he intimated it was the patronage of an Afghan warlord that had made his Herat camp possible.

But being in Herat put Zarqawi closer to the north-east corner of Iraq. This was an area protected from the regime of Saddam Hussein by the US-imposed no-fly zone. It was here that a small group of the so-called Afghan Arabs worked with local Kurdish fundamentalists to set up a Taliban-style fiefdom known as Ansar al-Islam.

Washington argued that this was in fact a fallback set up by Al-Qaeda in the knowledge that after the September 11 attacks it would not be able to work from Afghanistan. But when the camps were raided as a part of the US invasion of Iraq, the evidence was inconclusive. There was proof of experimentation in small-scale chemical terrorism but conflicting intelligence assessments on whether Zarqawi himself had been stationed in the camps.

People living near the Ansar al-Islam camps claimed Zarqawi arrived soon after the September 11 attacks and that he was an agent of Al-Qaeda. A farmer told Al-Jazeera: 'This house that you see behind me was built by the Ansar. Zarqawi, representative of Osama bin Laden, used to live here.' Mohammed Rumman, a brother of the journalist Abdullah Abu Rumman, is doing a doctoral thesis on the Salafi movement. He says his sources have persuaded him that from the arrival of Zarqawi, the camps were moulded into the sort of facility that might have turned out fighters who are now playing key roles in the Iraqi insurgency.

The US claims Zarqawi was close to Saddam's Baghdad and had been to the Iraqi capital to be treated for wounds from a US missile strike in Afghanistan. But Rumman believes Zarqawi remained in the north till after the fall of Baghdad in April 2003. Zarqawi has been so contemptuous of the Saddam regime and the Baath Party, which he dismissed earlier this year as 'infidels' and 'weaklings who can't fight for themselves', that it is difficult to see how they might have worked together. Laith Shubaylat, an outspoken Amman lawyer, who was in Swaqa prison with Zarqawi, told me: 'He can deal only in black and white. He is so utterly inflexible I'd say it's impossible for him to work with the Baathists—you'd have to show me the video of the gun to his head before I could see him working with Saddam.'

Jordanian security officials claim Zarqawi illegally re-entered his homeland through Syria late in 2002—about a year after September 11. A month later, US diplomat Laurence Foley was murdered. Three men were arrested, and all allegedly told investigators that Zarqawi had been the operation's instigator. It was his first entry into the Western media consciousness.

Five months later, Colin Powell made a now widely discredited speech before the United Nations justifying Washington's planned invasion of Iraq, in which he claimed Zarqawi was a bin Laden 'associate and collaborator' and part of a 'sinister nexus between Iraq and the Al-Qaeda terrorist network'.

Zarqawi's old Amman lawyer, Mohammed al-Dweik, told me: 'I stayed in touch with the client that I knew as Ahmad Fadil al-Khalayilah till he disappeared off to Afghanistan and it wasn't till last year, when Colin Powell told the United Nations, that I knew there was a terrorist called Zarqawi. And a couple of days later I had a call from his mother to tell me that my client was the man in the news.'

The United States was warned that its invasion of Iraq would create a terrorist honey pot—and this was just what Zarqawi had been looking for. The early targets in the resistance were conventional: the US military and those Iraqi institutions deemed to be collaborators, such as police stations. But the bombing of the Jordanian Embassy in Baghdad in August last year signalled a critical new turn—and that a new hand seemed to be at work.

The blast was so powerful it destroyed the vehicle in which it was planted—no one could tell if it was a car, a bus or a truck. As many as a dozen people died and in the chaotic aftermath an Iraqi crowd stormed the building, destroying pictures of King Abdullah and his late father, King Hussein. US forces raced tanks and Humvees into place, leaving a circle of about 100 metres in diameter littered with body parts from the dead and injured and their wrecked cars. I was in Baghdad at the time, and I climbed onto the roof of an adjacent building to get a better view. Looking down, the circle looked like the first ripple going out in a campaign that would claim many more lives and would be felt way beyond the dusty confines of Baghdad.

All the dead were Iraqis. And perhaps because no Jordanian diplomats died and the building was not so badly damaged, the realisation that this was the start of a brutal new campaign by a new player was reserved for a bomb two weeks later at the United Nations' Baghdad headquarters. Zarqawi became the only and immediate suspect, in part because the embassy strike was a gory and personal double-hit. Apart from being the first major insurgency bombing since the invasion of Iraq, it struck at the heart of the Amman regime, which Zarqawi hated for its lack of Islamic purity and alliance with Washington.

Now, Zarqawi either claims or is blamed for every atrocity in Iraq—and several beyond its borders. Moroccan intelligence believes he may have helped organise the Madrid train bombings in March; the Germans say they have sprung a cell whose members were trained at Zarqawi's Afghanistan camp; and the Jordanians claim he was behind a plot in April this year in which 20 tonnes of chemicals were to be detonated in Amman, producing a poison cloud that could have killed 80,000 people. Whether Zarqawi has the muscle to run such a terror network across the world is an open question.

Unlike bin Laden, who has positioned himself more as a head-office strategic operator, Zarqawi is a hands-on, in-the-field jihadist. US and other intelligence services have concluded from some of the beheading tapes that it is Zarqawi who is holding the knife and his voice making the announcements.

In a tape aired on Al-Jazeera, Zarqawi spelt out his agenda: 'We are invading them, just as they are invading us; and we are attacking them, just as they are attacking us; and we are hurting them, just as they are hurting us.' Soon after, he celebrated all that he claims as his work, and the rest of which he is accused, in another chilling audio recording: 'God honoured us and so we harvested their heads and tore up their bodies in many places: the coalition forces in Karbala; the Italians in Nasseriyah; the US intelligence in Al-Shahin Hotel; and last but not least, what God has honoured us with today, the Polish forces in Hilla.'

There are, however, signs of tension between Zarqawi and the dozens of Iraqi insurgent groups that have emerged since last year's invasion. There were internet death threats against Zarqawi after a wave of attacks on Iraqi police stations earlier this year. I was also told by sources in Falluja recently of an organised movement that hoped to drive foreign fighters out of the war-torn city.

But some insurgency groups claim to be inspired by Zarqawi, fighting in his name without a direct link, in much the same way as the bin Laden brand of terrorism has been franchised around the world. Fighters who took to the streets in Baqaba, north of Baghdad—as part of a wave of tightly coordinated strikes that killed more than 100 people in the days before the establishment on 28 June of Iyad Allawi's interim government—wore headbands proclaiming their support for the Jordanian. Meanwhile, one of the more hardline Sunni mosques in Baghdad has been renamed to honour the fourteenth-century Muslim philosopher Taqi al-Din

Ahmad Ibn Taymiyya, whose brutal religious justifications for war are the core of Salafi thought and the Zarqawi campaign.

Mohammed al-Dweik, Zarqawi's lawyer in Amman, has vivid memories of being lectured by his client on his conversion to the brittle Salafi thinking that now underpins his every move. In a recent, late-night meeting on the terrace at the Four Seasons Hotel in Amman, he recalled how Zarqawi showed off what he had absorbed during his time with Al-Maqdisi: 'He'd tell me that the Arab homelands were like fields, farmers' fields; that our leaders worked the fields for the United States and that we, the Arab people, were their cows and donkeys.' And like so many others in Jordan, Al-Dweik insists that Al-Maqdisi is the key to understanding Zarqawi, describing the scholar as 'the most dangerous man in the whole Middle East'. The lawyer said that what made Al-Maqdisi such a threat to the region was his single-handed revival of the warrior and religious teachings of Taqi al-Din Ahmad Ibn Taymiyya and the impetus that revival had given to the Salafi movement.

Zarqawi's agenda is not a simple demand that US forces leave Iraq. It is also about who should be allowed to run the country and even to live in it. Zarqawi believes the Allawi interim government must be eliminated, not just because of its association with the United States but because it fails his Salafi test of religious purity. That is why Zarqawi has already issued a personal threat against the life of the interim prime minister. But under the arcane principles of Salafi thinking, Shiite Muslims—who make up about 65 per cent of the Iraqi population and are determined to take over the running of the country—are also deemed to be 'infidel', and they, too, are Zarqawi targets.

Such are the strictures of this philosophical straitjacket that even though Zarqawi himself is a Sunni, he is opposed to the regime of the ousted Saddam Hussein and his Baath Party, both of which were also Sunni but far too secular in their outlook for Zarqawi's liking. The Zarqawi world view is ferociously fundamentalist and allows for the survival of only the few who embrace his extremist Salafi doctrine.

The core Salafi belief, best exemplified by the Taliban in Afghanistan, is that only those who knew the prophet Mohammed and the next three generations could have acquired a pure sense of what Mohammed understood of Islam. Any change outside that ancient narrow window is deviant behaviour that must be stamped out. But the philosophy divides again in terms of the perceived threats to Islam and, more importantly, the duty of individual Muslims to counter such threats. Do the threats reside only in a foreign, non-Islamic invader, like the United States? Or is there an internal threat to Islamic purity from Muslim governments, be they tradition-based, such as in Saudi Arabia and Jordan, or puppet regimes installed by foreign force, as in Iraq and Afghanistan? Or, as Zarqawi is arguing in Iraq, from whole classes of people, such as the country's Shiite majority?

None of these finer points was understood when Zarqawi first came to the attention of analysts and commentators, who conveniently bundled him in with Al-Qaeda. But within the relativities of Islamic terror, Yousef Rababa argues that bin Laden is less of an extremist than Zarqawi. To Westerners, it might seem like splitting doctrinal hairs, but the teacher told me: 'Bin Laden sees Americans and Jews as the enemy, along with the foreigners who are in the Arab homelands. But in prison, Zarqawi told me that anyone we think is not a believer is the enemy—and that can be Arabs, too, especially Shiites.'

Despite the ghoulish beheading tapes, Zarqawi is still much of a chimera. Given his philosophical opposition to so many of the factions around him, his support base in Iraq is not easily understood—other than that it is based on the old adage that 'mine enemy's enemy is my friend'.

Each tape he releases is pounced upon by teams of US experts who have concluded that most are genuine. But others take an interest, too. Many who did prison time with Zarqawi harbour doubts that this is the man they knew. The release of each tape sparks a ring-around among former inmates of Swaqa and others who have known Zarqawi, as they attempt to match the voice on the recording with the one they recall. There is much scepticism. His lawyer, Mohammed al-Dweik, pulled at his lower lip and tongue to mimic the sounds and patterns of his client's speech, which, he says, are absent from the recordings. Another added, 'How do you go from being almost illiterate to near-genius? Personal limitations would make it impossible for someone like him to carry on a war in a country he doesn't know.'

But perhaps the best insight into Zarqawi's thinking is a controversial letter recorded on a CD found in the possession of a suspected insurgency courier captured by Iraqi security forces in the north of Iraq in January. American intelligence has seized on the letter because it was addressed to Osama bin Laden, underpinning Washington's claim of a relationship between bin Laden and Zarqawi.

However, there is only a bare hint of a master–servant relationship in the letter, which reads more like that of one chief executive to another on how to take advantage of a market opportunity: 'We do not see ourselves as fit to challenge you . . . [but] if you agree with us . . . we will be your readied soldiers, working under your banner, complying with your orders, and indeed swearing fealty to you publicly and in the news media . . . if things appear otherwise to you, we are brothers, and the disagreement will not spoil [our] friendship.'

If it is genuine, this letter is of greater interest for what it reveals about Zarqawi and his plans to foment civil war in Iraq. The author uses classic flowery language to signal his plan to provoke an intra-Muslim civil war when he says of the majority Shiite population: 'They are the insurmountable obstacle, the lurking snake, the crafty and malicious scorpion and the penetrating venom . . . they are the enemy . . . the bone in [our] throats . . . if we succeed in dragging them into . . . sectarian war, it will become possible to awaken the inattentive Sunnis as they feel imminent danger and annihilating death at the hands of these Sabeans. The only solution is for us to drag the Shiites into battle . . . to strike the religious, military and other cadres among the Shiites with blow after blow until they bend to the Sunnis.'

When the letter is read with an understanding of the Salafi dogma so fiercely held by Zarqawi, it becomes truly frightening. It warns of the approach of 'zero hour'—30 June—which at the time was the date Washington proposed handing some power over to an interim government. It harangues: 'If we are able to strike [the Shiites] with one painful blow after another until they enter the battle . . . if you knew the fear [for their future] among the Sunnis, your eyes would cry over them in sadness.'

The emerging pattern of violence in Iraq is dishearteningly similar to the Algerian civil war of the 1990s. That was a conflict that claimed more than 60,000 lives in an unbridled application of Salafi-sanctioned intra-Muslim violence. The US-backed Algerian regime was attacked on the basis that it was a foreign lackey; Muslim civilians who sided with the regime or simply sat on their hands were deemed to be fair game because, as the Salafis would have it, by not defending Islam they were being un-Islamic; and the media, schools, missionaries and foreign individuals and companies all became targets.

Perhaps this is the challenge Zarqawi has set for himself in Iraq. The most sober intelligence assessments say he has a force of no more than a couple of hundred fighters—Jordanian and other Arab nationals. He can't do it all by himself, but there is a risk that the religious and other divisions that exist already in Iraq are so deep and treacherous that a campaign of well-targeted violence could provoke Iraqis into doing the job for him.

SEDUCTION OF AN UNWITTING SUICIDE BOMBER

Baghdad, Iraq
9 February 2005

Of all the savage stories of the twenty-month-long Iraqi insurgency, the story of how a young disabled boy was turned into a human bomb is one of the cruellest. His mother is unable to forgive herself for mistaking the intentions of the strangers whose promises of help for her desperately poor family ultimately led her nineteen-year-old son to his fate as a weapon in the war against America.

Fatima al-Zubaidi thinks long and hard. She stares into a darkened corner of her tiny room—but she methodically examines every last minute of her unfortunate son's life. It is night-time in Baghdad's Al-Askan quarter, and Fatima, 45, huddles on a cold floor, shrouded in black. Grief and guilt tear at her but, between bouts of quiet sobbing, she finds a firm voice to answer difficult questions.

She is trying to remember, with hindsight, if anything in her teenage son's behaviour might have hinted that he was being trained for a terrorist mission against his own people. Her strength is ebbing and, as she bites her finger, she finally whispers: 'No. I don't think so.'

Amar Ahmed Mohammed, a Shiite who had Down's syndrome, was a perfect target for the ruthless men of the insurgency. Unable to speak, because of the severity of the condition, he could not tell anyone he was being groomed for death; and, well-known from his daily wandering in local streets, he was beyond suspicion as he tried to penetrate tight election-day security with explosives under his coat.

While the family buried his broken body in the shrine city of Najaf last week, a relative speculated to me that Amar's abduction was an opportunistic snatch by total strangers from the insurgency while his parents were a couple of blocks away, celebrating their new-found right to vote at a family lunch. But, in an interview yesterday, the mother revealed the veiled brutality of an elaborately planned seduction, in which her family was made to believe Amar finally had found benefactors who could dramatically improve his lousy lot in life.

As the insurgents planned their campaign for the day of the Iraqi elections, it was clear the security shutdown would hinder the use of their weapon of choice, the suicide bomb. But a young boy known to neighbours and locals could wander the streets without attracting attention. And so it was that Amar's fate was sealed. He was preyed upon to turn him, unknowingly, into a human bomb.

The family spent the last twelve years of Saddam Hussein's rule on the run because Fatima's 50-year-old husband, Ahmed, was an army deserter. They fled to Baghdad from the southern city of Basra but, without local residency papers, Ahmed was unable to find work. Six years ago they found this room and opened a tiny shop at the front window; well-meaning local traders advanced them stock.

Accustomed to living on charity, they were not entirely surprised when, ten days before the election, two men got out of a car that pulled into their alley to announce that they were from the local Sunni mosque and they wanted to help Amar.

Fatima was overjoyed: 'They said they would organise a sickness pension from the new government, that they were arranging with the Red Crescent for a block of land on which we might build a house, and they gave me $300 for stock for the shop. They said that they would take Amar to a special school, and each day they collected him and drove away. They gave him sweets and clothes and cigarettes. He loved them. Sunnis had helped us before, so I didn't think it strange. It felt good that these men cared for us and they were so affectionate to Amar.'

Fatima was especially grateful because she thought that, with the downfall of Saddam, their lives were about to change—her first child, a daughter, had died at age twelve because, she says, they had neither food nor medicine for an illness she suffered. But she said that, after voting early on 30 January, she came home to be told by her other boys—Murthada, nine, and Ali, eight—that the Sunnis had driven away with Amar.

Distress makes her pull the veil more tightly around her face, till only her brown eyes can be seen. 'That was normal—we had come to trust them like family. I wasn't worried, and the rest of us went off to lunch at my sister's house. Then there was an explosion.'

She recounted painfully how a neighbour told her Amar was definitely the bomb carrier because he had recognised the teenager's decapitated head where it lay on open ground; how she had insisted on going to the scene, where she was able to identify him because his name and address was on his shirt in her handwriting—it was there so neighbours could bring him home when he wandered too far.

The Sunnis have not been seen again. Her husband has spent the days since the election either sedated in hospital or wandering the streets looking for the two men. 'He is sick with grief; he thinks he killed Amar,' she sobbed. 'We went to the Sunni mosque but the Imam was crying too. He said he did not know these men.'

So what does Fatima make of the new Iraq? 'The election was meant to be so exciting. But we've had to give Amar as a present for the new Iraq and we just hope that it will get better, as a victory for Amar and all the people.'

THE UNKNOWN
ZARQAWI LEGACY

Baghdad, Iraq
10 June 2006

Remember the other turning points in Iraq? When Saddam
Hussein was captured, the American brass assured us that
the rebels were 'on their knees'; and the subsequent siege of
Falluja supposedly 'broke the back' of the insurgency. The death
of Saddam's sons was another 'new dawn for Iraqis'. Then there
was an election, a constitution and another election; but through
all that time the liberated Iraq continued its slide into the mire.

So how then should we assess the death on Wednesday of
the Jordanian-born insurgency leader Abu Musab al-Zarqawi?
In short, cautiously. Anthony Cordesman, a terrorism analyst at
the Center for Strategic and International Studies, acknowledged
Zarqawi's demise as a political and propaganda victory for
Washington and Baghdad, but he wondered if it would have a
major impact over time.

The US president, George Bush, has opted to leave the 'mission
accomplished' banner in its locker at the White House. And

while there is a justified air of optimism, his Iraqi and American colleagues are wisely keeping their rhetoric in check. They finally seem to have grasped that one of the consistencies in this conflict has been the regularity with which a baffled shrug of the shoulder is the only sensible response to the inevitable 'What now?' question.

In the wake of the death of the Jordanian terrorist, the only certainty is more uncertainty. Zarqawi was a thug, a tyrant, a zealot. He is already being eulogised on Islamic websites and books will be written about how real he really was; and how much his profile, bad and all as it was, had been enhanced by US propaganda.

But, in a sense, Zarqawi's work was done. He took himself to Iraq to ignite a bloody sectarian war and his success can be measured by the rising flood of battered bodies arriving at Baghdad's central morgue every day. As reporters fanned out in the city to do their death of Zarqawi vox pops, Dhia Majid, a university professor whose brother and sister-in-law were gunned down last year, told the *New York Times*: 'Zarqawi is part of the story [but] the story will not end when he is finished. It's not Iraq—it's a slaughterhouse.'

Zarqawi's singular achievement was to make Iraq less manageable, stoking Balkan-like tensions, religious and ethnic, to the extent that a negotiated accommodation among Shiites, Sunnis and Kurds under a single government in a single nation-state may have been rendered impossible. In death, Zarqawi was reluctantly acknowledged by Iraq's national security adviser, Mowaffak al-Rubaie: 'There is a fracture between the two communities [Sunni and Shiite]. His work over the last three years has not been in vain.'

Too many Iraqis now have a taste for blood—Sunni and Shiite. The violence has its own momentum with Shiite death squads using the Iraqi security forces for shelter and their US training, arms and funding to roam the country, killing at will. And because it is now Iraqi-on-Iraqi blood sport, what was an insurgency war against US occupation has become a sectarian war.

The manner of Zarqawi's parting—unmanned surveillance drones and precision air strikes—displayed American technical superiority, but it also underscores their limited knowledge and understanding of the Iraqi resistance. Zarqawi became the personification of the insurgency; but he was never the leader of a unified resistance, fighting for the one cause.

There are dozens of insurgency cells which split into two broad groupings. The majority are believed to be Iraqi nationalists, fighting for power and resources within the existing Iraqi state; and then there is a lesser, foreign-led grouping that is fighting for varying shades of a fundamentalist, Taliban-like regime.

This second group is usually understood to be no more than about 10 per cent of an estimated 20,000 insurgents. And within this small but powerful rump, Zarqawi was merely the leader of one group. His Al-Qaeda in Mesopotamia organisation might well be set back by the death of its leader and it could even fracture over who in their ranks should replace him. But Anthony Cordesman cautions: 'Unless the United States captures information that reveals Al-Qaeda's overall organisation and cell structure, it seems likely that the impact of Zarqawi's demise will be limited. He may be treated as a martyr and his death may even be spun into a kind of victory.'

For now, all the other cells are expected to fight on and it will be up to the Baghdad leadership to break its habit of failing to capitalise on so many presumed 'turning points' since the ousting of Saddam.

US and Iraqi analysts can only hazard guesses at who Zarqawi's replacement might be and just how his sudden departure might play in shaping a viable post-Saddam Iraq. There is a presumption in some quarters that the loss of Zarqawi might weaken or fracture the insurgency. But while the insurgency will have lost one of its more brilliant propagandists, the reverse might also be the case.

That one of Zarqawi's confreres has turned US informer is just the latest evidence of splits within the Islamist world over Zarqawi's style, particularly his attacks on Shiite civilian targets. So his demise could prompt a tactical and strategic review that might be a unifying force, particularly if attacks were to be limited to American and Iraqi security forces rather than mosques and markets.

Arguing that much of Zarqawi's group has become Iraqi rather than foreign jihadis and that its structure is secure, Cordesman predicts it may become stronger: 'The end result might be that most of it survives and even moderates, expanding its reach in ways that Zarqawi's extremism prevented.' Such a shift might also shore up sympathy and moral support from those Sunnis opposed to Shiite control of Iraq but who just don't have the stomach for Zarqawi's brutal assaults on civilians.

The timing of Zarqawi's death means that capitalising on it will be the first major test of the new prime minister, Nouri al-Maliki. This week the Iraqi leader made two significant gestures to the once-powerful Sunni minority: he appointed a Sunni defence minister and he has promised to release thousands of Sunnis being held without charge in Iraqi and US-run prisons.

But the greatest challenge that confronts him is changing the environment in which the insurgency exists. That's a tall order—he has to put enough on the table that is acceptable for the Sunnis without drawing the ire of the Shiite majority.

And that's the dilemma. Too many Shiites, particularly those in leadership positions, want to see the Sunnis utterly defeated. Near total control of the government and national resources is not enough for them, so they happily dispatch the death squads to exact revenge for the atrocities of the Saddam era.

After so many failed attempts by imposed and elected administrations, too many Iraqis have lost faith in the ability of their leaders to lead. Morale is low and individual Iraqis complain that the national psyche is depressed.

And that is a great sadness, because three years ago there were no death squads and Zarqawi was a virtual unknown. Now tit-for-tat is the new dynamic and hatred is the national sport.

THE JUDAS KISS

Baghdad, Iraq
23 August 2006

There is a chilling intimacy when Khamis al-Obeidi surrenders to his fate as he is taken out to die. The lawyer leans in for a Judas kiss from one of his killers just before others bind his hands behind his back.

The last living minutes of the third of Saddam Hussein's lawyers to be murdered in Baghdad were captured by at least two of the killers on mobile-phone video cameras. I have seen what appears to be part of one of the videos being shown within a tight Shiite circle in the Iraqi capital. The clip has been edited, but the bruised and haunted face that dominates this 90-second segment seems to be that of the 49-year-old Mr Obeidi as he represented Saddam in his televised trial.

Sources in Sadr City, a Shiite stronghold in Baghdad, say Mr Obeidi's execution was the work of a ruthless new Shiite warlord, who emerged about three months ago to conduct his own missions of death against Sunnis in greater Baghdad. A stocky and bearded one-time fishmonger who walks with a pronounced limp, he is said to have taken as a *nom de guerre* 'Abu Dereh', meaning 'Father of the Shield' or 'Protective Father'.

Shiite leaders profess to know little about him. But as I made inquiries of a senior adviser to Abdul Aziz al-Hakim, one of the most powerful Shiite political leaders, Mr Hakim's twelve-year-old grandson exclaimed: 'Abu Dereh? He's the hero of the people!'

The men who knocked at Mr Obeidi's door early on 21 June wore police uniforms and produced paperwork which they claimed authorised them to escort him to the Ministry of the Interior. Instead, he was driven to a private home in Tarakh, a Shiite neighbourhood.

The video begins in a narrow alley outside the house, to which the lawyer was taken for 'interrogation'. As he emerges, Mr Obeidi appears to have been beaten about the head, but he makes a desperate plea based on the Iraqi sense of humiliation: 'If you want, I will lie down beneath your shoes.'

Despite what lies ahead, he is reassured. 'No, don't be afraid. We are brothers; you are my guest; there is nothing to fear.'

Mr Obeidi replies: 'I will do whatever you want. I'm ready.'

The ringleader, who is believed to be Abu Dereh, says, 'I need to ask you for a favour.' He then explains that he needs to tie Mr Obeidi's hands 'for his own safety' as he is transferred elsewhere in the city.

Helplessly, the lawyer inquires: 'Meaning?' A small boy looks on as Mr Obeidi puts his hands behind his back to have them bound with the same kind of plastic ties that US forces use to immobilise their Iraqi prisoners.

A source who claims to have studied the unedited video says that Mr Obeidi is then made to stand on the back of a white, Japanese-make utility as five men climb aboard. Two stand guard on either side and Abu Dereh takes up a position behind their hostage. Four other vehicles make up a convoy, which slows to walking pace as it arrives in the heart of Sadr City.

One of the guards is seen hitting Mr Obeidi twice on the back of the neck. Local traffic joins the procession as children and adults run alongside, chanting Shiite slogans and the name Abu Dereh. Others gather on rooftops and some in the crowd throw stones.

A voice, said to be that of Abu Dereh, is heard through a loudspeaker on one of the vehicles: 'This is a criminal. He is worse than Saddam Hussein because he defends the man who killed Iraqis. This is the destiny of a traitor.'

After parading their captive for about 45 minutes, the convoy stops in an open, dusty bazaar. Abu Dereh produces a Glock pistol from his pocket. Still standing behind Mr Obeidi, he steadies the lawyer by grabbing the clothing on his left shoulder. Wrapping his right arm around Mr Obeidi's upper body, he places the barrel of the pistol hard up under the lawyer's chin—three shots are heard.

As Mr Obeidi slumps he is caught by the guards and dumped from the back of the utility. Several produce their own weapons and, amid cheers by bystanders, they fire a volley of shots into the lawyer's body.

The father of six children, Mr Obeidi is the tenth person associated with the trial of Saddam to be murdered in eighteen months. His colleagues in Saddam's legal team, Sadoun Janabi and Adel al-Zubeidi, were murdered late last year. A judge and the judge's son were among seven court officials also murdered. There have been no arrests.

Just weeks before his abduction, Mr Obeidi explained to a reporter why he refused a US offer of accommodation in Baghdad's fortified Green Zone. 'If we withdraw out of fear, it will not be a shame for us as lawyers but for the entire Iraqi judicial system. The only weapon we have is praying to God to protect us from being killed.'

At the time, Mr Obeidi's death was attributed by his defence colleagues to Shiite death squads operating within the Iraqi security forces. Others claimed it was the work of the Mahdi army militia of the rebel Shiite cleric, Moqtada al-Sadr.

One of Abu Dereh's associates confirmed that the warlord had been a senior figure in the Mahdi army but claimed that Al-Sadr had disowned the killer because he could not control his violent sprees. But another said Al-Sadr had laughed as he sent Abu Dereh packing—as though he did not mean what he had said.

'He is the hero of the Shiites because he avenges attacks on us that are not dealt with by the authorities,' the associate said. The 40-something Abu Dereh is said to have been responsible for the abduction of scores of Sunnis whose bodies have been recovered from a garbage tip at Al-Sada, a lawless wasteland near Sadr City.

But the story the associate relished confirming was about the warlord commandeering a fleet of government ambulances with which he lured dozens of Sunnis to their death. 'He drove the vehicles into Adhamiyah [a Sunni-dominated quarter of Baghdad] and used the ambulance loudspeakers to make this announcement: "Please give blood for the insurgency! The Shiia are killing your insurgency brothers!"'

Sweeping his hand as if telling the tale of the Pied Piper of Hamelin, the associate gave the impression that he was among those with Abu Dereh: 'They piled in. They were mostly young people—between 40 and 50 of them,' he said.

The associate also said that, as a Shiite warrior, Abu Dereh had also declared the Americans to be the enemy. As proof, he produced a DVD compilation of what he said was Abu Dereh's fighters at war with US forces in Sadr City: close-ups of injured

Americans being rescued by colleagues or captured by Shiite fighters, and the destruction of what appear to be US tanks and other heavy vehicles.

Abu Dereh is thought to have masterminded the July kidnapping of Tayseer Najah al-Mashhadani, a Sunni woman MP, who is believed to be still alive. He also is said to have supervised the forced eviction of hundreds of Sunni families from Shiite-dominated areas of the capital and some outlying towns. He reputedly offers his victims a choice in the manner of their death—suffocation, shooting, or what was described as 'being smashed with cinder blocks'.

Authorities have not publicly revealed Abu Dereh's name, but Iraqi and US forces are hunting for him. The associate claimed that Abu Dereh had stood among onlookers watching a US attack on his own home in Sadr City in the first days of August.

Another source who claimed to be familiar with the warlord's activities told me: 'The next day Abu Dereh goes to the Ministry of the Interior and marches straight into the office of the Iraqi general who helped organise the American attack on his house. He warns the general not to go near his house again. There's nothing he can do, because before going to his office Abu Dereh kidnapped two of the general's sons. He released them unharmed later.'

There is speculation that after a recent series of attacks on Sunnis, Abu Dereh has crossed Iraq's eastern border, opting to lie low for a while in neighbouring Iran.

MISSION FAILED

Baghdad, Iraq
26 August 2006

The layout drawings are a state secret, so just where Starbucks and Krispy Kreme doughnuts will be is a mystery. But as the concrete hulks of a 21-building complex rise from the ashes of Saddam Hussein's Baghdad, Washington is sending a clear message to Iraqis: 'We're here to stay.'

It's being built in the Middle East, but 'George W's palace', as Iraqis have dubbed the new US embassy, is designed as a suburb of Washington. An army of more than 3500 diplomatic and support staff will have a sports centre, beauty parlour and swimming pool. Six residential blocks will each contain more than 600 apartments. The prime 25 hectares were a steal—actually a gift from the Iraqi government. And if the five-metre-thick perimeter wall doesn't keep the Iraqis at bay, then the built-in surface-to-air missile station should.

Guarded by a dozen gangly construction cranes, the site in the heart of the Green Zone is floodlit by night and is so removed from Iraqi reality that its entire construction force is foreign.

After almost four years, the Americans still can't turn on the lights for Iraqis, but that won't be a problem for the embassy staffers. The toilets are the same: they will always flush on command. All services for the biggest embassy in the world will be self-contained and operate independently from the rattletrap utilities of Baghdad.

Scheduled for completion in June next year, this is the only US reconstruction project in Iraq that is on track. Costing more than $US600 million, the fortress is bigger than the Vatican. It dwarfs the edifices of Saddam's wildest dreams and it irritates the hell out of ordinary Iraqis.

On a recent visit to the real Baghdad—outside the Green Zone—a deepening sectarian separation was immediately evident in the personal stories of everyday living. Abu Zamaan, a Shiite truckie who often updates me on life in the capital, had some very personal news: 'My daughter is upset because I blocked her wedding plans. He was a nice boy—rich and a good job—but he was a Sunni.'

Making fake identification papers has emerged as a thriving new business opportunity as Shiites and Sunnis try to blur their allegiances in a city where a name can be a death sentence. Men called Ali, Jafar, Moussin and Hyder are almost certainly Shiites—they face summary execution at Sunni checkpoints. Omar, Marwan and Khalid are Sunni names that cut little ice with the Shiite death squads.

The Shiite taxi driver, Salwan al-Robian, was unlucky. A couple of weeks ago he used his false papers for the first time to get through a Sunni checkpoint south of Baghdad. But, his companions told me, he gave himself away by invoking the name of Imam Ali, the Shiite saint, rather than that of Allah as a Sunni would, when he exclaimed at his good fortune in surviving the roadblock. The gunman heard him, and he was dragged off. His family recovered his body from the Tigris River a few days later.

Sunni graffiti artists now daub city walls with slogans such as 'Shiite families out' and 'Shiite dogs'. Meanwhile, Shiite men roar with laughter at DVD recordings of Shiite comics mocking Sunnis about their forthcoming outing to Al-Sada, a lawless section of the capital where Shiite death squads dump many of their victims.

In Baghdad, all roads lead to the morgue. Despite webs of spin from Baghdad to Washington and London about the nature of the violence in Iraq—is it an 'undeclared', a 'low-grade' or a 'nascent' civil war?—this establishment, on the city's northern side, comes from the pages of Dante. It reveals the unvarnished truth of this deepening conflict. The body count rises steadily: more than 1800 mutilated corpses were trucked in from across the capital last month, a significant rise on the June toll of almost 1600. Across the country, almost 3200 Iraqis died violently in June.

Coping with this flood of victims of suicide bombings and mass murders is an impossible task for morgue staff. The Iraqi police make an effort to be out before sunrise, to gather corpses from the killers' favourite dumping spots before the broiling heat of the day makes it an impossible task.

At the morgue, the bodies are divided along sectarian lines. The viciousness of the killings is sickening. Sunni victims of Shiia violence usually have holes drilled in their heads and joints, and are found near the Shiia slums of Sadr City; Shiia victims of Sunni violence are often shot in the head or decapitated and are usually dragged from the tepid waters of the Tigris. Up to 200 bodies are delivered each day. Sometimes there is the dignity of a body bag; but often body parts are delivered in banana boxes which have been discarded at city bazaars.

The Iraqi government threatens morgue staff with reprisals if they dare reveal information to reporters, because the data they hold is such a devastating indicator of the government's—and the Americans'—failure. But one of the doctors agrees to talk to me if his name is not published: 'It just gets worse, especially in this heat. The bodies have been in the sun for so long that they fall apart in our hands, just like that. It's a nightmare. At home I can't say anything about it to my family. And how can we believe it'll get any better—we don't have enough doctors to do the autopsies and we're getting more and more bodies every day.'

After almost four years of trying to build Washington's democracy beachhead in the Middle East, US defence officials concede the violence in Iraq is at its worst—by the body count, by public support and by the ease with which Sunni insurgents and Shiite militias exploit gaps in American forces, which are spread far too thinly to make a difference.

At most critical points the Americans misread the social, tribal, political and military landscape and have wrong-footed themselves by denying evolving realities that were all too apparent—the events they declared to be 'turning points' were actually 'tipping points'.

Distrust of Washington in all of the Iraqi factions has robbed the United States of what it believed was an easily won regional trump-card: control of Baghdad. But Iraq is a democracy in name only. The elected parliament doesn't function and, despite mouthing support for the niceties of the democratic process, it is hard not to conclude that Iraqi leaders have more faith in achieving their goals by letting the violence run than by taking part in any US-managed national dialogue.

The dynamic has changed. Sunnis who campaigned for US forces to leave Iraq now insist they should remain, to protect the

Sunnis because the Shiia majority has a taste for blood. Shiites who welcomed the American invaders now declare the United States to be an enemy bent on robbing them of their centuries-old dream of control of the country.

It's remarkable that George Bush has waited until now to—reportedly—vent his frustration at the failure of the Iraqis 'to appreciate the sacrifice the United States has made in Iraq'. Ironically, about the same time as the White House meeting on 14 August at which the president wondered aloud about the ability of yet another Iraqi government to turn the tide of violence, a Baghdad factory owner was mimicking the American president to me: 'We give them Pepsi, the internet and mobile phones and they're still not happy. What more do they want?'

The combined forces of the US and the Iraqi government number more than 400,000, but the country remains a lawless jungle. The Americans say they get thousands of 'actionable tips' from Iraqis; they kill or capture more than 500 insurgents a week and they are defusing twice as many roadside bombs now as they were in January. But graphs of car bombings, armed attacks and civilian deaths keep climbing. It's the same with the estimated ranks of the Sunni-backed insurgency—more than 20,000 and rising. And almost half the Iraqi respondents to a recent poll approved of attacks on US forces.

Iraqi and other agencies now estimate the death toll since the March 2003 invasion stands at 50,000 or more. But in a country trying to rebuild itself, there is another disturbing development: more than 40 per cent of its professional classes have fled abroad since the invasion. They include an estimated 12,000 doctors; they have been driven away by the murder of 2000 of their colleagues, the kidnapping of 250 more and salaries that stagnate at about $US400 a month.

The US Committee for Refugees and Immigrants estimates that close to 900,000 Iraqis have fled their country since 2003. Iraqi Airways has more than doubled flights to Damascus to cope with the exodus; bus services on the treacherous desert route to Jordan have gone from two to 50 a day; and taxi passengers who used to pay $US200 for a ride to Amman now are gouged for $US750.

Those who are stuck among the rotting garbage piles in Baghdad take what precautions they can. As statistics cry failure on so many fronts, Washington's stated plan for US forces in Iraq to 'stand down as the new Iraqi forces stand up' is being shredded daily, along with the lives of innocent civilian victims in the streets of Baghdad.

Much of the terror is organised by private militias that have infiltrated the Iraqi security forces. These militias are operated by the key political parties in Prime Minister Nouri al-Maliki's administration. His government would fall without the political support of one of the worst offenders, the radical Shiite clerical leader Moqtada al-Sadr and his Mahdi army militia.

In Basra, deep in the south, there is little Sunni insurgency activity, but there is much violence as Shiite militias and warlords fight for turf. British and American officers accuse neighbouring Iran (Shiite) and Saudi Arabia (Sunni) of arming the factions. The country's second-biggest city becomes more Islamicised by the day: music and liquor shops have been bombed out of business, women are made to wear headscarves and board games are being outlawed, much as kite-flying was criminalised by the Taliban in Afghanistan.

Whatever the Americans have done in Iraq has usually been too little, too late. The June death in a US bombing raid of Abu Musab al-Zarqawi, the Sunni insurgency leader and Al-Qaeda point man in Iraq, was a powerful combat victory, but the absence from the battlefield of the Jordanian-born terrorist has failed to staunch the blood-letting. Zarqawi's stated objective was to foment unstoppable sectarian war. In a sense his brutal work was done with the February bombing of a revered Shiite shrine at Samarra, north of Baghdad. Unlike Bush, Zarqawi could go to his grave rightly claiming: 'Mission accomplished.'

The two sides are dug in for the long haul. On one side are disparate Sunni insurgency cells, which now show great unity and common purpose: the religious rhetoric is the same, their leadership is Iraqi not foreign, and they have defeated a US counter-insurgency push to divide them.

On the other side, the Shiites use the well-stocked resources of the US-trained and funded Iraqi security forces. A senior figure in Al-Sadr's Mahdi army says: 'We can get anything we need. We are a professional force: we have proper command-and-control structures; organisation is strict; and after the victory for Hezbollah in Lebanon, we feel stronger and more powerful because we have seen what a Shiite force can achieve.'

He then took time to make clear who the enemy was: 'We will fight the Sunnis till they have a clean heart towards Shiites. But we have to fight the Americans too, because they are with the Sunnis against us.'

Despite all the hand-wringing in Washington and Baghdad, the new US-trained, funded and equipped Iraqi police service is riddled with corruption and sectarian murderers. The Iraqi army is not much better. On the flight into Baghdad, an American official told me of the challenge a colleague faced as he arrived to lecture the senior ranks of the Iraqi forces on military ethics. This, he said, is how an Iraqi general introduced him to the class: 'Don't worry, we'll do it their way while the Americans are here . . . and then we'll do it our own way.'

In a city of 7 million people, 25 or 30 violent attacks a day might sound insignificant. But the pervasive uncertainty and the randomness of the strikes has crimped the personal space of ordinary Iraqis much more tightly than was the case in the days of Saddam Hussein's dictatorship. Communities are barricading themselves and recruiting vigilante squads or pleading to the militias for protection. Children are kept indoors and few adults stray from the confines of their workplace, their houses and the nearby homes of friends. Simple errands become fraught logistical operations.

When I accompanied a Shiite resident of suburban Al-Salam City on a shopping expedition, we became trapped in gridlocked traffic for 90 terrifying minutes. It was impossible to move. Behind us was a mesh of checkpoints thrown up in the wake of a roadside bombing. In front of us chaos, because the police had set up a routine checkpoint just where a two-kilometre queue of cars waited for petrol at a petrol station that had run dry.

Barging through the middle of all this, sirens blaring and guns firing, was a convoy of police utes with heavily guarded prisoners on the back of each—except that in Baghdad, you can never be sure that the men in uniform are policemen or that their prisoners are not hostages being whisked off to a rubbish-dump execution. Neither can you be sure that while that 'police' convoy inches past you that it will not become a target for another bombing.

As we sat there, it was not just the 50-degree heat of summer that had our Shiite driver in a bath of perspiration. He angrily hurled a Pepsi can out the window, shouting: 'How can we be expected to live with all this dread and fear? Under Saddam all we had to do was keep our traps shut, but now we never know who will strike . . . or when. We used to have one Saddam, but now we have thousands and we don't know what their rules are.'

Increasingly, there is talk of dividing Baghdad—and the entire country. As the prime minister, Al-Maliki, shows signs of the same isolation and ineffectiveness that beset his predecessor, a senior government official articulated what many observers suspect, telling reporters: 'Iraq as a political project is finished—the parties have moved to Plan B.' The Tigris is a natural 'Baghdad wall'. Sunnis dominate to the west of the river; Shiites to the east and, in the minds of some, this would be a logical and manageable carve-up as those who are driven from their homes seek refuge on 'their' side of the river.

Washington trumpeted the new Iraqi constitution drawn up in 2004 as the glue that would bind the Iraqi nation, but the observers who warned that it was a recipe for partition, if not the disintegration of the Iraqi state, are being proved right. Powerful Shiite political figures now use the lack of security to justify a three-state federation in which each statelet would stand its own army to fend off that of the other two.

Abdul Aziz Hakim, leader of the Iranian-backed Supreme Council for Islamic Revolution in Iraq, is pushing a nine-province Shiite state in the south—with about 60 per cent of known oil reserves—along the same lines as the Kurdish fortress that exists in the north. The Sunnis would be left in the west and the middle of the country with virtually none of the country's rich resources and a festering, divided capital which would have only nominal control of the nation's affairs. American and British officials who, in the early days of the US-led occupation, touted the south as a model of post-Saddam stability, now complain that it is captive to Shiite warlords and militias who are laying the groundwork for Hakim's grand design.

The nominal enemy for the United States in Baghdad is the militias and criminal gangs, but the force they are up against is Iraqi indifference—if the centre doesn't hold, nothing holds. But the Iraqis didn't ask for democracy so much as an opportunity to slice and dice the country's people and resource riches according to their own agendas.

Perhaps one of the most dangerous signs of things to come in Iraq is the fading authority of the Shiite's reclusive spiritual leader, Grand Ayatollah Ali al-Sistani. Before the Samarra bombing in February, his fatwas were an effective restraint on Shiite revenge for Sunni attacks. Not anymore. Last month he called on 'all sons of Iraq [to] stand shoulder to shoulder [to] reject hatred and violence', but the killing sprees picked up a notch. 'We warned about this,' Hytham Husseini, the adviser to Hakim, explained. 'Young people will not observe fatwas when they want revenge for the suffering of their families.'

This is not the first Western intervention in the Middle East. But most previous efforts were about putting down money and arms to keep the home bowsers primed. This time the foreigners' gift of democracy has unleashed a perfect storm of nationalism, religious fundamentalism and a tribal war that threatens Washington's whole grand design for the region.

The neo-conservatives who urged the US-led invasion of Iraq in 2003 were convinced that if Saddam Hussein was eliminated, then Iraqis would instinctively default to the ways of democracy. If this is democratic Iraq, welcome to the new Middle East.

IRAQI JUSTICE

Baghdad, Iraq

26 August 2006

The lined face peers from shrouds of mourning black. Wabila Felehi Hussein is a 50-year-old grandmother, and her life is imploding.

Muthanna, her 30-year-old son, is dead; Adel, her eldest boy, has fled to Egypt; Hanoon, her husband, is in near-catatonic shock. After 35 years in the mixed community of Hoorijab, on Baghdad's southern rural fringe, they were driven out under gunfire. Now sixteen of them camp in a single room in the Shiite slums of Sadr City.

Even a short time spent with this family reveals the grandmother's towering strength. Until now, all the blood-letting has been laid at the door of organised insurgency cells, religious militias, death squads that operate within the national security forces and tribal gangs. But this woman is being hailed by thousands as the Shiite mother who spectacularly—and brutally—avenged her son's death.

197

US officials tick the boxes as they try to build a civil society: they have written a constitution, there have been elections, and new police and military services are in training. But it all collapses in a meaningless heap at the feet of Wabila Felehi Hussein. Iraq's democracy dream is being strangled at birth.

Wabila Felehi's home town, Hoorijab, is near the gateway towns to an insurgency stronghold to the south-west of the capital which has been dubbed the Triangle of Death. But the family insists that until just a few weeks ago the Shiite minority still shared meals and tea with Sunni neighbours.

Then suddenly the word *alasa*—traitors—was in the air as Shiites accused old Sunni friends of fingering them for an insurgency clean-out of Shiites. On 31 July, Muthanna, the fourth son of Wabila Felehi, was abducted from the makeshift shop where he sold ice, fruit and black-market petrol.

'The next day they started shooting at our house—we left in just the clothes we were wearing,' the grandmother says as she sits cross-legged on the marbled floor of a friend's home. 'We searched for ten days before someone told us that Muthanna's body had been dumped in the river at Arabjabour [which is inside the Triangle of Death]. I asked the police to get him back. They said it was too dangerous. The Iraqi army and the Mahdi army [a Shiite militia] refused to recover him, so I had to do it myself.'

Her adult sons—Adel, Saad and Mohanad—feared for their lives, so she organised sixteen other men, guns and cars. Saad explains how finally she shamed them into action, threatening to go alone if they would not go with her.

As the convoy set out for Arabjabour, Wabila Felehi was in the first of five cars. The family was armed with borrowed weapons—three rocket-propelled grenade launchers, a few AK-47s and a handful of pistols. 'At the last checkpoint before Arabjabour, the Iraqi police warned that if we went to the river we'd be killed,'

Saad says. '[The officer] got angry when my mother abused him for cowardice, but he stepped out of our way when she announced: "We are ready to die."'

The evening light was fading as they came to a point on the river bank where six bloated bodies floated face-down in waist-deep water. They recognised the clothing on one as Muthanna's and they confirmed his identity by two tattoos. The brothers used a blanket to haul his remains up the embankment, laying him at his mother's feet. His hands were tied behind his back, there were two bullet wounds to the back of his head and he had been beaten.

But there was no time for grieving. Suddenly the sky was lit by a parachute flare and they were under attack. Saad said: 'As we loaded the body onto a pick-up, they started firing mortars; they raked our cars with Kalashnikov fire.'

Saad attempts to explain that his mother's strength 'comes from the God' but she cuts across him: 'I couldn't wait—this was my son. Now I wait for God to avenge his death.'

Not quite. Wabila Felehi Hussein is already exacting her own temporal revenge with a cold-bloodedness that, even by Iraqi standards, is unnerving. Out of earshot of the family, the friend in whose house we meet admonishes me: 'You didn't ask who told them the body was in the river.'

He then explains that, after fleeing Hoorijab, the first task the mother set for her sons was to work their mobile phones, calling the few whom they could still trust in Hoorijab to get the name of the *alasa* who might have given Muthanna's name to the insurgency.

'They got the name of the son of a local tribal sheikh who lived near their house,' he says. 'When she sent the boys, she insisted he must be brought back to Sadr City alive, because no one was to be killed unless they had proof of their involvement in Muthanna's death. He was interrogated and gave up nine more names. Eight of them were abducted and brought back for interrogation . . . and then they killed them with guns, knives and by bashing some of them. Adel killed six; Saad killed three.'

So then, if this is democratic Iraq, Wabila Felehi Hussein is unimpressed with the new Middle East. But as she slip-slapped her hands in disgust, she was contemptuous. 'This is not democracy . . . We have no stability, no future. It would be better if we all were dead . . . Get me out of Iraq.'

Tears streaming down her face, she hit bottom. 'We were happy when the Americans came. They lifted the Saddam darkness, but now they have led us into a new, blacker darkness.'

THREE INTO ONE
PROVES AN ODD FIT

Baghdad, Iraq
4 November 2006

Cartography is such jolly good fun. Take this river, slash a pencil across the map till it hits those mountains, and we'll give it a flag and call it a country. Stop! Go back—the oil fields are meant to be on 'our' side of the line.

That's pretty well how it was done in the early 1900s. Fabled names from the British Colonial Office stomped the marshes of Mesopotamia: Percy Cox, Gertrude Bell and T.E. Lawrence. Especially colourful was the pipe-smoking St John Philby, the father of the English spy, Kim, who careered around the deserts on a motorcycle, drawing borders as he went.

That's how we got Iraq. They threw together three loosely affiliated provinces of the collapsed Ottoman empire: Mosul, Baghdad and Basra. But they had no regard for the lack of national or even communal interest between the three provinces.

Fast-forward to 2003. The Americans, like the British before them, refused to go to their libraries and archives, where shelves groan with sociological and political studies dating from the thirteenth century, warning that the geographic putty they wanted to mould as the new Iraq was treacherous stuff for would-be colonisers.

Down the centuries, the regional landscape has changed dramatically—politically, commercially, militarily—but the missing ingredient has always been any real sense of nation. To the extent that the people we call Iraqis were bound at all, the cohesive forces have been the tribe, the clan and—more recently—the mosque. Attempts to centralise power were met with contempt and, inevitably, they failed.

Ironically, the most successful was that by the ousted dictator Saddam Hussein. But even he could manipulate the tribes and clans for only so long, and only with the brute force for which he is likely to be sentenced to death tomorrow.

The high point for Saddam was 1991, when tribal chiefs assembled at his presidential palace in Baghdad. They laid at his feet banners that represented their mini-statehood and they removed their headdress as a tribal sign of their deference and allegiance. This was not about love and respect for Saddam, so much as the dictator's ability to strike the right price—in money and jobs, power and influence—as he played the tribes against each other. Saddam even took to calling his Baath party the 'tribe of tribes'. But by 2003 the sheikhs had had a gutful, so they stepped back as their 'chief of chieftains' was taken down by an American-led strike.

Amid the excitement of a successful military invasion, acknowledging the tribes was too much like anti-democratic mumbo-jumbo for the predominantly Republican evangelicals who swarmed into Baghdad on an American mission to rebuild Iraq as a model of democracy. But the tribes' renewed sense of entitlement was a time bomb left for the Americans by Saddam.

Today it is exploding and, as Iraq falls apart, we are witnessing the birth of at least three new nations: already we know the mountains of the north as Kurdistan; the resource-rich, southern triangle likely will become Shiiastan; and a barren, central belt could become Sunnistan.

Now that the US rhetoric of 'stay the course' is starting to mean 'cut and run', advocates of breaking up the country are getting traction in the Iraq discourse in Washington. Britain is falling into line and Australia doesn't matter. American leverage— diplomatic, economic and military—is just about exhausted and, despite all their vital interests, none of the neighbours will help. Except to stir the pot.

There are many recipes for attempting to unscramble the Iraqi eggs. 'Hard' partition, 'soft' federalism, 'loose' confederation and, try this one, 'Quebec-like asymmetrical decentralisation'. But all entail stepping down the road towards dismantling what the British built in the years after World War I.

Incredibly, against the backdrop of so much suffering in liberated Iraq, some US analysts still believe they have the luxury of choosing between the break-up of Iraq and a full-blooded civil war, seemingly forgetting that one is usually born of the other and, invariably, at huge and painful cost to the local population.

A few cheerfully fall back on the Vietnam-era policy of bombing villages to save them. In an essay circulating on the internet, Major Isaiah Wilson III, a former military planner in Iraq who now lectures at West Point, brims with enthusiasm as he answers his own question: 'Should we give civil war a chance . . . ? For Iraq, as ironic and illogical as it may seem, a true and sustainable future may come in the aftermath of the very sectarian-based civil war we have been striving to prevent.'

The partition massacres in India–Pakistan and, more recently, in the Balkans are either forgotten or factored in as just another price to be paid, with numbing suggestions such as retired US Colonel T.X. Hammes's offering to the *Washington Post*: 'We will have to develop and fund some kind of displacement agency to move the families . . .'

The Brookings Institution's Michael O'Hanlon also masks the inevitable further suffering by Iraqis in chillingly abstract terms: 'the international community and the Iraqi government could help offer housing and jobs to those wishing to move as well as protection en route. Houses left behind would revert to government ownership, to be offered to individuals of other ethnic groups who wanted them, in what would largely become a program of swapping.'

How might the new new Iraq look?

The noise you hear is the back door slamming as the Kurds quit Iraq. Since 1991 they have had virtual autonomy and they have managed to preserve and strengthen it in the new Iraqi constitution. They have a booming economy. They have their own language and now have adopted English over Arabic as the second language to be taught in their schools. They have their own military and their own laws; they refuse to fly the Iraqi flag and staff of the Baghdad ministries and the Iraqi military are barred from entering Kurdistan.

Shiites are now demanding that they be allowed to have in the south what the Kurds have in the north. The Shiite factions have taken to shooting at each other in recent weeks but, while their divisions are voiced as support or opposition to partition, they are read by some analysts more as tests of numerical strength and a contest for control of oil and funds. The imposition of strict Islamic codes across the south suggests the government of Shiiastan would be a version of the neighbouring Iranian theocracy. That would be deeply disappointing for Washington.

The main Sunni players in Iraq are fighting any break-up, principally because Iraq's vast oil wealth lies beneath the Kurdish strongholds in the north (40 per cent) and the Shiite strongholds of the south (60 per cent). But Al-Qaeda had already declared a Sunni Islamic emirate through central Iraq. And if the Kurds and the Shiites go their own way, it would amount to a lock-out—the Sunnis would have been forced into a sad and sullen state, sandwiched between their runaway neighbours to the north and south.

Secular and Islamist factions could well end up fighting for control of Sunnistan; a contest that Rend al-Rahim, an Iraqi community leader in the United States, predicts would make it a radical, Taliban-style regime and a potential breeding ground for regional, if not global, terrorism. This would be even more bitterly disappointing for Washington.

In Baghdad recently, I asked one of the architects of the new Shiiastan about the Sunni fears of abandonment and impoverishment in their new statelet. He replied dismissively: 'So what?'

War has neutered Baghdad as a central authority; the Iraqi parliament has legislated for the first steps towards dismemberment of the country; and the new Iraqi constitution, which Washington hailed as a victory for democracy, also happens to be a break-up blueprint. The constitution reduces Baghdad to a shell of a capital—it might end up with control of foreign affairs and some fiscal powers, but tax-raising, much security and all new resources royalties would go to the new regional capitals.

There is hardly a nationalist bone among the new Iraqi leadership. Instead of running the country for all Iraqis, they fight for sect and ethnic control of ministries, which many of them then rob blind. The security forces are the same—they too have splintered into ethnic and religious fiefdoms, with little regard for the national good.

The dissolutionists gloss over the intense inter-mixing of Shiites, Sunnis and Kurds in Iraq's biggest cities, arguing that Baghdad could be a Canberra- or Washington-style capital state, or that the population in Baghdad and Mosul could be shunted to whichever bank of the Tigris River they already dominate. The United Nations estimates that since the US-led invasion, 1.6 million Iraqis have fled the country and another 1.5 million have been internally displaced. In other conflicts we gave this process a name: ethnic cleansing.

The oil-rich, north-eastern city of Kirkuk is an explosive element in the new equation: the Kurds want it; the Shiites and Sunnis insist they can't have it. The Kurds argue it is Kurdish; but local Arabs, many of whom were trucked in as part of Saddam's program of Arabisation, and a sizeable Turkoman population, disagree. And on another front, no one seems to have given any thought to the fate of Iraq's significant Christian population.

The likeliest aftermath of partition would be continuing war. The Americans would be safer in bases in the new Kurdistan and Shiiastan, whose respective militias could be enlisted as security forces to man their borders. Territorial disputes would leave stretchmarks the length of all the new borders and Sunnistan, inevitably, would be home to terrorist elements and to Sunni nationalists refusing to concede the loss of what was their share of Iraq's natural resources—oil, in particular. That means a lot more war.

If the Sunnis were starved of foreign reconstruction aid, they would soon fall into line, some of the dissolutionists claim. 'Let them rot,' argues a retired US Army officer, Ralph Peters.

The regional consequences are dire, too. Do the Shiite theocrats in Tehran put Shiiastan in their pocket? Will the Shiites of adjoining north-eastern Saudi Arabia, whose territory holds much of the kingdom's oil wealth, want to join in? How much

Kurdish autonomy would Turkey tolerate? How much Sunni dispossession could Saudi Arabia and Jordan stand? And whatever the Americans do in Iraq now, they can hardly move without being accused by at least one of the three main factions of siding with one of the other two.

One of the darkest warnings from analysts on the hopelessness of Washington's position is their underscoring of a deep lack of trust in the new Iraq. No matter how watertight any deal on power- or resource-sharing might seem, there are scores to be settled, so there is no reason for the Sunnis to trust either the Shiites or the Kurds in the long term.

Another of their warnings is not to think just of three regions. Some analysts predict volatility and fragmentation within each of the three regions; there are two Kurdish factions, and numerous Shiite and Sunni factions that are capable of turning on each other as they jockey for supremacy in the respective regions.

So, as civil war and disintegration continue apace, what might we learn from the history of conflicts around the globe? Stanford University's Professor James Fearon had sobering news for a US congressional committee in September. He told them the average duration of post-World War II civil wars around the globe is more than ten years; the chances of a successful power-sharing agreement ending such conflicts are less than one in six; and the presence of foreign forces merely delays the inevitable. Whether they stayed for one or five more years, the likely scenario on the departure of US forces is a Lebanon-style civil war.

Those archives of advice that were ignored by Washington also hold the ruminations of John Glubb, a 1920s British colonial officer who, in his diaries, railed against the US and the British establishment and media. He wrote: '[They] continue to demand that the nations of Asia and Africa should make a clean cut with their past and, at one fell stroke, adopt the mentality and traditions of the Western democracies . . . Would it not be more practical, as well as more polite, if we left these nations to govern themselves in their own way?'

At that time, Glubb was seen as a captive of the romance of the desert tribes. In these politically-correct times, some will dismiss his suggestion that the desert is no place for democracy as racist. But as the Americans try to backtrack out of a hell of their own making and Iraq disintegrates into something like it was 80-plus years ago, it seems that, despite his romance and racism, Glubb actually wrote what his successors might belatedly call an 'exit strategy'.

THE OIL GUSHER

Basra, Iraq
16 October 2010

The tension is exquisite. Iraq is a political, security and economic basket-case, but it's also the world's last energy bonanza. So, desperate for a piece of the hottest hydrocarbon action on earth, oil executives come to prostrate themselves—offering to pump Iraq's runny black gold for a pittance.

There is another tension, equally exquisite. As the politicians fumble their efforts to create a government that might harness oil wealth so colossal that it could catapult Iraq to among the globe's leading economies, they are in a race against time and rising anger in a marginalised and disenchanted population.

All of that is topped off by a remarkable turn of events. After waging a trillion-dollar war of liberation, which at home and abroad was cited often as a measure of Washington's determination to kick in Baghdad's door for the Texas oilmen and their kin, American companies were left in the wash by more determined competitors from across the world in the grand auction of development licences in Baghdad. 'Paltry' is how the *Washington Post* described the performance of the American firms.

The Chinese are in in a big way; so too the Russians and Europeans. Companies from Malaysia and Angola have a stake in five of the winning consortia. Petronas, state-owned in Kuala Lumpur, is a partner in three; Luanda's part-state-owned Sonangal is a partner in two.

Seven US firms registered for the Baghdad auction, but only one—Exxon Mobil—came through as a senior partner. Of the rest, only Occidental Petroleum Inc. won a minority stake in a single project. By comparison, the state-owned Chinese National Petroleum Corp [CNPC] is the senior partner in two developments, and two Russian firms—including the Kremlin-owned Gazprom—are in there too. Big American oil houses like Chevron and ConocoPhillips, which industry observers expected would stay in the mix because of their close ties to the Iraq oil ministry, were left with nothing.

When the BP–Chinese joint-venture became the first to test the Baghdad waters—offering a deal by which it would be paid just $US2 a barrel to lift oil, as it promised to push the 'super giant' Rumaila oilfield's output to just under 3 million barrels per day—some in the industry saw the bid as a crazy, self-defeating lowball. But in the wake of the BP–CNPC negotiations with Baghdad, two hard realities emerged for the rest of the industry. One, Baghdad was deadly serious about retaining sovereign ownership of its resources and so would hold the international oil companies to being paid a flat per-barrel fee, meaning that all the upside from rising oil prices will flow to Iraq; and two, that the $2-a-barrel fee for Rumaila was a first-bidder's reward for BP–CNPC and that most who came after them would be screwed just a little bit harder by Baghdad.

Despite the feigned scepticism of the oil majors when confronted by this hard-nosed stance in Baghdad, the December auction at which the development licences were sold was seen as the best last chance to be a player in the world's last energy casino. Despite a wave of terror bombings, which were intended to frighten off the bidders in the run-up to the auction, a senior oil man told me: 'Those last days were the tipping point for companies deciding they just had to be in.'

Alluding to the low profile of the American firms that were expected to lead the charge, he explained: 'The people you don't see are Chevron, who did a lot of work on West Qurna, which is the second or third biggest oilfield in the world. ConocoPhillips also is significant by its absence.'

Ben Lando, Baghdad bureau chief for *Iraq Oil Report*, explained: 'American companies aren't involved to the extent everyone thought—which was utter domination. Instead, the Americans are providing drilling and other services, [a level of participation] that does seem a bit tepid for the country that actually gave birth to the oil industry.'

Another international executive, whose company failed in the Baghdad bidding, explained the American reluctance as cautious business decision-making. 'You look at the security and political madness in Iraq,' he said. 'And then you look somewhere else, maybe Brazil or Australia's North West Shelf—secure environment, stable government and hungry markets nearby—and you say "go for it". Instead of the US domination that many expected in Iraq, you have an Iraqi oil sector that is essentially Chinese, European, British and Malaysian.'

Another explanation puts the countless uncertainties of Iraq in a different light, highlighting the extent to which bungling by Washington in the years since the September 11 attacks on New York and Washington has diminished US power as a global force.

Noting how the United States choreographed the drawdown of its troops from Iraq as another 'mission accomplished' moment in August this year, an international oil executive in transit through Amman, Jordan, made this point to me: 'They thought conquering Iraq would be easy, but they are leaving without having created the kind of environment that would have better positioned US companies to exploit the vast wealth of Iraq.'

When I quizzed the Baghdad government's chief energy adviser, Thamir Ghadhban, he pointedly recalled the live national telecast of the auction of the licences. 'It was all done in a very transparent manner,' he said. 'I can't explain why the Americans are absent . . . but it does prove that the Iraqi government did not deliver its oil on a gold platter to anyone, doesn't it? And what is good about the outcome is the diversity—companies from Europe, South Asia, North America, Japan and Korea.'

At this point in the interview, Thamir Ghadhban became positively smug, outlining his take on the deals struck by Baghdad. 'Analysts say that under the contracts we have signed, the government's take will be almost 95 per cent and that the companies will get only 5 to 6 per cent of the revenue. The deals the companies wanted would have given them about 20 per cent of the revenue.'

At that kind of discount, it needs to be said that the risks for the international oil companies are huge. Quite apart from continuing security and corruption crises, the failure by successive administrations in the new Iraq to agree to a new legal framework for the industry exposes it to the risk of a repeat of Saddam Hussein's 1972 nationalisation of the whole industry. Local trade unions are antsy about any foreign participation; some of the tribes are up in arms over the extent to which revenue is to be centralised through Baghdad; Kurds in the north want to run their oil sector as a separate entity from the rest of the industry; and there is jockeying in the oil-rich south for even greater retention of oil revenue in the areas in which it is generated.

But the potential rewards for the companies are huge too, because they have an inside running in one of the boldest expansions of the industry ever contemplated. In 2007, *Harpers* magazine did a rough and ready calculation; assuming an oil price of $US60 per barrel and proven reserves of 115 billion barrels, it priced Iraq as a $US7-trillion energy bonanza. Fast-forward to the present; the oil price is up around $US80 and industry 'guesstimates' put Iraq's total oil reserves at double that 115 billion barrel figure referenced by *Harpers*.

At its most modest, Iraq presents its plan as a 'doubling of output in a few years'. Stated more boldly, however, regional and global security and economic imperatives kick-in. Baghdad wants to overtake Tehran, to its east, as a major producer before knocking over the world's number-one producer, Riyadh, to its south. Jealous of its historic standing as the world's biggest gas station, Saudi Arabia has already revealed plans to push its own capacity—currently about 11 million barrels per day—beyond the 12 million barrels-per-day mark.

Driven by its hunger for revenue, Iraq is desperate to use any growth in its production capacity to the maximum, but that will require deft diplomacy with its neighbours and with more distant energy producers. Still to be resolved are the terms on which Iraq returns to the ranks of a global powerhouse it helped to form 40 years ago: the Organization of the Petroleum Exporting Countries (OPEC). Calculating production quotas for member countries—using a formula based on total reserves and production capacity—OPEC works to keep the ever-sensitive oil price in a band within which all can live. The objective is to stay the hand of individual producers who otherwise might flood the market and force a price-cut, which would compel other producers to pump more oil to maintain their earnings, which would in turn force prices even lower.

The realpolitik here is that Iraq's planned mega-barrels cannot be sold into the market unless capitals from Moscow to Caracas are prepared to take either a production or a revenue hit. Iraq's pre-Gulf War quota was 3.1 million barrels per day, roughly the amount by which OPEC forecasts world demand will increase by 2015. Currently producing 2.5 million barrels per day, but with the world's third biggest reserves of oil, Baghdad wants to arrive at a massive 12 million barrels per day, all in a matter of just seven years.

Restoring Iraq's quota would, alone, account for all OPEC's forecasted market growth, requiring other producers to forego any quota increases. But on top of that, Iraq's plans for massive expansion would position it to dump three times the OPEC growth forecast onto the market. Something has to give. Advanced economies might welcome a market awash with low-priced Iraqi oil. No doubt they would call it 'price moderation', but other oil-producers might see it as something else . . . perhaps a pricing war.

Apart from acknowledging a need for 'market cooperation', Baghdad has yet to state its quota expectations. Oil politics were the root of Saddam Hussein's back-to-back wars—his decade-long conflict with Iran and his short-lived but costly invasion of Kuwait. At a security conference in Bahrain last year, Iraqi Foreign Minister Hoshyar Zebari rattled Baghdad's sabre: 'Iraq is a powerhouse in the region and it will regain its place, its rightful place [in OPEC].'

That insistent tone was present as Oil Minister Hussein al-Shahristani revealed to me an outline of Baghdad's thinking. Other producers had been making hay during Iraq's two-decade absence from the market, and Iraq now expects them to step back. 'All the countries realise Iraq has been deprived of its fair share over many years and [that we] need revenues to rebuild our economy and infrastructure,' he said when we met in Baghdad. Suggesting that some had degenerated into global gamblers, he went on: 'Many countries have finished the requirements of reconstruction and a lot of their additional revenues are going for external investment and not internally absorbed by their economies. We expect them to understand Iraq's requirements and to accommodate our wish to increase production.'

At the same time, Al-Shahristani embraced the OPEC strategy of producer countries maximising revenue as 'a product of exports and market prices'. Acknowledging OPEC's concerns, he added: 'So we'll make sure that the world energy market is supplied with all the oil it requires, but not flooded so that the prices will be adversely affected.'

Beyond locking horns with its competitors or, if it is lucky, schmoozing its way through the gaps in OPEC's ranks, there is a pressing need for Bagdad to settle explosive domestic differences. In the past seven years, the country's sects and creeds have not been able to finalise the terms of their cohabitation in the absence of Saddam Hussein's vice-like grip. At a time when they desperately need leadership and a government that can confidently get on with business, Baghdad's political wannabes have spent seven months since national elections in March mind-numbingly failing to agree on who should be the new prime minister. These are the fragile early days of a new democracy born in fraught circumstances; in the absence of a firm governing authority, the promise of oil billions alongside the existence of a US-trained and funded Iraqi military machine could tempt some in the military or political classes to consider a coup—it would not be the first time.

Historically, the only countries that have managed to ramp production as dramatically as Iraq intends have been the former Soviet Union and Saudi Arabia. In the 1960s and 1970s, Moscow and Riyadh pushed through the 10 million barrels-per-day barrier. 'But in today's Iraq it's not just about getting oil out of the ground, it's about building pipelines and ports and roads,' a sceptical foreign diplomat told me. He then dispensed with diplomacy entirely: 'Look, the country is stuffed. In some cases the only thing holding the pipelines together is the sludge in them.'

Thamir Ghadhban, the Baghdad energy adviser, concedes that such a huge industry expansion has never been attempted in the past, certainly not in the timetable envisaged by Baghdad or in such an uncertain political, administrative and security environment. He skates over the embarrassing fact that seven years after the US-led invasion, crude oil production is less than it was in the last days of Saddam—2.32 million barrels per day now, compared with 2.5 million back then—and that in this supposedly new era, output has surpassed the pre-war mark in only four of the 90 months for which we have production figures.

'There are many papers that cast doubt on our expansion target,' he conceded during a long interview in his office in the Baghdad Green Zone in September, before enumerating the challenges that Riyadh and Moscow did not face in the decades it took them to achieve similar goals: 'Political instability, insecurity, logistical difficulties and having to fit within the OPEC view of world supply and demand.' He treads carefully, resorting to the diplomatic euphemism of Iraqi politics and security being 'very much related to the geopolitics of the region' to convey the extent to which neighbours like Shiite Iran and Sunni Saudi Arabia contribute to the instability that feeds into everything in Iraq.

In the comfort of his embassy office, a Western ambassador to Baghdad spoke more frankly, albeit anonymously. 'The problem is that no one in the region wants Iraq to succeed,' he said. 'Iran wants a Shiite Iraq, but not a strong one; and Saudi Arabia doesn't want a Shiite Iraq at all. And the others including Syria, Jordan and the Gulf States . . . everyone is very conscious of Iraqi history and no one wants a powerful Shiia Iraq.'

After a crippling seven months since the elections, during which the bureaucracy has existed in cryonic suspension, Thamir Ghadhban speaks as though logic and common sense will prevail tomorrow. 'We expect that the new government will focus on improving services, employment and the standard of living, and on improving the security and intelligence services. Once all this is handled, and I'm an optimist, there will be a rapid improvement in the environment that will be more conducive to working.'

Ishmael Mohammed Hussein, the head of one of about 70 families who are squatters in what was a government office block in Baghdad, is far less optimistic. 'Today's Baghdad is such as miserable place,' he tells me. 'We hoped on getting rid of Saddam that we would have wealth and happiness, but most of the people in power have come from outside the country and they think only of themselves.' His 56-year-old wife, Zaheda Saleh, agrees. 'Iraq is like a milking cow and these people steal all the milk.'

Hussein worries for the future of his country. 'You should not think that Iraq will be stabilised. Yes, there will be more fighting and it will be worse than what we have seen in the past. There is no reason why this country should not be one of the top-twenty economies in the world—but we are still oppressed and this makes us very angry.'

This squatter couple might be dismissed as not necessarily representative of Iraqi public opinion, but according to a Baghdad-based diplomat, there has been a 'steady deterioration' in the ordinary Iraqi's faith in government. 'The politicians just look after themselves, failing at the same time to make agreements or decisions that might be in the interests of their people,' he told me. 'And the people will become more disenchanted—wouldn't you if you got just three hours power a day at the same time as you knew that chronic corruption extended to the top of government?'

The implications of the stalled effort to form a government are as grave for ordinary Iraqis as for the oil industry. Speculating on the ability of politicians who believe that the winner should take all to see the sense of forming an inclusive government, the diplomat was cautious in articulating hope. 'If the eventual government is genuinely inclusive, you'll likely continue with simmering popular resentment instead of outbursts of hostility.' Perhaps skating too lightly over the consequences of America's mishandling of the occupation, he added: 'They have all this wealth and a history of education and training. You think to yourself, how they could get it wrong? But looking at their own history, sometimes it is the Iraqis who are the most pessimistic. They see 1000 years of violence and they say it will never change.'

This is a country that should be up there with the most prosperous nations in the world. By rights, its 31 million people should be enjoying the fruits of the single biggest energy reserves in the world and Baghdad should be driving one of the world's more high-octane economies. But the political classes have yet to demonstrate a willingness or an ability to put the greater good of their country ahead of vested interests and petty squabbles.

It remains to be seen if they can. Revealing more of the pessimism that gnaws at the diplomatic corps in Baghdad, a

Western ambassador told me: 'If they can get it right, Iraq will be like Turkey; get it wrong and they'll be another Libya.' He paused before wondering aloud at the potential for a serious eruption of public anger. 'What are Iraqis to think when they see Dubai—and it doesn't even have oil!'

THE LEVANT

THE MATZA BOMB

Haifa, Israel, and Jenin, the West Bank

2 April 2002

Terrorism. It just walked off the street on a Sunday afternoon and into the crowded Matza restaurant in the northern city of Haifa. I was back at the St George in East Jerusalem when the news flash came up on the *Haaretz* website. Though I had to drive more than 160 kilometres up the coastal freeway, the crowd was still there, screaming their anguish and their anger, much of it directed at Palestinian leader Yasser Arafat. Some were draped in the Israeli flag, many clutched mobile phones and a few were lighting votive candles. On the radio, police chief Shlomo Aharonishky stated the obvious: 'We're doing everything we humanly can, but it is impossible to be everywhere.'

The secretive arrival of the suicide bomber, the shocking deaths and the outrage that followed had become a well-practised ritual. It emerged that no one took much notice of the bomber as he slipped into Matza's because, despite an unprecedented wave of bombings, there was no security guard. One eyewitness said the bomber had been talking on a mobile phone as he walked in at about 2.30 p.m.; another said that he wore a black bulky jacket to conceal more than a kilogram of explosive taped to his stomach. In hindsight all this sounds careless, but there were good reasons for the false sense of security: this was cosmopolitan Haifa, where Jews and Arabs got on better than they did in other towns and cities; the Matza was owned by a Jew and managed by an Israeli Arab; and the hummus was so damned good it lured its enthusiastic clientele from both sides of the community.

When I arrived, special volunteers trained in forensics and strict Jewish burial rites were painstakingly gathering body parts from what was left of the rafters, floors and walls of the restaurant. As a Chevrolet Savana wagon wheeled in to take away the bagged remains, dumpsters were being loaded with debris and tradesmen were hard at work stabilising the wreckage. The building was a crumpled mess. The roof was peeled back and rubble was strewn around for 100 metres. The glass-fronted drinks cabinets were skewed and fractured and air-conditioning units hung precariously from the neat wall cavities into which they had been built. The steel frames of tables and chairs were mangled and a spaghetti-like mess of wires and plumbing hung from where the ceiling had been. Off to one side, a media battalion had its cameras lined up on the apron of an adjacent service station, filing reports which, together with another suicide bombing near Jerusalem during the afternoon, would bookend the evening's new threats from Prime Minister Ariel Sharon. In a five-minute television address in which he used the word 'terrorism' fourteen times, Sharon told Israelis: 'We must fight this terrorism in an uncompromising war to uproot these savages.'

The Matza restaurant was on Rupin Street, a broad sweep of bitumen running through a deep gully on the slopes of

Mt Carmel, a wooded limestone mountain that dominates the port city. A shell-shocked Miki Matza, the owner of the restaurant, said that about 30 people were having lunch when the bomber struck. I interviewed him as he sat on an upended plastic crate near the bowsers at the adjacent service station. He described the scene: 'I was ten metres away when it went up; I was just walking away. Terror doesn't have eyes—it doesn't look at Arabs or Jews.' Propped up in his hospital bed, Ali Adawa, a member of the Arab family that ran the restaurant, was incredulous when he spoke to a local TV station: 'I am an Arab and I should get a guard? Believe me [these attackers] don't make distinctions. There are five of us Arabs in the restaurant—my brothers, my relatives. We're all one family there.'

The Matza had become a halfway house for Arabs and Jews. Miki Matza said: 'Jews and Arabs have been coming here for years. They could have fun here; we had something like a brotherhood—Jews, Muslims and Christians from all levels of our society.'

Fifteen people died: fourteen Jews, one Arab. They included the husband and two teenage children of Rachel Koren, who attended the burial of her family on an ambulance stretcher so that she could hear a government minister ask for forgiveness for failing to protect them. And there was Moshe Levin, who had stopped at the Matza only to pick up some hummus to take home. His daughter, who chose to wait for him in the car, watched the restaurant erupt. There was sixteen-year-old Orly Ofir, who was a talented young woman soccer player, and another victim was the niece of Avraham Menchell, a big local soccer star. Suheil Adawi, another member of the family that ran the restaurant, died because he came in on his day off to fill in for one of his brothers.

At the funeral of another of the victims there were heart-breaking exchanges as the sons of 67-year-old Dov Chernevroda continued an old family argument with their father—even as they put him in his grave. Chernevroda was a Jewish left-winger, a champion of the peace process. He helped out at a cultural centre, the charter of which was peaceful coexistence. He urged Israeli Arabs to contest municipal elections, he helped the Muslim community on planning matters and he had organised speaking engagements for his old friend, the Palestinian leader Faisal Husseini, who died in 2001. In a hillside cemetery that looks over the Mediterranean Sea, Chernevroda's tearful son Shaul chastised his father's naivety: 'How could they kill you, especially you who tried for a Palestinian state even more than the Palestinians themselves? Father, do not say that I didn't tell you so. Thanks for your values, which I took and then went in the opposite direction. You used to ask: "How did I produce such a monster?" And to laugh about it—because you loved me anyway.'

But a second son, Yaov, defended his grieving father: 'It is so wrong that you were killed by a cruel fanatic during a period in which this country has lost its way. You were a torch of hope. Everyone called you naive, but you showed that every human is created in God's image. You showed us that there is one way, to believe in the worth of every human even in this difficult hour.'

Dozens were killed or wounded, but these are just statistics. It is the account of survivors like seventeen-year-old Yuhuda Aigzer that conveys the horror of this attack: 'I was just about to go into the Matza when I was thrown to the ground by a massive boom. Everything was on fire. I saw one man with his hair on fire. A young boy with his face covered in blood. There was blood and glass everywhere.' Shimon Sabag chanced to be driving past when he heard the explosion. He pulled over: 'What I saw was horrible. I went into the gas station and I started to deal with the injured people. I couldn't deal with the critical injuries so I tried to help those with lesser injuries. I saw a mother holding on to her daughter as I was putting out the flames . . . there were pieces of flesh everywhere.'

When I found Haifa's new mayor, Amran Mizna, at the edge of the crowd, he was devastated: 'Innocent people sitting in a restaurant, and this comes out of the blue—I don't recall anything in the history of mankind that would make people send us suicide bombers.'

There was a lot of understandable hard talk and calls for immediate revenge but, as darkness softened the jagged edges of what remained of the Matza, a lonely voice in the confusion that is life, war and politics in Israel struggled to be heard from a bed at the nearby Ramban Hospital. Twenty-seven-year-old Sinjana Wakid was being treated for minor injuries received in the blast. She said: 'I came to this country seven years ago and I am Christian, Jewish and Muslim. My grandmother on my father's side was Jewish, and her husband was a Muslim and my mother was Christian. The person who blew himself up was not crazy. They say the Arabs are crazy but it's not true. It's someone who saw the same pain that I saw today, and he did it out of what he saw. They also feel pain. Those who blow themselves up are not terrorists; they are soldiers. They come to take revenge. I don't justify them. They make a lot of mistakes. I have all three religions in me and I don't want to stay here. Sharon's old and doesn't care that young people are killed, and Arafat is the same—he doesn't care if the young people commit suicide. It's well known that what's done to Muslims, like in Chechnya, brings revenge. And a Jewish boy who cries on his father's grave will grow up with hatred and seek revenge.'

Some Israeli authorities accept Palestinian claims that Yasser Arafat does not have control over the bombing activities of

Hamas or Islamic Jihad, both of which claimed responsibility for the Haifa bombing. But despite claims by the Al-Aqsa Martyrs Brigade that they plan and execute their activities in isolation, their membership is drawn from Arafat's own Fatah faction of the PLO. Sharon holds Arafat entirely responsible for all the bombings. He and US president George W. Bush have demanded that Arafat appear on the Arab TV networks again and make a more convincing appeal for a halt to the bombing than he has done in the past.

As the Israeli emergency crews cleared the Matza rubble, calls of celebration went out from the mosque loudspeakers in the refugee camps at Jenin, an impoverished West Bank town about 50 kilometres south-east of Haifa. They announced that the suicide bomber was eighteen-year-old Shadi Tubasi, a resident of the town's teeming camp who had acquired an Israeli identity card by marrying an Israeli Arab. On the night of the bombing I stayed in Haifa and rose early so that I could go on to Jenin and file both sides of the bombing story as a single report in the next day's edition of the *Herald*. There was fierce tension in the camp as hundreds crowded into the local youth centre to celebrate the martyrdom of Shadi Tubasi. This was a ritual too. Driving to the youth centre I had to avoid mounds of earth on the road, which the locals told me had been mined in advance of an expected Israeli incursion; and overnight new graffiti had been drawn and special postcards printed to honour 'the one who did the heroic Haifa explosion'.

But 52-year-old Zakaria Tubasi, the father of the bomber, was feeling anything but heroic. He said: 'I thank God that my son is a martyr, but I'm not happy that he is dead. No one thought he would do such a thing. I don't know if he left a message, but he was not politically active and I did not see anything in his behaviour to tell me he might do this. His life was difficult because of the way we live—he had no job and he was depressed.'

And the dead in Haifa? Tubasi shrugged in resignation: 'They are the same as us—they too are human beings.' His son had been dead for less than 24 hours and the nearest Tubasi came to making a political statement was this: 'If there is peace, everything is possible.'

GUIDED MISSILES

Gaza City, Occupied Palestinian Territories

13 April 2002

The coffee was bitter. Intentionally. As hundreds of Palestinians poured in to give their condolences, Shadi Tubasi's family formed a greeting line, handing each new guest a postcard celebrating the 'hero of the Haifa explosion', a reference to the Matza restaurant bombing. Off in a corner, 31-year-old Walid Fayad watched proceedings, unsmiling as he clutched an M-16 rifle. He explained to me the unusual absence of sugar in the cardamom coffee, which was served in tiny china cups: 'Today we drink it bitter, so that we can share the Tubasi family's bitterness for the Israelis.'

Fayad waved away the revulsion and horror of young Tubasi's Haifa outing. We were in a cinder-block youth centre in the fetid Palestinian refugee camp at Jenin, at the northern end of the West Bank. Fayad was more interested in talking about the violence to come. He spoke with disturbing relish of the terrible fighting he expected would soon engulf the camp. 'It'll be a massacre,' he

said. 'But we're ready to be martyrs. All of us await our fate . . .
we want to go out with bombers' belts strapped to our bodies,
because that is better than sitting at home, waiting for them to
kill us. So before they kill me, I have to do something—I must
explode myself with some Israelis. We want our turn to die . . .
it will be good to be with God.'

My exploration of the unprecedented wave of self-destruction
in the Middle East in the spring of 2002 started with Shadi
Tubasi's bombing in Haifa on 1 April. It became a tour of what
the Israelis called the terror towns of the West Bank and the
Gaza Strip: Tulkarm, Jenin, Nablus, Ramallah and Gaza City.
It was a week of clandestine meetings, some to which I was
whisked late at night, some at which those interviewed would
allow no identifying information to be recorded. I came face to
face with two bombers who had been trained and were awaiting
instructions on their bomb missions; I spoke with the trainers
of others and those who dispatched them, with the military and
political leadership of the Palestinian factional cells that justified
the carnage, and with the man whom they said lit the ideological
fuse for this bout of brutal death, the ailing 61-year-old cleric
who is the spiritual leader of Hamas, Sheikh Ahmed Yassin.
He told me: 'The Jews attack and kill our civilians. We will kill
theirs. When the first drop of the martyr's blood spills on the
ground, he goes to paradise. His victims, the Jews, go to hell.' So
for Sheikh Yassin the suicide bomb was an 'exceptional weapon'.

Khalid, my fixer, spoke in awe of a martyr's encounter at the
gates of heaven, as though the new arrival would actually have
his file checked: 'There will be blessings for 70 of his family and
friends. The 72 virgins are real—their skin is so pale and beautiful
that you can see the blood in their veins . . . If one of these virgins
spits in the ocean, the seawater becomes sweet . . . the martyr is
so special he does not feel the pain of being in the grave and all

that his family has to do to cleanse his file thoroughly is to repay his outstanding debts.' Surely, I asked, this view of the Koran should be seen as philosophical? A parable, perhaps? But no, there was a chorus of disagreement from a gathering of Khalid's friends—workers and students—in the Jabalya refugee camp near Gaza City. 'No. This is real . . . this is as it will be,' said Khalid, as much for himself as for the younger Palestinian generations who now talked endlessly of the benefits of death over life in a bombing campaign that was the focus of a war which had taken more than 1500 lives on both sides in eighteen months.

Until late 2001, the suicide business was monopolised by two organisations: the militant and hugely popular Hamas and the smaller Islamic Jihad. Both were vehemently opposed to the peace process and to the very existence of the state of Israel. But then they were overshadowed by a new group—the Al-Aqsa Martyrs Brigade, which emerged from the impoverished Balata refugee camp on the outskirts of Nablus late in 2001. The brigade was not a fringe militia—it sprang from Yasser Arafat's Fatah faction of the PLO in an effort to retain the allegiance of frustrated younger members who were switching to the more radical Hamas and Islamic Jihad.

In the past, groups like Hamas had to work hard to cultivate candidates for suicide, but all three militia groups now said they were inundated with offers from eager teenagers, young women and fathers in their forties who were prepared to die. Instead of a calculated process of indoctrination, which the sponsors of suicide bombing used to outline as though it somehow legitimised their operations, they only had to give some of the volunteers a pat on the back and point them at their target.

The Palestinians achieved a rare breakthrough—instead of operating from the fringe of society, as the IRA and so many other terrorist organisations have done, they were at the heart of it, swamped by volunteers who were ready to die, as opposed to merely agreeing with them. Even Dr Rabah Mohanna—whose Popular Front for the Liberation of Palestine claimed its own share of the violence, including the previous year's assassination of a minister in the Israeli government—was confounded by this lunge for the grave. He told me: 'Thousands of young men and women are ready to be blown up. It is a new phenomenon; you have no idea how big it is.'

For the Israelis, the twin cities of Nablus and Jenin are the fount of the terror that haunts their daily lives. Israeli authorities say that the cities' refugee camps, their slums and the aggressively hardline Al-Najah University in Nablus are the chaperones of terror. By some accounts, the university has produced as many as 30 suicide bombers in the current crisis, and one of the targeted assassinations most celebrated by the Israelis was that of Qais Adwan who, at 25 years of age, was a member of the Al-Najah student council and one of Hamas's master bomb-makers.

Political change at the university—where classrooms are adorned with signs that read 'Israel has nuclear bombs, we have human bombs'—explains the imperative behind the decision by Arafat's Fatah movement to set up the Al-Aqsa Martyrs Brigade. Traditionally, Fatah had total control of the university's student council and academic staff, but in 2001 Hamas and Islamic Jihad swept to power. But it is not just students who have been radicalised. Their parents are being pulled to Hamas and Islamic Jihad because of general distrust of the faltering peace process through the 1990s and disgust with rampant corruption and human rights abuses in Arafat's Palestinian Authority. Opinion polls in recent months found that while Westerners might see the suicide bombings as grotesque, Palestinian support for the renewed violence ran as high as 80 per cent, a huge rise on support levels of about 20 per cent when Hamas mounted its first suicide bombing in the mid-1990s.

The bombings have become threads in the fabric of Palestinian life. Take the girls at the Ahmad Shawquin Secondary School in Gaza City. They are regularly drilled in emergency preparedness: rescuing the injured, fighting fires and administering first aid. And when the head of civil defence in Gaza, General Mahmoud M. Abu Marzourg, dropped in to give them a pep talk, he did not spare their innocence: 'Surely you have heard of your sisters who blow themselves up to defend the dignity of Palestine? Anyone who kills and struggles for the sake of their land, and dies doing so . . . is alive with a new life, because as a martyr you will be alive in heaven.'

Some of the children can't wait until they are old enough. The three smartest kids in their class at a Gaza school, all of them only fourteen years of age, stole away from their homes one night in June 2002. They were armed with knives, a crude pipe bomb and a hoe to dig under the fence of a Jewish settlement. An Israeli patrol saw them—all three were shot dead. Recently, the Israelis arrested a twelve-year-old boy who they insisted was planning a suicide mission; eleven-year-old Palestinian children talk about the joys of martyrdom on TV chat shows; and in the playground, according to a distraught parent I interviewed, small children played a game called 'being a martyr'. This was a local version of cowboys and Indians in which, she told me, the children used to fight to play the role of the Israelis because that was where they saw the strength, but these days they all want to be the Palestinians—no one wants to be the Jew.

Many of the bombers are instructed not to tell their parents that they have volunteered for death. And the families that do know say they are running out of arguments against their children. As 21-year-old Dareen Abu Aisheh planned her death in February 2002, she argued every which way with her family: 'Aren't we being shot down like dogs? Do you feel like a human being when the Israelis control your every move? Do you believe we have a future? If I'm going to die at their hands anyway, why shouldn't I take some of them with me?' Her uncle, Jasser Khalili, said that finally he had to admit that he could not argue against his headstrong niece. She had been angry and depressed after the suicide-bomb death of a cousin, and about being spurned by Hamas and Islamic Jihad when she had volunteered as a bomber—because she was a woman. But eight months after her first approach to Hamas, the Al-Aqsa Martyrs Brigade strapped her up with explosives and pointed her at an Israeli military checkpoint.

At about the same time, in Tulkarm, the parents of fifteen-year-old Noura Shalhoub were trying to lift her out of her depression—showing her where her new bedroom would be in the extensions to their home—when she took a kitchen knife and rushed a soldier at a checkpoint near her town. He shot her and she bled to death where she fell. When Izzedin Masri blew up a Jerusalem pizzeria in August 2001, the neighbours in Jenin celebrated. But his father, Ahmed Masri, was more circumspect: 'If I'd known he belonged to Hamas, I would have pressed him to stop his activities.' The young Masri had taken over the running of the family restaurant, but the old man lamented the hard-heartedness of the younger generation: 'Israelis used to come to the restaurant . . . now no one looks at them as human. [My family] is desperate only in the way that all Palestinians are—we have got to get rid of the Jews from around us.' And eight months later he told *Newsweek*: 'I lost my health. I wish I still had my son around . . .'

But for those who plan the bombings, Mariam Farahat is the model terrorist mother. A video she made with her nineteen-year-old son, Mohammed, as he prepared for a shoot-out in which he killed five Israeli military students before he was gunned down has made her a celebrity across the Arab world. She has been dubbed *Um Nidal*—Mother of the Struggle—and she doesn't seem to mind that her family is being torn apart, literally, by the intifada. One son is dead; another blew three fingers off when he tried to throw a grenade at some Israeli soldiers; and her husband was fired from his job as a Palestinian policeman, presumably because of the family's deep Hamas connections. Talking about the special lunch she made for her son the day before his attack—kebabs and cucumber salad—this woman said: 'He was filled with hate for the Jews. He told me he wanted to carry out an operation against the Israelis. I told him it was a good idea and wished him luck. I knew that almost no one comes back alive from such operations, but I kept those thoughts to myself.'

In the 1990s the militias had difficulty finding volunteers for suicide bombing and often they were accused of seducing—or brainwashing—impressionable young men who hung around mosques, faction meetings and checkpoint riots. But as Nassar Badawi, the Al-Aqsa Martyrs Brigade commander I interviewed in Nablus, said: 'Because the situation is so bad now, many people are ready to explode themselves. We do not have to pick them—they come to us, ready to die. After training by our martyrdom unit, they know what they are going to do and they are convinced that they are dying in defence of their country.'

We sat either side of a desk in his Nablus office. A copy of the Koran lay on the desk and a martyrdom poster of Badawi's dead brother shoulder-to-shoulder with Yasser Arafat hung on the wall in a gilt-edged frame. Why attack Israeli civilians? 'In Israel there are no civilians—they're all soldiers and fighters. When the Israelis started the targeted assassination of our leaders, we decided that if any of our martyrs could get into Israel and reach a target where people were gathered in a restaurant or in a street, then that was where they should explode themselves. We are sending two messages: telling the Israeli security forces that we can still reach them, and that all their security is meaningless; and telling the Israeli public that this is the result of Sharon's policies against us.'

When I enquired about the ruthless efficiency and expertise revealed in the brigade's work, he said: 'We draw on the warriors and fighters who have served in other Palestinian armies, like those who were deported from Lebanon in '82 and who trained in the PLO camps in other Arab countries.' Badawi is a chronic doodler, and even as he explained his wish for maximum civilian pain and damage in Israel, the pen was working furiously. 'The Israelis kill Palestinian women and children in our streets, so we try to maximise their losses because blood is for blood, violence is for violence and suppression is for suppression. We will do to them what they do to us . . . so no, we will not be throwing flowers at them.'

Before the onslaught of suicide bombs in the spring of 2002, the factions claimed that they had rigidly enforced rules. No suicide volunteers under the age of eighteen—but now sixteen-year-olds are sent out. Women were discouraged—now they are lionised. Married men with children and anyone who was a family's sole breadwinner were rejected—not any more. The trainers said that normally a volunteer was subjected to a period of covert observation by the martyrdom units before being approved on grounds of religious observance, temperament and an ability to dress and act as a Jew. The head of Islamic Jihad in Jenin, Mahmoud Tawalbi, told how 24-year-old Rafat Abu Diyak cried tears of joy when he heard he had been selected to bomb a bus on which seven Israelis died. Tawalbi said: 'He started crying like a child; he started kissing me, saying, "Thank you, thank you, thank God." He said he wanted to make every Israeli cry like the Palestinians cried.'

The factions used to stress the seriousness of their undertakings with a lot of talk about the training of suicide bombers. But now there are missions in which freelancers seem to have taken over, and anything goes. They talked about the bombings being an act of faith, not revenge. But the families of dead bombers and a few bombers who have been caught before detonating their bombs often talk of revenge. A bomber who was trained and awaiting his mission told a reporter that he carried the deeds and keys to the Jaffa home from which his family was driven when Israel was established in 1948.

Early reports that avenging the death of a relative was not allowed and that women were discouraged make the tale of 21-year-old Arien Ahmed disturbing reading. She balked on the way to her target late in May 2002 and ended up in Israeli detention. She told the *New York Times'* James Bennett, who was allowed to interview her in prison, that she wanted to avenge the death of her fiancé, who she believed had been killed by the Israelis. Within five days of volunteering she was called out of a marketing lecture at Bethlehem University, shown a backpack and how to detonate the bomb inside it, and then driven to the area of her target dressed to look like an Israeli woman.

The logistics of a suicide mission are a tightly held secret. About six or eight volunteer cells are involved, and each is kept ignorant of the identity and location of the others. They groom the bomber, religiously and tactically; they make the bomb; they transport it and the bomber; they select and monitor likely targets; and they organise accommodation and disguises. Where careful planning still holds, the bomber is instructed to quietly disappear from his or her home and place of work a few days before the mission. Some have gone off to visit families and relatives. Friends of Nabil Arir told of how he took them out for a lavish dinner—without saying that it was a farewell. All pay off any loans because the indebted may not enter paradise. Ahmed Ayam even set aside five shekels ($US1) that he owed his father before detonating a bomb in Netanya in March 2001.

Then begins a period of immersion training, of intense periods spent with a father-figure minder. The bomber is coached into great psychological dependence, both to please the father figure and to follow his every instruction. One of the last acts is the recording of a celebratory video to be released after the bombing—a good propaganda tool but in some cases more important as an act of commitment that helps to lock in the bomber at a point where he or she might have second thoughts. The student is told to read the chapters of the Koran that deal with jihad, the birth of Islam, war, Allah's favours and the importance of faith. Often, details of the target and the nature of the attack—whether it is to be a body bomb, grenades or firearms—are withheld from the bomber until only hours before the attack. And more often than not, the first that the family and friends of a bomber will hear of the mission is after the fact—a news bulletin, a message on the mosque loudspeakers or a volley of celebratory shots fired into the air outside their home.

Some of the people I spoke to said a bombing mission could be set up for as little as $US150: gunpowder or a mix of readily available chemicals (sugar or fertilisers), a battery, a light switch, some wire, a belt to hold the bomb and transport to deliver the bomber close to the target. But a Hamas operative who insisted on anonymity said the price of a complete mission was more likely to be about $US4000. Israeli authorities say that after they demolished parts of Yasser Arafat's Ramallah bunker in April 2002 they found a document which they call an 'invoice of terror' putting the cost of a tailored bomb belt at 700 shekels (about $US150).

Late on a Monday night a taxi came to my hotel, collected me, and raced by a circuitous route out of Gaza City and into the silent depths of the Jabalya refugee camp. Here I met a guide who took me up to an apartment. In the time that it took to make Arabic coffee there was a quiet knock on the door and two young men came in, accompanied by a silent minder. Nervously, they shook hands and said that they were from Islamic Jihad, but there would be no names. They apologised for breaching an understanding arrived at with the intermediary who had set up the meeting—that they would bring their bomb belts. 'It's too risky,' the taller one said. 'The drones are in the sky.' This was a reference to the pilotless Israeli surveillance aircraft that were on constant patrol over the Occupied Territories.

The young man wore a heavy navy jacket and a five o'clock shadow, and he quickly revealed himself to be an agitated and excitable 29-year-old English teacher. His more relaxed associate, a 22-year-old student of Islamic studies, wore military fatigues and heavy boots. Even before a question was asked, the nervous one broke into a religious rant: 'I trust in God and I am ready to sacrifice my life for the defence of my nation and my people.' His colleague supported him: 'Jihad is the highest form of Islam . . . I have seen the occupation and the massacres here and I know of Sharon's massacre at Sabra and Shatila.' The first one continued: 'This highlights the depths of our faith. This is not terrorism . . . we are not murderers. My obligations are to my God and to my people.'

Asked what training they had been given to be suicide bombers, the older one again turned to religion: 'We pray and we wake in the middle of the night for special prayers; we fast on Mondays and Tuesdays, we are at peace with our neighbours and we attend the mosque for all prayer sessions. After that we were delivered to Islamic Jihad's military wing. We have been trained in how to use the bomb belt.' He went through the motions of strapping it on and used his thumb to press an imaginary detonator. 'But I have chosen that my mission will be with a machine gun on a settlement or a military post'—this is where the Palestinian assailant opens fire on his Israeli targets and keeps shooting until inevitable Israeli reinforcements kill him—'so I have had weapons training at a farm. We also have been taught how to dress and walk so that we will not stand out among the people at our targets. We'll either look like tourists or Israeli soldiers. The military wing is assessing targets and they have told me to be ready. They will show me the target to make sure that I can do it, and we will practise, maybe many times, to make sure that we do it right.'

Asked about Western revulsion at the crude terrorism of becoming a human bomb, he said: 'I will answer your Western question with another question, why do you look at us with just one eye?'

The younger, shorter man said that he had elected to die with a bomb belted to his waist. Both of these young men were married and had discussed their decisions to die with their wives—and had received their blessings. The short one added that, but for the fact that she was pregnant, his wife would also volunteer to be a suicide bomber.

They spoke briefly—and, in a way, dismissively—of life before the intifada. 'We married and we wanted to have children, we'd go to the computer centre and play games, we'd watch television,' said the taller one. And then, quickly and quietly, they disappeared into the night.

The profile of the typical suicide bomber is constantly changing and observers of the crisis are frequently required to reposition their arguments. Labib Kamhawi, a political analyst in Amman, Jordan, who had studied the bombers, posed a question for reporters: 'What prompts a twenty-year-old to blow himself up and kill as many Israelis as possible in the process? It definitely takes more than belief in God to turn a boy into a martyr. It takes desperation, anger and loss of hope. It's believing that your life is not worth living anymore.'

A Hamas military leader in Nablus, who gave the *nom de guerre* of Abu Saed, told me: 'When someone asks to be a martyr, it's because they can't live in freedom or because their father or brother is dead, or in Israeli detention, or their family land has been taken. He knows that the Israelis are the cause of his suffering. And if, because of all that, he doesn't know how to live, then he does know how to die. This is good.' Sitting cross-legged on thin mattresses on the floor as a dark storm raged outside, he went on: 'God imposed jihad on Muslims as a duty to fight the enemy. And if the martyr is absolutely convinced that life after death will be better than this life, there is no doubt that he will go to paradise and that he is doing what God has asked him to do. So when the bomber arrives at this conviction, death for him is better than this life.'

As I discovered in Tulkarm, there is a significant financial reward for the bomber's family. Iraq's Saddam Hussein sends a cheque for $US25,000 and the survivors of those who are sponsored by Hamas get either a lump sum of $US10,000 or a pension of $US150 to $US300 a month and the health and education costs for their family are usually taken care of. But many, including members of several families I interviewed after they had been presented with their Iraqi cheque, said it was the tension and suffering in their day-to-day existence that drove their sons and daughters to be suicide bombers, not the speeches of their political and religious leaders and not Saddam's money.

A typical suicide bomber used to be male, seventeen to 22 years of age, single, footloose and uncertain, with few prospects and deeply religious. But in the past year they have come from upper-middle-class families, from businesses and colleges, and now women were joining their ranks. Izzadin Masri abandoned a promising future in his father's successful restaurant to kill himself and fifteen Israelis at a Jerusalem pizzeria in August 2001; Daoud Abu Sway, an apolitical 47-year-old, walked out on his eight children to kill himself and injure two Israelis when he exploded a bomb outside a luxury Jerusalem hotel in December 2001; and eighteen-year-old Ayat Akhras, a straight-A student who was about to graduate and marry, killed herself and an Israeli girl of about the same age at the entrance to a Jerusalem supermarket in April 2002. Mahmoud Bakker Nasser resigned from the Palestinian prison service before signing up for death with Islamic Jihad to avenge the death of Iyan Hardan, an Islamic Jihad militiaman he had befriended who, on his release from prison, became a victim of the Israelis' targeted assassinations when a bomb exploded in a Jenin telephone booth as he made a call.

Palestinian researchers say that they are discovering a genera-tion of young people who don't see a future. Rita Giacaman, who is examining the attitudes of students at Bir Zeit University, explained: 'We found that our students generally have an inability to dream, or to visualise a better future than their miserable current life.' Dr Eyad Sarraj, a Palestinian psychiatrist, knew the background of a young Palestinian who spoke only in terms of nationalist pride and his belief in God when a reporter asked why he had volunteered for suicide. But Sarraj filled in the blanks in the boy's story: 'What the young man did not say was that he was burning with a desire for revenge. He was a tearful witness, at the age of six, to his father's beating by Israeli soldiers. He would never forget seeing his father taken away, bleeding from the nose. Ours is a nation of anger and defiance. The struggle today is how *not* to become a suicide bomber.'

For all that, Jerrold M. Post, a researcher at George Washington University who worked as a psychological profiler with the CIA for more than twenty years, argues: 'It's really important to emphasise that these are not crazed people. Nor are they unhinged loners or embittered outcasts. They are rational, logical, above-average in intelligence, and suffer no major psychological problems. And they are just utterly convinced that they are right.'

Some moderate Islamic scholars have branded suicide bombings as illegitimate and anti-Islam. But given the anger and frustration in the Palestinian community, there has been little oxygen for any debate on the rights and wrongs of suicide bombs as a tactic. Dr Sarraj argues against the culture of glorification which he says draws young Palestinians to death. And almost lost in the fury of battle in June 2002 was a newspaper advertising campaign by 55 politicians and intellectuals attempting to force a debate on the effectiveness of suicide bombing. After running for several days in *Al-Quds* newspaper, it had 500 backers. But when Sheikh Yassin, the spiritual leader of Hamas, was asked how he reconciled the bombings with Islam's teaching, he said: 'First, these are not suicide operations. We do this to protect ourselves and you are talking from the situation of people who live normal, peaceful and convenient lives. You don't understand our lives and our day-to-day suffering.'

Ironically, Yassin has been half-dead for most of his life. Paralysed from the neck down since a soccer accident at age sixteen, the head of the militant Hamas faction sits in a wheelchair, draped in an apricot-coloured shawl. Perhaps from lack of use, his skin has a death-in-life pallor about it. As we talked, he tired visibly just from the effort of raising his shrill voice to be heard above the incongruous shrieks and giggles of his grandchildren at play outside.

His Hamas colleague Dr Abdul Aziz Rantisi seemed genuinely hopeful that the Israeli military would maintain a permanent presence in or around the Occupied Territories. He told me: 'If they do that, they will be presenting us with thousands of targets.' And he then proceeded to turn arguments of innocence on their heads, insisting that it was the 26 Israeli victims of the Passover massacre at Netanya in March 2002 who had committed suicide, 'because they have accepted the word of their Zionist leaders who told them that our land was theirs'.

As I did the rounds in Gaza City, the only Hamas leader who ducked an invitation to openly endorse the Netanya bombing— the horror that sprang the hair-trigger for Israel's re-occupation of the West Bank—was the surgeon Mamoud al-Zahar. Asked for his response, as a father and as a doctor committed to saving lives, to the death of 26 people, he said: 'I'm not here to speak as a private person . . .' Later in the interview he said, 'They didn't mind us throwing stones in the last intifada or holding peaceful demonstrations. But now they are feeling a deep sense of loss because the methods we are using are destroying the integrity of Israeli society. They still think they can suppress us and stop the martyred bombings. But let's wait and see if their big campaign stops the resistance.'

Small children excitedly collect pictures of the martyrs. And when the news of their deadly exploits gets back to their towns, villages and refugee camps, there are street parties and their families turn on spreads of coffee and lollies with all the festivity of a wedding. The young in particular invest great meaning and symbolism in the lore of the bombings, like the story of a bomber who had a change of heart at the last minute. Abu Saed, the Hamas commander in Nablus, told it to me. 'When he was given his belt and details of the target, he said: "I don't want to die." Another man who was with us jumped in and said that he would take the bomb. He had had no training, but he did it, he exploded himself. And the man who said he couldn't do it was killed by the Israelis a few days later.'

And they hang on the words of Salah Othman, who is called the 'living martyr', the man who 'gave his life to Allah' and whom 'Allah brought back to life'. After a botched 1993 suicide mission during which he was shot in the head and the back by Israeli soldiers, Israeli doctors pronounced him brain-dead and sent his vegetable-like body home to Gaza. But he made a remarkable recovery. Today he has a wife and three children and, despite having been to the brink, he rhapsodised on the appeal of martyrdom: 'The power of the spirit pulls us upward, while the power of material things pulls us downward. [As we prepared for the mission] we were floating, swimming in the feeling that we were about to enter eternity. We had no doubts. We made an oath on the Koran, in the presence of Allah, a pledge not to waver. This jihad pledge is called *bayt al-ridwan*, after the garden in paradise that is reserved for the prophets and the martyrs. I know that there are other ways to do jihad, but this one is sweet—the sweetest. All martyrdom operations, if done for Allah's sake, hurt less than a gnat's bite.'

Like Othman, the young Palestinians who were toting guns and marching out with bombs strapped to their bodies cut their teeth as stone-throwers in the last intifada. It is frightening to think of what they might do in the next one.

MARKED MEN

Nablus, the West Bank
15 April 2002

Suddenly, Palestinians were killing Palestinians. An orgy of death by mutilation and humiliation broke out across the West Bank as vigilantes pulled men off the street or from their prison cells and executed them before cheering, mocking crowds. This was not justice as we expect it; it was not humanity as we know it. But with the collapse of law and order and the weight of occupation, just the mere suspicion of collaborating with the Israelis meant a death sentence. And much of the killing was being done in the name of the Al-Aqsa Martyrs Brigade which, as the second intifada started late in 2000, issued a warning: 'We promise that we are going to teach the spies a lesson in patriotism that they will never forget, which will lead them to think twice before doing such evil acts. Death to collaborators.'

The rain was pouring down and the streets of Nablus were deserted—except for my car, on which I had balanced the risk of going into a Palestinian town with yellow Israeli registration plates by using coloured tape to shape a big T and a V on all sides of it to tell any snipers that I was a foreign reporter. My instructions were to go to a particular street corner and wait. It turned out to be two blocks from a ragged pile of rubble that had been Yasser Arafat's local residence until it was demolished in an Israeli missile attack. There was a tap on the window and Tacsin, my interpreter, got out to talk to a heavy-set man who had materialised by the car. They headed off, calling for me to follow—around the block, through a set of heavy security gates, around the back of an apartment block and into an office where I was ushered into the presence of Nassar Badawi. Eight months earlier he had stepped into his brother's shoes as one of the leaders of the Al-Aqsa Martyrs Brigade, an offshoot of Arafat's Fatah faction of the PLO. Yasser Badawi died in a car-bomb attack that Nassar Badawi said was part of an Israeli campaign to eliminate key Palestinian leaders. When I went to see him, he was justifying the killing of Palestinians by Palestinians.

There were twelve executions on the day we met. At Tulkarm, in the north of the West Bank, two masked gunmen went into a building used as a temporary prison (the old prison had been demolished in an Israeli attack). The prison guards did nothing as the gunmen herded eight suspected collaborators into the street. As a crowd gathered, the prisoners were executed and their bodies left on the street as a lesson to others. Earlier in the day, in Qalqilyah, a few kilometres south of Tulkarm, the bodies of two young men jailed twelve months earlier for collaboration—Abu Ishab, 20, and Walid Radwan, 22—were found dumped in a side street riddled with bullets. Their deaths were said to be the handiwork of their prison guards. Another killing was reported from Beit Jala, a community near Bethlehem.

The last killing of the day was loaded with symbolism and sinister intent. It took place in the heart of Bethlehem, near

Manger Square, reputedly the birthplace of Jesus Christ. The killers, again members of Badawi's Al-Aqsa Martyrs Brigade, blindfolded and bound 21-year-old Mahmood Rahamie, whom they accused of using email to send information to his Israeli operators. They were so pleased with themselves that they allowed a Reuters film crew to record the execution, but then they thought better of it. They demanded that the cameramen hand over the tape; they destroyed it on the spot and then threatened the journalists, warning them that they would be held personally responsible if any images of the incident were published.

Nassar Badawi did not flinch as he told me: 'These are not random killings. They are limited to just one kind of person: those who give the Israelis the information they need to assassinate our leaders. They have killed many of our people, like my brother. So this is our message to the Palestinian people: don't talk to the Israelis. And also, we had to kill these people before the next Israeli assault on us, because we can't have the Israelis rescuing them.'

The Israelis have exacted a heavy toll on the Palestinian leadership since beginning a program of systematic assassination late in 2000. Dozens have died in what the Israelis call 'pre-emptive self-defence' and what Amnesty International calls 'extra-judicial execution'. The first such attack was on a deadly accurate Palestinian sniper, 37-year-old Hussein Abayat. As he drove through the hills near Bethlehem, three Apache attack helicopters circled in from the rear and four Hellfire missiles demolished Abayat's Mitsubishi pick-up. Months later Abayat's younger brother Nadji drove me along the route of his brother's last journey, creating in me a feeling of great exposure as he explained that he had served time in an Israeli prison for attempting to blow up a bus and that now he was being hunted by the Israelis on suspicion of being behind the revenge death of an Israeli soldier on the day of his brother's funeral.

The Israelis admitted that they have an extensive network of informants and that they need detailed and timely information to mount operations such as the one that killed the older Abayat and, a few weeks after I met Nassar Badawi in Nablus, Marwan Zaloum. He was a fellow leader of the Al-Aqsa Martyrs Brigade in Hebron whom the Israelis blamed for a suicide bombing that killed six and wounded 85 in Jerusalem. Zaloum died as Abayat did—a midnight missile attack on his Mitsubishi sedan as he drove through the heart of Hebron, the site of Abraham's tomb.

The call for revenge was immediate, brutal and misplaced. Within hours three men who were doing time in the local prison on charges of collaboration, and who presumably could not have helped the Israelis in the attack on Zaloum, were dragged to open ground close to a mosque and near where the charred wreck of Zaloum's car still smouldered. They were given a show trial that lasted only minutes, declared guilty, stoned, beaten and then shot in the head. And in an appalling act of communal savagery, the bodies were then strung from lampposts and mocked and mutilated by a cheering, jeering crowd. One of the bodies hung upside down by one foot; another was almost decapitated and the third was dumped in a garbage truck. As women and young girls looked on, small boys stubbed cigarettes in wounds that older men had hacked in the bodies with knives.

Assassination by missile strikes, helicopter-gunship attacks on homes and cars, and the placement of concealed bombs in phones that the targets were known to use—none of these could have happened without the likes of Munzer Hafnawi, a Nablus clothing merchant who Palestinian investigators say admitted to signalling to Israeli gunmen via a mobile telephone the precise moment that a Hamas activist could be gunned down as he left a mosque; or the collaborator who avoided suspicion by disguising himself as a melon vendor on the streets of Nablus to collect information on the movements of senior Palestinians. Talal Dwakat, the head of Palestinian intelligence in Nablus, was disturbingly pragmatic: 'It's an open war, and every side tries to get information in this battle.' But it was hardly surprising when an Israeli intelligence officer observed that the Palestinian authorities were more efficient at arresting and punishing those accused of collaborating than they were at dealing with their own who were blamed for the suicide bombings.

The rate at which Palestinian collaborators were being killed was unprecedented. In the seven years of the first intifada, which began in 1987, about 800 Palestinian collaborators died. In the eighteen months since the start of the second intifada late in 2000, only 24 were executed, but ten of those were in March. And now they have hit a dozen in one day. As the crisis escalated, so did the volume of the message sent by vigilantes. In March 2002, Palestinian police prevented the street executioners from hanging a collaborator's corpse above Manger Square in Bethlehem. But now it was okay to leave the remains of Raed Naem Odeh swinging by the ankles from a traffic circle in the centre of Ramallah.

The informants' network dates back to Israel's seizure of the West Bank and the Gaza Strip in 1967, when it took control of community records that told it who the petty criminals were and who might be susceptible. Usually they were blackmailed and the price was mostly cheap—drugs, sex, food or small amounts of money, or just the freedom to move within the straitjacket that Israel has imposed on Palestinians who want to move around the Occupied Territories and Israel. In 2001 a reporter asked Abu Sharif, an adviser to Yasser Arafat, about the execution of collaborators. Sharif candidly confirmed the deaths and explained them this way: 'When [the Palestinian Authority was set up] in 1993, all these people who were collaborators—there were around 5000 in all—fled to Israeli security. Gradually, the Israelis forced them back to our areas so they could use them again . . . sometimes they were accompanied by Israeli Special Forces who speak good Arabic and who dress like us. They were promised protection in our areas.'

And to explain how the Israelis cultivated new informers, Sharif gave the example of a butcher in the town of Tulkarm. Israelis regularly bought lamb from Abu Mohamed. But then they complained about the quality—why didn't he buy better meat that was available from Jordan, they wanted to know. The butcher said that to do that he needed a licence from the Israeli authorities. So in time the Israelis offered Abu Mohamed such a licence, and from the moment his hand closed on the piece of paper that would allow him to import meat, to move through the West Bank, to go to Israel or to travel abroad, he was capable of being suborned by the Israelis.

To the outsider, the treatment of the collaborators is appalling and so destructive of Palestinian claims to decency and nationhood, but on the West Bank and in the Gaza Strip paranoia, frustration, anger and helplessness gnaw at people who every day become a little less like people. The collaborators do not get justice and they are denied a Muslim burial, their families are shunned and their businesses are boycotted. A man watching the acts of butchery in Hebron told a reporter: 'They are no longer Palestinians.'

DEEP IN THE HEART
OF LEBANON

Nabatieh, Lebanon
4 August 2006

odies are still being dug from the rubble at Qana. So it seems
odd that 32-year-old Samira Sabah is cheerful as she fossicks
among the wilting fruit and vegetables at a makeshift stall in
the desolate streets of Nabatieh. Utterly unshaken by the death
just hours earlier of dozens of women and children in the Israeli
attack on nearby Qana, she dallies over the crated produce. She
tests and talks as she goes.

Sabah is wearing wraparound sunglasses and a military-chic
jumpsuit. She totters on sequined high-heels. Are they appropriate
in a time of war?

'I don't run.'

What about the daily bombardment, which so far has killed 30,
wounded 250 more and forced about half of her townspeople to flee?

'It's just like someone banging on a barrel.'

The stallholder, Bassam, calls for coffee, which a boy brings on
an engraved brass tray. As they sip this muddy brew, Sabah articu-
lates a statement of faith that is one of the most potent weapons

in the Hezbollah militia's arsenal: 'God will protect us. As long as we have Allah and [Hezbollah's leader] Hassan Nasrallah we will stay here. We are not afraid. We are all Hezbollah—our men, women and children are the resistance.'

At the Hykmat al-Amin Hospital on a chalky hill above the town, a local gynaecologist makes the same claim on behalf of the newborn. Explaining that one in three were stillbirths, Leyla Noor Eddine says of the survivors, 'They are the new resistance.'

This is the rhetoric from one side in an asymmetric war, an act of faith that eclipses United States and Israeli charges that Hezbollah (literally, 'The Party of God') is a terrorist organisation, just as it renders meaningless all Western condemnation of a force that Lebanese see as freedom-fighters.

It also is a hymn of praise for a force that is fracturing the myth of Israel's military invincibility. On Wednesday they stepped up their attacks dramatically, lobbing more than 230 missiles into Israel just as its prime minister, Ehud Olmert, was declaring that all Hezbollah's infrastructure had been destroyed and that Israel was 'victorious'.

By maintaining a daily strike rate of about 100 missiles and not crumbling in the face of a powerful Israeli ground and air attack, Nasrallah is fast becoming the next-best Arab hero since Egypt's Gamal Abdel Nasser nationalised the Suez Canal 50 years ago. And just by continuing the fight, Nasrallah's men have exposed sloppy Israeli intelligence. In less than a week, the Israelis killed four United Nations peacekeepers, the women and children who were sleeping at Qana, and a Lebanese army soldier who they believed was a Hezbollah kingpin.

With no let-up in Hezbollah's punishing, indiscriminate missile strikes after three weeks of fighting, with the loss of dozens of Israeli soldiers and the failure to take substantial territory in the border region, Israeli commentators are making their own judgements. Zeev Schiff, a respected military analyst, wrote in *Haaretz* last week: 'Israel is far from a decisive victory and its main objectives have not been achieved.'

And that's Israel's big problem. To win this war it must win; but, in the best tradition of guerilla war, Hezbollah merely has to ensure that it is not wiped out. Or as Nasrallah puts it, he 'needs only to survive to win'.

Lebanese civilians lucky enough to escape the line of fire or who emerge from the rubble of the latest strike invariably thank Allah and Nasrallah. The ruthlessly efficient Hezbollah machine—military, political, social and corporate—is often described as a 'state within a state' in Lebanon. But more importantly, it is a state of mind for most in an idolising population and all the more so because Hezbollah's highly secretive guerilla fighters are thwarting the might of Israel's conventional forces.

Inspired by the 1979 Iranian revolution of Ayatollah Ruhollah Khomeini and funded, trained and armed by Tehran ever since, Hezbollah emerged in the early 1980s from what one of its founders describes as 'a scuffle of desert camels' among competing Shiite groups in Lebanon.

When they wanted a military base for training, the fledgling Hezbollah commandeered a Lebanese army barracks. When they needed military instructors, Tehran bussed in 1500 of them. When the Lebanese military and other militia groups tried to block them, they shot their way through. But the making of today's Hezbollah was the appointment in 1992 of the enigmatic Nasrallah as its secretary-general. The young Iranian-trained cleric has built a near-invisible military structure of self-contained and semi-autonomous cells.

Last week the Lebanese president, Emile Lahoud, told me: 'As commander-in-chief of the Lebanese Army in the 1980s, I knew that my forces could not oppose the Israeli occupation of

Lebanon, so I allowed Hezbollah to do it . . . they are respected here and throughout the Arab world because they drove the Israelis out.' Surrounded by three urns of freshly cut red roses and dressed in a shiny pale-blue suit, Lahoud added: 'But most people don't know who the Hezbollah people are, where they are, or where their weapons come from.'

A senior political adviser in Beirut explained Hezbollah's organisational tightness with an anecdote: 'An expatriate Lebanese called us from Paris because he was anxious about his 73-year-old father, who lived in a southern village that was being bombed. We made extensive inquiries before we established that his father was alive and well and fighting for Hezbollah. The son was shocked—he knew nothing of his father's part in the struggle.'

The exile's father is among small Hezbollah units that come together for just minutes at a time to fire missiles into northern Israel from Hezbollah's hidden launchers, confident in the knowledge that they can be back in their homes within the ten to fifteen minutes it takes for the Israelis to identify their location and return fire. They do not wear uniforms and are impossible to pick from among their neighbours who may—or may not—be aware of their activities. They can invoke the protective silence of their local communities or hide behind their women's skirts at the same time as they can throw their weight around because of the political and military weakness of the central government.

In today's Lebanon, they are the biggest kid on the block. They have been trained to operate new-tech missile launchers; they are computer-literate. Their only armour is their faith and everything is positioned in the south—they don't have supply lines that might be targeted by the Israelis.

Seemingly unaware of the firepower of Israel's sophisticated US-made weapons and its command-and-control structures, a US military observer complained about Hezbollah's six-year preparation for this war, including the stashing of an estimated 12,000 Iranian-made missiles along the border. He told a reporter, 'They dug tunnels, they dug bunkers, they established communications systems: cell phones, radios, even runners who are not susceptible to eavesdropping. They divided southern Lebanon into military zones with many small units that operate independently, without the need for central control.'

Military experts have coined a name for this kind of conflict: network war. In a network war, the rigid hierarchical structure of a conventional army has difficulty engaging the flattened structure of a hybrid force like Hezbollah, in which all the sophistication of a conventional force is packed into a horizontal cell structure.

In the judgement of Anthony Cordesman, an analyst at Washington's Center for Strategic and International Studies, Hezbollah has the Israelis foxed. Of the Israeli performance, he writes: 'It may simply be too late for Israel to react in this war. It entered it based on deeply flawed grand strategic . . . and tactical principles. [Non-state armies like Hezbollah] compensate for . . . conventional military superiority by using populations and civil facilities as a shield, and constantly finding and exploiting new ways to use civilian casualties and collateral damage as ideological, political, psychological and media weapons. It is a duel that favours [Hezbollah]. It is easier and cheaper to disperse, shelter and hide, and then exaggerate and lie if civilian casualties and collateral damage occur.'

This invisible, below-the-radar structure has defied attempted infiltration by Israel's intelligence services. Mocking their efforts to co-opt Hezbollah's strictly disciplined fighters, Nasrallah told a reporter in 2000: 'But they were always confronted with rejection because . . . Hezbollah is a group seeking the heavenly world, martyrdom and death. So members cannot be easily drafted by the enemies.' Every Hezbollah fighter goes through deep-immersion spiritual training and, leaving nothing to chance, an extensive internal party security apparatus also vets every member and maintains a file on their movements and contacts.

Nasrallah heads a standing army of about 3000 paid fighters, which includes an elite commando force reportedly trained in Iran. But he also has thousands more reservists. Such are the lines of organisation that some, like a group of reservists interviewed by the *Guardian* in the south this week, were still biding their time, waiting for explicit orders to join the fight.

In the 1980s and 1990s, Hezbollah or its associated groups mounted a series of menacing suicide missions. The most lethal were six months apart: the death of 90 Israeli soldiers in Tyre, in the south in 1992, and six months later the death of 80 Americans in an attack on the US embassy in April 1993. In the 1980s, Hezbollah or its front groups were involved in the abduction of dozens of foreigners. They were also implicated in several aircraft hijackings—charges the group has denied.

But despite Israel's outrage at Hezbollah's claim that the kidnapping of two Israeli soldiers, which sparked the present crisis, was to set the scene for a prisoner swap, that is precisely what both parties have done in the past. In a remarkable German-brokered exchange in 2004, Hezbollah won the release of 435 Arab prisoners from Israeli jails in exchange for the bodies of three captured Israeli soldiers and a former Israeli army colonel who had been abducted in Lebanon.

After the Israeli withdrawal from south Lebanon in 2000, Nasrallah set about the meticulous planning for this war, with help from Iran and, to a lesser extent, Syria.

Despite US and European prodding on the need to disarm Hezbollah, few in the Beirut political establishment seem to take the idea seriously. An adviser to one of the Christian leaders says the only way to disarm the party's military wing would be to co-opt it into the Lebanese security forces.

For now, Hezbollah's military leadership has gone underground. But other senior figures go about their political, welfare and media work seemingly with little regard for their security. One non-military leader told me: 'At a time like this you feel there is an element of risk, but we have this sense of sacrifice.'

But they also have time on their side—to fall back, to regroup, to plan new attacks. Elaborating on the claim by a Taliban captive in Afghanistan that 'the Americans have watches, we have time', the Hezbollah fighters who spoke to the *Guardian* said that part of their training entailed spending days at a time alone in an empty building. Their leader was quoted: 'Patience is our main virtue. We can wait for days, weeks, months before we attack. The Israelis are always impatient . . . I know them very well.'

Hezbollah's followers take Nasrallah's word as gospel. Talal Salman, editor-in-chief of *As-Safir* newspaper, told me: 'In this war Hezbollah is showing that it can do what it says it will do.'

The unique aspect of Hezbollah is that while it keeps one foot in the resistance-militia sphere, it keeps the other in national and local politics; its two cabinet ministers were among the signatories last week to Prime Minister Fouad Siniora's ceasefire proposal. Their shift into democratic politics in 1992 was highly strategic. The possibility that a strong central government might emerge meant that Hezbollah needed to be a part of the process to protect its interests and, with all this talk of disarmament, its very existence.

The party takes its name from a verse in the Koran: 'Those who accept the mandate of God, his prophets and those who believe, Lo! the Party of God, they are the victorious.'

On these early summer evenings in Beirut, television sets sound from apartment to apartment, blending into a chorus of warlike anthems from Hezbollah's Al-Manar satellite channel. The Party of God is still at work.

WAVES OF DESPAIR

Gaza City, Occupied Palestinian Territories
2 September 2006

It could be anywhere in the world. Colourful umbrellas, flags taut in the breeze and the lifesaver's shrill whistle. It's late on a hot, humid day and no one wants to leave the beach. School holidays are almost done and small boys squeal in delight as they dart away from languid family picnics—off again to conquer the foaming surf with all the fearlessness of youth.

It is picture-perfect. But this is Gaza City, and it's too good to be true. Beneath this veneer, more than 1.3 million Palestinians are trapped in deep misery. For six months now, they have been squeezed in a global vice of collective punishment.

First, the United States and the European Union cut virtually all aid funding because the Palestinians elected a government that refuses to explicitly recognise Israel and to eschew violence. More recently, Israel launched a campaign of Lebanon-style destruction because the local militias captured an Israeli soldier in a cross-border raid.

If all of that is not cause enough for anxiety, sour-grapes infighting between the Palestinian factions since the surprise election in January of the Islamist party Hamas threatens to erupt into what many fear will be a cruel civil war. This is the context that makes the Gaza beach scene so surreal.

There is not a bikini to be seen. Some mothers move their plastic chairs to the water's edge, revealing only their naked toes. In the 40-plus heat, there is great hilarity when a few plunge right in, still dressed head-to-toe in swathes of black cloth as white water washes over them.

But my comment on the size of the crowd elicits an early explanation of the grim reality of civilian life in a tiny strip of territory that has become an Israeli shooting gallery. Over coffee on the terrace at the Beach Hotel, the chef, Abu Omar, explains: 'Most families come here now because they are frightened of Israeli shelling on the other beaches.'

'Now' began in June, when pictures flashed around the world of a distraught 10-year-old, Huda Ghalia, as she fell weeping beside the body of her dead father on one of Gaza's popular northern beaches. Nearby lay the mangled remains of the girl's step-mother and five of her brothers and sisters. The Israelis admit their tanks were in action at the time, but they deny firing the killer shell. Eyewitnesses, foreign reporters and Marc Garlasco, a former Pentagon battlefield analyst now working for the New York-based Human Rights Watch, disagree. 'My three-year-old saw the images on TV and now she freaks out at the suggestion of any of us going to the beach,' says Abu Omar.

Apart from their toes, the women on the beach also reveal their hands—and paler-skin reminders of wedding bands that have been sold, either to feed their families or to buy clothes and books for children, who started the new school year yesterday.

It's a measure of the intractable nature of this conflict that the United Nations Relief and Works Agency is now in its fifty-sixth year of caring for Palestinians who became refugees when the state of Israel was established. So the agency's director, John Ging, draws on official records when he declares: 'It's dangerous and miserable. This is the largest, most enduring crisis of modern times.'

Since the West cut funding to the Palestinian Authority, as many as 170,000 families in Gaza are without an income and there is little else to prime the local economy. About 90 per cent live below the poverty line; as many as 85 per cent are said to be jobless; and close to 1 million individuals depend on United Nations handouts of oil, flour, beans, rice, sugar and milk. The shelling has driven hundreds from their homes and forced farmers to abandon crops in the fields.

When my driver takes a wrong turn in the traffic, we are caught amid stone-throwing and wild gunfire as police try to break up a mob of protesters outside one of the city's main banks. They are government workers venting their anger at a decision by the banks to unilaterally deduct loan arrears from a one-off, partial salary payment that the Palestinian Authority has deposited in their accounts. The Jordan Bank caves in, leaving the loan repayments for another day.

Elsewhere, housewives such as Um Fatima complain they can no longer save by cooking in bulk because they cannot rely on refrigeration—an Israeli attack on the main power station has reduced them to a few erratic hours of power each day. And no power means no domestic pumps, which means no water. One hand instinctively covers the other when Um Fatima catches me observing her band-less wedding finger. But this woman still has dignity and she declines to discuss her last visit to the Gaza gold market.

Plying their trade against the stone walls of the seventh-century Great Omari Mosque, the 25 gold traders are idle after a surge in business in April and May, when they each were buying as much as 15 kilograms of gold a day as families first began to feel the pinch.

No customers are buying gold these days. Traditionally, Arab women hold as much solid gold as they can afford, which they sell in bad times—but when they come offering their light wedding rings for sale, the traders know their families have hit bottom. The gold trader Hamdi Basal says: 'Usually, summer is a time for weddings and brides buying their first gold in great excitement. Now the women only come to sell.'

Back at the beach, there is more excitement as children rush in to help six men haul in their nets, but it's a mistake to conclude the fishermen are spared from the hardship. Abu Omar explains: 'They net from the beach because the Israelis enforce a navy blockade along the coast—the fishermen get shot at if they take their boats into deep water. There's not a lot of fish in the shallows.'

As if on cue, there is a combat chorus to prove that Israel has this place covered. A destroyer heaves into view, the thump of its turbines pulsing through the water as it carves a south-bound course. A series of thuds signals more artillery in the north of Gaza, and overhead there are twin sounds—the lawnmower squawk of a surveillance drone and, much higher, a growling fighter jet. Such is the level of infrastructure bombing now that European aid officials have concluded that rebuilding any of Gaza in the absence of a viable peace process is a waste of good money—the roads, bridges and buildings will only be bombed again, they say.

One of the fishermen says he has been too scared to venture out since the capture of the Israeli soldier on 25 June. But when other boats pull in, three take their combined haul to market on the back of a single bicycle.

Darwesh Abu Mustafa still ventures out, despite three past incidents in which he says his small boat was confiscated for months at a time by the Israeli navy. His friend Ahmad, who has just returned from five hours of casting his nets in the shallows, fumes because his haul of sardines does not even fill a plastic bucket and when he sells them at the dockside, he gets only 30 shekels ($9). 'How does he feed a family on that?' Darwesh demands. 'It's God who feeds our children. But we can't forget the martyrs, so this is the tax we all have to pay for the resistance.'

The ability of the Palestinian people to keep paying that 'resistance tax' is being tested yet again. And Raji Sourani, head of the Palestinian Centre for Human Rights, warns that Israel should take account of what he calls the local 'camel' psychology. Mindful of a United Nations estimate that about 9000 Israeli artillery shells have been lobbed into Gaza in the last year, he explains: 'You can make the camel so thirsty and hungry and you can make it carry too great a load; you can beat it and insult it. But watch out when the animal revolts—it will kill you.'

ON THE VERGE
OF CIVIL WAR

Gaza City, Occupied Palestinian Territories

6 September 2006

The power fails. Abu Annis stabs at the keys of his mobile phone, sparking a glimmer of light as he and six fighters for Islamic Jihad talk about life on the Gaza Strip—bombs, death and the daily grind.

Anxious that the group might be detected by the Israeli surveillance drones which are overhead constantly, they straggle in one at a time to this cinder-block home in Gaza's Jabaliya City. All defer to Abu Annis who, at just 22, is their appointed spokesman.

The stern-faced young man demands light so that nothing will be lost when he addresses an ominous new twist in the turmoil of the Middle East—the threat of a Palestinian civil war.

The Palestinians have been isolated since early this year, when they elected a government controlled by Hamas, an Islamist movement with ties to regimes in Iran and Syria. Now, in Gaza and on the West Bank, many cower in their homes as Hamas gunmen clash almost daily with loyalists of the regime they defeated.

It is their worst nightmare. Caught between the secularists of the late Yasser Arafat's failed Fatah movement and the fundamentalists of Hamas, they fear that the dream of their own separate state might shrivel in the continuing clash between radical Islam and the West.

Amid the distractions of the Iraq war and, more recently, the new Lebanon war, little attention has been given to overlapping efforts by Washington, Europe and Israel to weaken or destroy an Arab rarity, the democratically elected Hamas government of the prime minister, Ismail Haniya.

Since late June, when militiamen from Hamas and other factions tunnelled under the Gaza–Israel border to capture an Israeli soldier, Gaza has been subjected to unrelenting Israeli retaliation. Aerial and tank bombardments and border skir-mishing have killed almost 200; more than 30 Hamas cabinet ministers and MPs have been snatched in Israeli raids on the West Bank; and border closures have made Gaza a virtual prison.

Earlier in the year, Washington, Brussels and Tel Aviv paralysed the working of the new government and the local economy when they cut vital funds transfers to back their demands that Hamas abandon its refusal to recognise Israel and renounce violence. And other US-friendly but anti-democratic Arab regimes sit on their hands as Palestine burns.

This is how the stage is set. The popularly elected president, Mahmoud Abbas, is from Mr Arafat's long-dominant Fatah faction, a secular nationalist movement that traditionally had a mortgage on Palestinian power and which has committed itself to a negotiated peace settlement with Israel. Despite the swing to Islam, Mr Abbas retains control of Palestinian negotiations with Israel and the world. More importantly, Mr Abbas commands the loyalty of much of the 35,000-strong security forces, almost exclusively Fatah loyalists, who have launched armed attacks on government buildings because they have not been paid for six months due to the funding freeze.

Embittered by defeat, Fatah refused an invitation from Hamas to join a government of national unity in the aftermath of the January poll, prompting the International Crisis Group to conclude: 'It's a question of power, pure and simple. [For Fatah,] allowing their main rivals to exercise it is inconceivable and too great a threat to their own positions.' Despite its legendary corruption and abuse of power in office, Fatah was unable to accept electoral defeat. The inexperienced Hamas did not expect to win government and has been slow to grasp power decisively. In response to Mr Abbas's grip on the security forces, Hamas has started setting up its own parallel forces.

At the mobile-phone-lit meeting at Jabaliya, the seven from Islamic Jihad set out their own unambiguous position. They are fighting to the death for the liberation of all of historic Palestine: 'This is a religious war against the Jews.'

The showdown between Hamas and Fatah is an unnecessary distraction. Among the ruins of Netzarim, utterly destroyed by the Israelis last year when they abandoned their fortified settlements in Gaza, I chanced upon the brothers Rubin and Khalid Khadoura, who were picnicking with their families. As the children fossicked in the rubble that had been Israeli settler homes, the brothers complained about the new siege and Rubin had words of caution for the Hamas leadership: 'If I was the prime minister, I'd be thinking about the plight of the people without salaries because Hamas will never change the ideology of the people unless we have a good life.'

Amid another pile of rubble, not far away in Beit Hanoon, 65-year-old Mohammed Hussein affirms his commitment after what he claims has been almost 30 years as a resistance agnostic. The new fire in his belly is caused by an Israeli air strike that pulverised a four-storey building in which his children lived and from which he ran one of the biggest supermarkets in the area.

'I worked for 22 years in Saudi Arabia for the money to build it,' he says. 'The Israelis call at one o'clock in the morning on my seventeen-year-old son Hussein's mobile, saying everyone must be out of the building in fifteen minutes. Minutes later two missiles hit one side of the house. Neighbours rushed in, trying to help us get stuff out of the rest of the building but the Israelis call again, saying to get the people away because there will be another strike—six minutes later two more missiles knock down the rest of the building.'

Surrounded by several of his sons, the old man bounces his one-year-old grandson, Osama, on his knee. 'They oblige us to join the resistance,' he says, before he delivers the Palestinian distillation of decades of failed diplomacy and ineffectual war: 'We have made agreements with Israel, but it doesn't respect them . . . they don't want peace, they just want to drive us from our land. Do you really think things would be any different if they could bring Fatah back?'

Then Ribhi, the father of little Osama, demands silence because he has something to say: 'You see this one-year-old? He will grow up to be a bomber in Tel Aviv if the Israelis keep killing our people. He is my boy, but he is not as priceless as Jerusalem.'

To another house on a rise overlooking the Mediterranean north of Gaza City, a palatial residence that has not been bombed. It is the home of Dr Nabil Shaath, who was foreign minister in the former Fatah-led government. Here the swimming pool, the manicured gardens and the Asian household staff are read by ordinary Palestinians as proof of the rampant corruption that caused voters to turn against Fatah.

A pistol-packing bodyguard hovers as a seemingly contrite Dr Shaath canvasses his party's options: 'We've made many mistakes. We were angry after the election, so we refused to be a part of a Hamas government . . . but now they need partners and we might be able to help. But we can't make the government that [President George] Bush wants; that is not how democracy works. The United States dictated that there had to be an election, but it can't dictate the outcome.'

The former minister acknowledges, but denies, allegations that Fatah has been instrumental in US–Israeli efforts to bring down Hamas. He insists: 'Not true. Our president is a good friend of the United States, but he has not been clubbing together with Washington and the Israelis . . . Our interest is in destroying the occupation, not Hamas. But these stupid sanctions and the jailing of their leaders are helping Hamas. . . . Hamas doesn't suffer one bit; it gets funds from Iran and the Arab world and they make sure that their own people don't suffer.'

Despite Israel's round-up of Palestinian officials on the West Bank, Hamas's minister for refugee affairs, Professor Atef Odwan, tools around Gaza in a beaten up Volkswagen Passat. The presence of just a single bodyguard supports the view of many Palestinians that the Israelis have snatched none of Hamas' Gaza-based ministers or MPs because they see the whole strip as an effective prison. 'They control our borders, the sea and the air, so why would they bother coming back in to face hatred and resistance? So I can move around,' Professor Odwan says.

In his spartan office, the minister sets out the various elements of an emerging Hamas compromise that remains unacceptable to Israel and the key international players: 'We have offered a 30-year truce in exchange for a Palestinian state within the 1967 borders, freedom for Palestinians held by the Israelis and complete sovereignty.' He acknowledges the glaring omission: there is no explicit recognition of Israel.

So what does the Islamist professor make of democracy when Washington is leading a charge that has paralysed the Hamas government? 'We have discovered that the Americans are liars; the Europeans too. They are not the democracy lovers they claim to be. They all just push their own interests.'

On the sidelines, there is a loud 'We told you so' from Islamic Jihad. Their political leader Khalid al-Batsh says: 'The worry now is, after their debacle in Lebanon, the Israelis will be looking for a quick victory in Gaza to prove to their people that they are not as weak as they were revealed to be in Lebanon. And the United States will push for superficial movement in the peace process as a gift to those heroes in Riyadh, Cairo and Amman'—he is referring to Washington's key Arab allies—'for keeping their mouths shut during the destruction of south Lebanon.'

Dr Ibrahim Ibrach, a political analyst at Gaza's Al-Azhar University, comes at the crisis from a different angle. 'This place wasn't ready for a vote. How do you have proper elections when the country is occupied and instead of political parties, we have militias? And now Israel wants internal Palestinian friction. It doesn't want to give Mahmoud Abbas a peace deal, and it doesn't want Hamas to falter completely.'

Dr Ibrach agrees that the current crisis has eroded some of Hamas' popular support. But he predicts that, if the elections were held again tomorrow, Hamas would win again. 'A government of national unity might work. But if Hamas fails, or if it is made to fail, Palestinian voters will not rush back to Fatah's corruption and its failed peace efforts. The voters will be looking for someone else—that's why the risk of civil war is so real.'

In May all sides in the Palestinian equation seized on help from an unlikely quarter—Israel's jails. Five revered Palestinian inmates, representing the key factions, drew up their own plan for national reconciliation and demanded that it be adopted. Intended more to bring Palestinians together than to appease Washington, it called for an independent state on all of the land seized by Israel in 1967, a right for the millions of Palestinian refugees around the world to return to their homes in the Occupied Territories and in what now is Israel, and for resistance by all means within the Israeli-occupied territories—not in Israel proper.

The prisoners' document acknowledged the role of the Palestinian Liberation Organisation, a bastion of Fatah power, but argued that Hamas must be brought into the PLO. Importantly, it urged the formation of a coalition government of Hamas and Fatah. Grasping the opportunity, Mr Abbas said that, if Hamas did not accept it, he would put it to a referendum within 40 days. Amid the squabbling, the Hamas signatories to the prisoners' document withdrew their signatures.

When Israel assassinated a key Hamas figure on 9 June, and blame for the death of seven members of a Palestinian family in a strike on a Gaza beach was laid at the Israelis' door, Hamas announced that its military wing was abandoning its ceasefire of sixteen months. Hamas had demonstrated that it could put its missiles on hold, and now it was sending a message through one of its senior MPs who told an International Crisis Group researcher: 'The alternative to our government is a resumption of suicide attacks.'

Finally, in the last week of June, virtually all the factions signed off on acceptance of the prisoners' initiative, but hardly anyone noticed because on the same day Hamas and two other militias kidnapped Israeli Corporal Gilad Shalit, bringing down the wrath of Israel on all of Gaza.

Corporal Shalit remains a prisoner. And under constant Israeli fire, it is virtually impossible for the Palestinian leadership to deal with the immediate internal political challenge: the shape of a unity government. Even more difficult will be Hamas and

Fatah finding sufficient common ground to work together, even in the short term.

Instead of joining forces to fight Israel, the Palestinian factions have turned on each other: the president and his Fatah backers try to undermine Hamas, while Hamas accuses them of treason because of their support for the international effort to isolate the Hamas government. These days, their separate rallies condemn each other as often as they condemn Israel.

With all sides on a hair-trigger, the only identifiable circuit breaker is fear of the consequences of internal war. But despite local anger at the new levels of hardship, Hamas is judged by most Palestinians to be the stronger and more popular party, as well as the victim of foreign interference.

Fatah might regain power but, beset by its own internal factional and generational wars, the party's resurrection would do little to break the new hand of radical Islam in the Palestinian equation. Like Hezbollah in Lebanon, Hamas is probably here to stay. Much is made of its refusal to explicitly recognise Israel, but local and international players can hardly be shocked: Washington's autocratic friends in Riyadh still refuse to do so; likewise Rabat; and Amman and Cairo both stonewalled on recognition until they negotiated their respective peace treaties with Tel Aviv.

After watching Israel's destruction of Lebanon, the Beirut-based Arab commentator Rami Khouri upbraided the Americans and the Israelis for their obsessional interest in symptoms rather than root causes. Noting that the Middle East crisis predated the arrival of both Hezbollah and Hamas on the scene, he writes: 'Every tough issue in this region—Lebanon, Iraq, Syria, Iran, terrorism, radicalism, armed resistance groups—is somehow linked to the consequences of the festering Israeli–Palestinian conflict.'

THE MAN WHO WOULDN'T DIE

Damascus, Syria
7 September 2008

A black Mercedes-Benz eases up to the curb and stops momentarily to pick up a passenger. Black curtains are drawn across tinted windows; a muffled thump signals the reactivation of the central locking system as the vehicle pulls away from the Al-Majed Hotel and glides back into the fumes and chaos of a Damascus afternoon.

The driver is Miqdad. A cheerful young man dressed in Hamas black, he keeps one eye on the rearview mirror as he hangs loosely over the wheel. He adjusts the audio control and fills the car with the techno-tribal thump of Hamas anthems, interspersed with hectoring snatches of fundamentalist oratory, the crack of heavy arms, and an occasional bomb blast.

Miqdad drives south away from the heart of the city, passing a rock massif on which the palatial home of Syria's leader, Bashar al-Assad, is etched against the sky. Straight ahead, another massif is adorned by a crop of spiky communications antennae.

At first the streetscapes are uniformly drab and dull, but here and there, curved Moorish mosaics and grim, angular facades of glass and steel break the monotony of box-like, Soviet-style architecture. Led by the purveyors of mobile phones, Syria's advertisers have run amok with garish billboards.

After about twenty minutes, Miqdad swings the Mercedes hard right, into a secured enclave reserved for high officials of the Damascus regime, foreign diplomats and NGOs. This is a journey to the sanctuary of Khalid Mishal.

A United Nations agency is signposted. Diplomatic missions or residencies are identified by various national flags. But no signs point the way to a nondescript bunker that functions as the headquarters of Hamas, the Islamic Resistance Movement in Palestine. The dusty four-storey complex has the appearance of a residential apartment block. Festooned with swivelling security cameras, it is hard up against a broken hillside on a street at the rear of the diplomatic enclave. Through-traffic is light.

The first indication that this might be the home of one of the regime's most high-security VIPs is the presence of three leather-jacketed Syrian guards who juggle firearms and walkie-talkies as they prowl the pavement outside. Less obvious but more powerful is the anti-aircraft battery concealed in a concrete shelter dug deep into the hillside, just across the street.

Miqdad has said little. But now he issues a blunt instruction for his passenger to remain in the car. Slowing the Mercedes, he jumps it onto the pavement, coming to rest under an outstretched awning that hangs from the perimeter wall. House guards, moving with practised precision, seize the loose end of two bunched canvas flaps suspended from the awning and pinned to either side of the wall. They draw them quickly out to the edge of the pavement and then along the gutter to fully envelop the car. Miqdad releases the central locking only when the Mercedes is fully concealed in its anonymous canvas bubble. No one sees in and no one sees out.

The arrival of an outsider is a major exercise for the attentive security detail that hovers around Khalid Mishal inside the complex. Each of his guards wears a smart suit and dark tie. They wear earpieces and all speak into the cuffs of their jacket sleeves from time to time. Courteous enough, they apply themselves with the discipline and thoroughness of men who understand that their boss is a constant target for a determined enemy.

Visitors' cell phones are confiscated at the door. The ground-floor vestibule is filled with a walk-through metal detector and an airport-like baggage scanner through which all bags are processed before being taken away for a microscopic physical search—in the absence of their owner.

At the top of a flight of stairs that turned sharply to the right halfway up, and behind a heavy, double-locked door, is the sprawling first-floor room where Khalid Mishal receives visitors. In the style of a traditional Arabian *diwan* or meeting place, the long walls are lined with plump sofas and armchairs, upholstered in a muted Hamas green. The carpet on the floor is another shade of green. Retainers glide in with welcoming trays of muddy Turkish coffee, sweetened tea, sodas or mineral water, and with small individual plates of Arabic sweets.

But there's more in this room than Arab hospitality. Confronting all who enter through the big double doors are portraits of about twenty Hamas 'martyrs'. In a mural that takes up much of the space between two imposing windows, each cell of a honeycomb pattern holds the face of a Hamas cadre who has been liquidated in Israel's campaign of targeted assassination. A shrine to the assassinated Sheikh Ahmad Yassin is in one corner of the room. Off against the far wall is an elaborate scale model, in polished timber, of the Dome of the Rock, the revered Islamic shrine in the heart of Jerusalem's Old City, over which so much blood has been spilled.

Khalid Mishal is shouting in Arabic. Holding the whole phone in his hand, with the loudspeaker on, he paces animatedly and angrily as the gaze of his aides alternates from his bulk to a television in the corner of the room. Several people—all talking at once—are on the other end of the phone line, barking back at Mishal. The TV images are graphic, coming in from Gaza.

At a time when Hamas desperately needs to show a less violent face to the world, Al-Jazeera is broadcasting footage of battles in the streets of Gaza between Fatah crowds and a slew of Hamas fighters. It is Friday, 7 September 2007.

With some courage, the remnants of Fatah have taken to organising Friday protests outside the bigger mosques. While prayer sessions continue inside, Fatah activists hold open-air services that double as anti-Hamas protest rallies. When prayers are over, Fatah provocateurs taunt Hamas's forces—chanting slogans, throwing stones and tossing homemade noise grenades. Hamas's Executive Force has taken the bait.

Armed with guns and batons, the Executive Force is roughing up the crowds that have ignored orders to disperse. Shots are fired in the air; rifle butts and batons leave welts on flesh. Some Fatah officials have been detained; journalists attempting to cover the unrest have been beaten. On the phone, Mishal is laying down the law in very precise terms, trying to curb the violence. He shouts the names of Yassin and Al-Rantisi, the long-dead leaders of Hamas in Gaza.

Sprawled on a nearby couch, Hamas's old media spokesman, Mohammed Nazzal, is nursing a fractured arm—the result of a traffic accident, he says. With a close-cropped beard adorning his several chins, the thickset Nazzal wears an old-style safari suit. *Sotto voce*, he offers advice as Mishal angrily demands restraint from the Hamas security forces running in the streets of Gaza. Among those on the other end of the phone is Said Siam, the interior minister in the Hamas government that was in power in the Occupied Territories until the appointment of the Mecca unity government in March 2007.

'I'm talking to our people to keep things calm,' Mishal says with evident exasperation. 'They must understand that we will not deal with Fatah as they dealt with us in the past. They put Yassin and Al-Rantisi in jail—we'll not treat them like that.'

The violent clashes abate quickly enough and Gaza, ever on a hair-trigger, calms down again. In the absence of any updates in the next hour, Mishal relaxes a fraction, claiming a degree of success. In this case, no news is good news.

'Now it's like any other Friday in Gaza,' he says. 'Okay, so there's a bit more tension.'

At age 56, Khalid Mishal has lost the lean Carlos-the-Jackal look he wore in photographs that appeared in the Israeli press at the time of Mossad's attempt on his life ten years earlier. In filling out physically, Mishal has taken on a burly aspect, accentuated by his height. The hair that was Arab-black a decade ago has turned silver-grey. His beard is neatly clipped.

Mishal dresses in what many Arabs refer to as 'Iranian style'. Usually, it is a grey or dark-blue suit with an open-neck shirt, sometimes white, often a pale blue. He seems comfortable in his solid frame, although he announces with a degree of locker-room pride that he has just shed 25 pounds after four months of rigorous dieting and exercise.

Ordinarily Mishal observes the Arab tradition of abandoning his shoes at the door and padding around in socks. But as autumn sets in and a chill rises through the concrete-slab floor, he has dispensed with custom, advising visitors to follow his lead and stay warm by keeping their shoes on.

He sits next to the portrait of Yassin and the flags of Palestine and Hamas, crossing his legs as he lounges in a big armchair. From time to time he rises on an elbow to make a point, before folding back into the depths of his chair.

Constantly hovering around Mishal is Abu Sayf, the same strapping bodyguard who ran the Mossad hit men to ground back in 1997. Like a coiled spring, Sayf is Mishal's shadow. Jet-black hair follows the contours of his skull in a number-three buzz cut. As trim as he was ten years earlier, Abu Sayf now wears button-down collars and a silver pin holds his tie in place. The ubiquitous pistol is shoved into his belt.

Years of anonymity behind the facade of the Hamas political bureau has left Mishal with a one-dimensional profile in the West—that of a hardline zealot bent on the destruction of Israel. But Hamas's election as the government of the Occupied Territories and the factional ruckus that followed has brought more studied attention to a man who has long played a shadowy role in regional affairs.

Mishal is a complex individual with a personal charm that belies the caricature and his cut-throat reputation. He has a broader interest in world affairs than his remorseless public rhetoric suggests. The man who presides over a killing machine has the fastidious personal habits of a hospitable Arab chieftain. He polishes grapes one at a time with a tissue, or he produces a knife to slice pieces from a ripened peach, before passing the fruit to a visitor. If the visitor's eye wanders, he interrupts his delivery, which is principally in Arabic, and switches to English to command eye contact with the words, 'Excuse me!'

In fact, Mishal has a sound understanding of English. Although he is reluctant to use it, he swiftly corrects a translator on nuances of meaning, thus revealing his own keen grasp of the language. In discussing the so-called Jordan Option, by which Palestinians might be driven from the West Bank to live among their eastern neighbours, he jokingly calls it the 'Jordan Cucumber' because the Arabic word *khiyar* translates as both 'option' and 'cucumber'. And he plays on words to make political statements: 'Ah! I have "sage" in my tea; "siege" is how the Palestinians live.'

On the narrow policy spectrum within Hamas, Mishal lines up in the pragmatic centre. But having observed how compromise and corruption have almost destroyed Fatah, he is hard-headed in his pragmatism, and some close observers of the movement argue that in recent years he has toughened in his policy outlook.

By Mishal's book, his championing of Hamas's participation in the political process ought to have appealed to the West. However, that endorsement has never come because of his determined stand on the prime issues: the ongoing violence, the rocket attacks, and the cornerstone commitment in the movement's charter, its call for the destruction of Israel. Mishal has no intention of compromising on what he sees as the movement's legitimate right to resist Israel violently. Hamas might run for election, but it does so as a resistance movement that keeps its finger on the detonator.

In the aftermath of the June war between the Palestinian factions in Gaza, Mishal knows Hamas has reached a historic crossroads. Despite the strained circumstances, he is enthusiastic about the responsibility of government, but he also warns that a 'third intifada' is on the cards. Hamas is open to an accommodation with Israel, but not at the expense of either the movement or the rights of the Palestinian people.

Like a chess player, Mishal steps carefully around speculation about the circumstances in which Hamas might enter talks with Israel. If he were to acknowledge Israel, what would Israel do in return for Hamas? What might the American and European reactions be? He continues to dismiss any knowledge of the ceasefire proposal Israeli sources claim to have received from Hamas in 2006. 'That never happened,' he insists. 'It's not correct, I'm sure. I'm the leader here—I know what's happening.'

While Mishal holds the muscular power in Hamas, his old rival and colleague Mousa Abu Marzook is established nearby in his own Damascus office. These two men still work closely in the Hamas leadership team, but Abu Marzook's fortunes have faded over the years as Mishal's grip has tightened. The relationship between the two men and what it says about the shifting balance of power at the peak of Hamas is a subject of considerable interest to the United States and to Israel.

A native of Gaza, Abu Marzook is a lifelong disciple of Sheikh Ahmad Yassin. He rebuilt the grassroots leadership of Hamas in the Occupied Territories in the early 1990s after the Israeli campaigns to round up and deport the movement's activists by the hundreds. By contrast, little has emerged on Mishal's activities in the same period, which some colleagues still cryptically refer to as Mishal's 'clandestine years'.

Anointed by Yassin, Abu Marzook was well-positioned as the man most likely to assume the leadership of Hamas. Instead, it was Mishal—who hastily denies that his father's role as imam to a senior member of the Kuwaiti royal family has conferred any privilege on his family—who rose inexorably. During Abu Marzook's incarceration in America from 1995 to 1997, Mishal cemented his own position in the hierarchy.

When Abu Marzook was released, he returned to the Hamas political bureau to find he had been demoted and would serve instead as Mishal's deputy. At every opportunity in the Hamas electoral cycle, Abu Marzook signalled his ongoing rivalry by standing as a leadership candidate—to no avail. At least three such efforts ended in failure and the most recent of them in ignominy, when he was unable to muster enough support even to retain his post as deputy, much less to dislodge Mishal from the top job.

But senior figures in Hamas explain that, in the interests of internal peace, Mishal proposed that Abu Marzook continue to serve as an appointed deputy. 'Brother Khalid carries the stick in the middle,' as one puts it.

These days Abu Marzook works from his hillside den above Damascus. The views are spectacular, but his accommodation has more the air of a barracks room than the stylish, corporate headquarters he enjoyed in the old days in Amman, back in the mid-1990s. From time to time, he emerges publicly to talk to the Western media, but Abu Marzook has the look of a man who has fallen on hard times. His sagging frame carries excessive weight, and the dapper dress sense of a former chief who saw merit in colour-coordinating his coffee cups with his office fittings has surrendered to a more pedestrian attire.

Outside the Hamas inner circle, some were surprised by Mishal's effortless rise to the frontline leadership team. Observers like the Gaza-based historian and non-factional political player Ziad Abu Amr argue that the authority and strength of Hamas provided the springboard for Mishal's ambition. 'You must remember that sometimes a powerful and credible movement makes the leader—not the reverse,' he explains.

In Amman, the well-connected journalist and analyst Ranya Kadri attributes Mishal's elevation to the Israeli assassination attempt of 1997. 'The day they tried to kill him was the day Mishal the leader was born,' she observes later. 'The man who died that day was Abu Marzook. Nobody wanted to talk to Abu Marzook after that—it was Mishal, Mishal, Mishal.'

Over the years there have been oblique references to a Muslim Brotherhood 'council of war' in Amman in 1983, which is said to have laid the foundations of Hamas. The official mythology has always pinpointed the legendary meeting on the evening of 9 December 1987, at the Gaza home of Sheikh Yassin, as the occasion on which the wheelchair-bound preacher and six others spontaneously gave birth to Hamas in an effort to channel outrage over a fluke traffic accident in which several Palestinians were killed.

But by Mishal's own account, the plotting began much earlier—first in distant Kuwait and subsequently at the secret conference in Amman. The plan for the creation of Hamas had been locked into the Muslim Brotherhood's strategic planning as much as four years before the fatal traffic collision near the Erez border crossing, which heralded the onset of the first intifada. Mishal's version suggests that the powerful imagery of the crippled Yassin, almost single-handedly working the length and breadth of the Gaza Strip in the name of Hamas, was a clever exercise in public relations.

'It would have been impossible for the Yassin operation to succeed in Gaza and on the West Bank without the outside project [instigated by Mishal],' a source close to the Hamas leadership says. 'Even when Yassin was focused on *dawa* [as opposed to armed resistance], it was funding from the Muslim Brotherhood [outside Palestine] that kept him going.'

Mishal's own explanation is that work on a new armed resistance was well under way when the Erez accident occurred, in which a truck driven by an Israeli ploughed into oncoming traffic, killing four Palestinians; the accident became the trigger that activated a pre-conceived plan.

'The decision by the Gaza Seven in 1987 was not a spontaneous or momentary event happening out of context,' Mishal says. 'Hamas's founders inside and outside the Occupied Territories had taken steps to prepare for the launch of the movement.

Anger and rage over the traffic accident made that December the opportune moment.

'We were ready. From the outside, it might have looked like a reaction [to the accident]. But the project envisaged in 1983 was on the verge of coming to fruition, and for us this was its crowning moment. This was the appropriate environment for Hamas to come into being and to go public.'

Mishal's years as an exiled Palestinian in Kuwait, seemingly intent on his new career as a physics teacher, were an effective veil behind which he dreamed of another destiny. 'I was a man with a mission, a cause, a project. I'd been dreaming of it since I was a kid! I'm proud that God bestowed on me the bounty of being a founder and a soldier for a project of which I've become leader. It's a position entrusted to me by my brothers. But what is personally important for me is that this is my project.'

Mishal now straddles the organisation, albeit from exile. By deft management or manipulation of each crisis in the organisation's history—including the assassination of Yassin—he has steadily consolidated his control over an intellectually and organisationally cohesive but geographically far-flung network.

The various wings of the movement—the military and political arms; the local leadership in Gaza and the West Bank; the powerful prisoners' leadership, which manages to function inside Israeli jails; and the government team, over which Ismail Haniyah presides in Gaza—can only interact through Damascus. Mishal keeps an iron grip on both the flow of funds and Hamas's extensive links with the Arab and Muslim worlds.

Mishal has the support of the more hardline elements within the movement, particularly in Gaza. He adopts the language of violence with ease, using rhetoric and propaganda to motivate his forces and to stand Hamas apart from Fatah's chequered efforts to achieve a negotiated settlement with Israel.

But, with an eye on Western perceptions of resistance and his own role as the movement's chief diplomat, Mishal seeks to play down his personal role in suicide bombings, contending that the separation of power between the military and political wings of Hamas is real. 'I have not personally authorised a suicide bombing,' he says. 'That is the prerogative of the military wing. They're the people who authorise and plan them.'

Adopting a distinction that worked for the Irish Republican Army and Sinn Féin in Ireland in the days before September 11, Mishal explains: 'The policy of the movement is to engage in resistance. The military wing decides what form it takes and it's the role of the political wing to defend and explain the resistance.'

Mishal, of course, does not deter the suicide bombers either; rather, he has urged them on and taken public satisfaction in the aftermath. But by 2004, the continued use of suicide attacks turned international opinion decisively against the Palestinian cause and prompted a reassessment within Hamas. Mishal holds to his view that there is still a strategic advantage to be gained by the use of such a catastrophic weapon. By his calculation, each attack undermines Israel's sense of security and unambiguously conveys the message that the Palestinians are not giving in; this, he believes, greatly outweighs the negative publicity.

It has taken more than a year of intense debate within the movement, driven by Hamas's supporters in diaspora communities in the United States and Europe, for the internal lobby against suicide missions to win the argument that there has to be another way to 'make Israel bleed'.

Mishal does not accept that the numbing violence Palestinians and Israelis inflict on each other has a brutalising effect on all who are trapped in the conflict. 'We don't believe that instinctively insisting on our rights dehumanises Palestinians. He who defends himself, his people and his country does not lose his humanity,'

Mishal argues, choosing to frame the decision to back away from suicide missions as a sensible exercise of the movement's *shura*, or consultative processes, and not as a personal defeat for himself. 'There'll be times when I feel restrained [by the internal debate], but it doesn't limit my ability to manoeuvre or to come up with new ideas.'

After a decades-long struggle that has defined not just his people but the whole region, the Khalid Mishal who has risen through the ranks to speak with such authority on the fate of millions of people is a Palestinian enigma. It is difficult to pigeonhole him. Mishal runs a huge, complex organisation that functions both as a government and as an army in a daunting environment. He has an international support network and a following in the Occupied Territories, which demands that he fill the roles of president, commander-in-chief, treasurer and ambassador to the world.

Mishal is branded a terrorist by the United States and the European Union. His oratory is rich in the rhetoric of jihad, but Mishal himself has never thrown a stone, much less fired a shot in combat. For him, there has been none of the resistance schooling of the prison cell or the guerilla camaraderie of the campfire.

Mishal is a hybrid mix of the pious and the worldly. He is deeply immersed in Islam, devoting an hour a day to learning to recite the Koran from a *qari*, a tutor who is the last in a rare and unbroken chain of teachers that goes all the way back to the prophet Mohammed. At the same time Mishal reveals few of the traits of the stereotypical fundamentalist: the myopic, insular and intellectually stunted extremist of Western perception.

'I've met him three times now and I still have not heard him say the word *Islam*,' an American analyst noted, almost in exasperation, after his most recent meeting with the Hamas leader.

The public Mishal projects himself as a hard man. In private he is prone to sudden, unexpected displays of emotion. Mishal indulges in misty memories of village life and the fare at his mother's table. He becomes morose when he recalls the death of Yehiya Ayyash, the master suicide bomber after whom Mishal named a son, born on the day that Israeli forces assassinated Ayyash in 1996. And he sheds a tear when he speaks of the mystery bomb attack in Pakistan in 1989 that killed the preacher-warrior Abdullah Azzam, the mentor Mishal shared with Osama bin Laden. 'Azzam was a great man and we owe him a lot,' Mishal observes, without elaborating on the nature of the debt.

Diplomats, mediators and analysts invariably emerge from the Damascus bunker talking more about what Khalid Mishal is not than about what he is. His critics in the West and in the Arab world are legion. They can cite a litany of his mistakes, but against the din of the rejectionist rhetoric from Washington and Jerusalem, a small but influential body of Western and Israeli support is building behind Mishal and his ability to wrestle tempest-like forces in a crisis that unfolds as a geopolitical psychodrama.

Senior analysts and former administration advisers and officials in the United States and the Middle East warn of the risk of underestimating Mishal, of denying him a seat at the table. By late 2007, it is possible to hear a former senior government adviser in Jerusalem describe Mishal as an 'authentic nationalist leader', or to hear a former White House official in Washington judge him as a leader destined to play 'an essential role' in the Middle East crisis.

Arab intelligence officials are troubled because, despite the Hamas leader's claims to the contrary, Mishal is the first figure in Hamas to take control of both the political and military wings. In Israeli military intelligence, the analysis is more about the qualities that make Mishal such a formidable enemy for the Jewish state.

'He understands power and the use of violence. Even if he doesn't do it himself, he understands clearly what it's about,' says a former Israeli military-intelligence officer who has studied Mishal from afar for fifteen years. 'He steadies the Hamas boat. He's not a great ideologist and he did not invent the Hamas ideology, but he understands it and what it allows him to do. But we have to understand that Mishal is a very dangerous person. He's not crazy; he is down to earth, or at least that's what he wants us to think. Remember this—he heads a terrorist group with its bombs and rockets and with people being hurled from fifteenth-floor windows.'

The same caution is couched in different terms by a key Fatah activist who has observed Mishal's increasing dominance of Hamas. 'He didn't win internal support for the leadership with charisma alone,' he argues. 'There were reasons for them deciding that Mishal would be a strong, determined leader. To get up, he had to sell the idea to Hamas and the Muslim Brotherhood that this posture of his can win important friends and neutralise significant enemies.'

An Israeli agent taps into a different, but equally potent, reservoir of resistance sentiment to define the forces driving Mishal. 'He wants to be like us, like the Zionists in historic Palestine,' he says. 'As a homeless people, they succeeded in carving out a new state that today is home to more than 40 per cent of the Jews of the world. Mishal sees himself being responsible for all Palestinians—inside *and* outside—and he wants to bring them all together in their historic home.'

In an era of instant communication, Mishal keeps the TV remote control handy to monitor more than half-a-dozen satellite news channels that feed real-time news from the Occupied

Territories to the bunker in Damascus. He has a basement television studio from which his speeches are beamed into Palestinian homes, either by Hamas's Al-Aqsa channel or by Hezbollah's Al-Manar. His principal tool of trade is the phone, though he rarely touches a cell phone—the Israelis are proven masters at tampering with them. Instead, he is a creature of the old-fashioned landline. His staff handle his email, but his personal connections are based on the handwritten lists he has compiled over a lifetime. When aides are unable to produce a phone number he requires, one of two little black books are brought to him. Small and dog-eared, these are Mishal's who's who of the world of politics, Islam and jihad. 'It's all in here—my links to the world,' he says.

Mishal has access to a secure military base in Damascus, where he can walk for exercise. More often, however, he spends an hour a day on a treadmill in the bunker. As he clocks up his daily four-mile walk on the machine, he devours newspapers, magazines and, sometimes, the Koran.

He has just finished reading the controversial memoirs of former CIA director George Tenet, *At the Center of the Storm: My Years at the CIA*, which he describes as a 'brave effort to open a window into the Iraq war'. He is reading Jimmy Carter's *Palestine: Peace Not Apartheid* and John J. Mearsheimer and Stephen M. Walt's *The Israel Lobby and US Foreign Policy*. At the same time, he is wading through the fourteenth-century Muslim intellectual Ibn Kathir's fourteen-volume history of Islam, *The Beginning and the End*. Mishal's bedside cache of reading includes one of the Ibn Kathir volumes; a biography of Saladin, the Muslim warrior-king who recaptured Jerusalem from the Crusaders in 1187; the Koran; and Al-Adhkar, another Islamic prayer book.

Mishal has finally curtailed his travel after years of being on the move. In an increasingly hostile environment, he remains in this shuttered bunker or in other secure locations in Damascus, which he alludes to with cryptic caution as 'my other places'.

'It's my destiny,' he says, explaining the inevitable constraints on his household. 'The family adapts. They are convinced of the nobility of the task, so they too shoulder the responsibility. It's their cause as much as mine.'

Mishal's seven children attend 'normal' schools and university in Damascus. At home his sons drift in and out of his meetings, including the three who witnessed Mossad's attempt on their father's life in 1997. Since this time, most of the key figures in the Middle East crisis have moved on. Jordan's King Hussein is dead and Samih Batikhi, his powerful intelligence chief, has been cast out by the new regime. The Palestinian leader Yasser Arafat too is dead, and Israel's Ariel Sharon is suspended in a deep coma. Bill Clinton is long gone from the White House. Of them all, Mishal is the one who was the marked man. In Hamas, they call him 'The martyr who did not die'.

In the aftermath of the civil war, Gaza wears two kinds of war wound. Locals can easily identify whether damage has been caused by Israeli weapons or Palestinian factions. Where a building teeters or has been reduced to a pile of rubble spilling into the streets, clearly it was targeted by Israel's high-calibre, laser-guided weaponry. But a building that still stands, with its walls scorched, masonry pitted and windows smashed, is likely to have come under small-weapons fire in the fighting between Palestinians.

For their attacks on Israel, Palestinian rocket crews are beginning to use a new targeting tool. Previously they relied on conventional maps of their enemy's terrain, but now they cross-reference them against satellite imagery downloaded from Google Earth, which can be accessed with a laptop and a simple internet connection from anywhere in the world.

On the second day of the new school year, 2 September, a barrage of nine rockets is launched in the direction of Sderot, the border community that took the brunt of the rocket fire from Gaza. A dozen small children are treated for shock after one of the devices lobs into the courtyard of an Israeli day-care centre.

Nine days later, a Qassam rocket fired by Palestinian Islamic Jihad has the potential to take the crisis over the edge of the abyss—again. Launched in the early hours of 11 September, the rocket crashes into Zikim, an IDF training base on the Gaza fringe. It hammers into an empty training tent, but dozens of young soldiers sleeping in adjacent tents are injured, one critically. With an additional 68 injuries, it is the most successful Qassam strike in the six-year campaign.

In Gaza, they expect the worst. A spokesman on Hamas Radio welcomes the strike as a 'victory from God', but the leadership is rushed to safe houses and into underground bunkers. Expecting their official compounds and security complexes to be targeted, Hamas evacuates all staff. When the ministerial teams move, they take their computers and walk-through metal detectors with them to their next, temporary quarters. Overnight, great mounds of earth are dumped at intersections, as protection for Palestinian fighters as much as barriers that might slow an Israeli incursion. These berms appear first in the northern communities of Beit Hanoun and Beit Lahiya, but with the passing of each day the dump trucks work their way deeper into the Strip.

Israeli military and public opinion urge a major attack. But, still shaken by the failure of the previous summer's invasion of Lebanon and reluctant to 'give Hamas what it wants', the politicians resist.

Bracing for an onslaught, Hamas conducts nightly military exercises, which include planting explosive devices on the roads and tracks into Gaza from Israel. Senior figures in the government take heart in the knowledge that Israel is aware of Hamas's recent haul of new weapons and the fighting prowess its men showed in routing the foreign-backed Fatah forces in June. 'They don't want to push us into a corner,' said Khaled Abu Hilal, the former Fatah commander who has gone over to Hamas. 'It's not that we are more powerful—but they know we have nothing to lose.'

The crisis over the Qassam strike on the Israeli training base collides with the euphoria of the holy month of Ramadan. It will begin on the first sighting of the new moon, which was expected two or three days after the attack on Zikim. As eyes turn heavenward, a cartoonist on the Hamas-run *Felasteen* newspaper portrays a hapless Gazan peering into a sky in which hangs not one but two slivers of new moon—one is for Hamas, the other for Fatah.

Spying on the tableau of grim city life is Israel's own eye in the sky—a great white, unmanned spy blimp that is tethered at an altitude of about 1000 feet on the northern border of the Gaza Strip. Ordinarily during Ramadan, it is the duty of prominent figures to host and to attend *iftar*—the breaking of the daily fast—up and down the Strip. But that has become impossible because of their fear of reprisal after the Qassam rocket attack on the Israeli training camp. There is a reasonable suspicion that the blimp and drones overhead are tracking their movements.

Despite being underground, the Hamas prime minister of Gaza, Ismail Haniyah, emerges to lead prayers at the Al-Gharbi Mosque, near his home in the Shati refugee camp. Five black-clad bodyguards form a tight cordon around the raised platform from which he speaks. Cradling AK-47s, they scan the mosque crowd until Haniyah has finished—at which point he is hustled through a side door and back into hiding.

Like many of his senior colleagues, Haniyah speaks of the ruptured relations with Fatah as a breach that can still be remedied, despite the huge cost in blood and trust. This is the first year in four decades under Israeli occupation in which a greater number of his people died in inter-Palestinian violence (over 490) than were killed in Israeli attacks (at least 396). Seven of the deaths, along with 90 woundings, took place at a huge Fatah rally in Gaza in November, after which Hamas announced that 38 members of the Executive Force had been jailed, sacked or demoted after accusations that they indiscriminately opened fire on the Fatah crowd, which was throwing stones and taunting them.

Others in the movement in Gaza speak in more revolutionary terms than Haniyah, as though a line has been crossed. 'This is what happens in a national power struggle,' a senior figure explains. 'It's not easy, but at some point you have to make decisions in the knowledge that some will not accept them, but the majority will. Go into the streets—there's not exactly a revolution against us out there! Today Iraqis are bombing each other and Lebanon has colossal problems, but here the majority is calm.'

In Gaza there was no overt or heavy-handed religious crackdown in the aftermath of the June conflict with Fatah. But, in a society that is already deeply conservative, there is a degree of self-policing. Tailors report women requesting even lower hemlines. More men are letting their beards grow and the barbers of Gaza confirm that 'the sword', a thin beard running from the sideburns and along the jaw line, has become a tolerable compromise between clean-shaven and the bushy undergrowth preferred by hardline Islamists.

Cinemas closed way back in the first intifada, and the last bar to sell alcohol in Gaza was bombed out of business in the weeks before the 2006 election. But shops selling music and DVDs—one of the first targets of fundamentalists elsewhere—are still trading in what now is derided in Israel and abroad as 'Hamastan'.

However, the last economic lifeblood is being drained from Gaza as the Israeli and international siege enters its twentieth month. With the exception of locally grown fruit and vegetables, stores and markets are increasingly bare. Grown men almost cry for cigarettes, which are still smuggled through tunnels from Egypt, but at such a mark-up as to make them unaffordable for most.

Hamas does control the territory of Gaza, but it is finding that, by remote control from Ramallah, Mahmoud Abbas resorts to what is perhaps the most divisive weapon of the inter-factional conflict. He continues to pay the wages of tens of thousands of mostly Fatah public servants in Gaza, but only on condition that they do not go to work. Overnight, he has created a two-class society in Gaza.

In the absence of a formal police force, Hamas volunteers—in yellow fluorescent jackets and Hamas-green baseball caps—direct traffic. Apart from an occasional flashpoint, there are no factional gang wars, no clan feuds, no car thefts. The release of Alan Johnston, a BBC reporter held hostage for four months by a local radical group in Gaza, is celebrated with new street banners in the city. *No more threat for our foreign visitors and guests*, they declare.

Essential goods are still trucked through Israeli-controlled border crossings, but at a finely calculated, minimal rate. 'After three months they have not collapsed,' an Israeli intelligence figure explains. 'We're letting just enough stuff through. We're Khalid Mishal's safety net—not because we like him, but because we don't want a full crisis either.'

•

Israel is between what ought to be grand celebrations. June 2007 marked the fortieth anniversary of the Six-Day War, in which Israel conquered both the West Bank and Gaza in 1967. Now great planning is under way to commemorate the sixtieth anniversary of the founding of the state of Israel in May 2008. For Israelis these are meant to be great monuments to centuries of Jewish struggle and survival.

But after 40 years of blood and summitry, Israel has achieved neither the security it craves nor all of the land to which its people feel entitled. By clinging to its illegal settlements, it has created the justification for the harsh security regime that encircles millions of embittered Palestinians and leaves many of its own citizens living a reality tinged with fear and anger. Forty years on, Israel is still fighting the last day of the Six-Day War.

Sandwiched between the two Israeli anniversaries is Hamas's twentieth anniversary. In those two decades, Hamas has withstood everything that Israel, Fatah and the world has thrown at it. And yet the Islamist movement of late 2007 is a very different movement from the angry group that emerged at the start of the first intifada in 1987.

Hamas has defied the early predictions of its demise. Israel's deportation of hundreds of senior figures in 1992 does not seem to have even dented Hamas's succession planning. Fatah powerbrokers have always claimed that the movement will splinter as pushy young militants overrun the cautious old guard of the Muslim Brotherhood—but they are wrong. Israel's targeted assassinations and Arafat's crackdowns have broken neither the spine nor the spirit of Hamas. On the death of Sheikh Ahmad Yassin, Israeli commentators insisted that there would be a leadership void, in which the young Turks would tear the movement apart. They too were wrong.

Despite the focused strategic efforts of Israel and America, and the overwhelming impact of worldwide sanctions backed by London and Paris, Hamas has held together. 'Obviously there'll be differences of governance and effective control,' says a senior Fatah leader well-placed to observe Hamas in the Occupied Territories. 'But in Hamas it does not go to dissent or mutiny. I'm looking—and I just don't see it.'

Authoritative voices in the United States have added their weight to the view of former Mossad director Efraim Halevy that Hamas needs to be brought in from the cold. They include former national security advisors Zbigniew Brezezinski and Brent Scowcroft, and former US ambassador to the United Nations Thomas Pickering. Bush's former secretary of state, Colin Powell, has cautiously voiced his position. 'Hamas has to be engaged,' he concludes. 'They won the election we insisted upon having.'

The emphasis in the Hamas discourse has shifted subtly from jihad to *hudna*, or a truce. Its territorial claims have shifted from a resumption of the land that runs from 'the river to the sea' to a two-state solution based on the 1967 border. The target has become the Israeli occupation, not Judaism.

Hamas has proven it can fight, but it has also demonstrated that it can hold its fire. The movement still has a foot firmly planted in resistance, but it has stamped the other firmly in the democratic political process. Hamas refuses to recognise Israel, but it has moved the bottom line. It can accept a Palestinian state adjacent to the Jewish state, and leave to future generations the question of Palestinian claims to all of the land that has become Israel.

The Hamas Charter of 1988—with its offensive language, its anti-Semitism and its incitement to battle—has become largely redundant. However, it survives in its old form. An internal Hamas committee spent much of 2005 working on a revision, but their work has been shelved in the aftermath of Hamas's unexpected election victory in the Occupied Territories. But, until such time as the charter's call for the elimination of Israel is finally revoked, Israel and the West can point to it as Hamas's defining credo.

Mishal himself still holds to the hardline Hamas commitment to armed struggle as the only source of Palestinian power in any negotiations with Israel. He will not renounce violence in the absence of substantial concessions. Marking Hamas's twenty-year anniversary at a rally in Damascus in December 2007, he declares, 'Land is only liberated by the gun.' It is a potent echo of the defiance he displayed in an earlier BBC interview, where he warned, 'Negotiation without resistance leads to surrender.' The ideology might be in the process of transformation, but the rhetoric of resistance is far from dead.

There is no end to the advice Khalid Mishal receives. Worried by the depth of the new Palestinian schism, his younger brother Maher has been on the phone from Amman to insist that Hamas needs to reverse out of its new-found control of Gaza.

The next broadside comes during a visit to Damascus by Mishal's old university lecturer, Asad Abdul Rahman, who warns his former student that he has to make a choice. 'You can't rule a country with sermons, welfare associations and guns,' Abdul Rahman tells him. 'You can't be a Muslim fanatic and, at the same time, be a politician . . . especially in a modern world with gigantic enemies—the US globally, Israel regionally!'

The point of Abdul Rahman's lecture is that Hamas should acknowledge that the 1967 border will inevitably become the basis of a two-state solution and that, therefore, it is time for the Islamists to publicly accept the existence of the state of Israel.

This likely outcome is accepted by most Arab states, he says, and many Israeli voters have come around to the belief that there should be a dialogue with Hamas. 'But you have to decide,' Abdul Rahman tells Mishal. 'You can't be half-pregnant. Either you want to engage in the peace process or not, and if you don't, there is a price to pay.'

Typically, it is late at night in Damascus when Abdul Rahman unburdens himself. Mishal's enigmatic response is brief. 'When the time comes,' the Hamas leader replies.

Mossad has a new plan to kill Khalid Mishal. The Hamas leader's security detail is alive every day to the prospect that the next attempt might be imminent. The execution will depend on a cost–benefit analysis that is as chilling as the reckoning behind the next suicide bomb. They have tried and failed once, and Mossad's mission is to eliminate Israel's enemies. If Mishal were to present himself in the right circumstances, a strike might simply be irresistible. Such are the opportunistic gambles on which wars have been won and lost. No one knows when it might come.

Mishal's predecessor and dozens of his comrades have already been assassinated by Israel, and he has been warned often enough that he remains in the crosshairs, notwithstanding the debacle a decade earlier in Amman. Hunkering in Damascus does not put the Hamas leader beyond the reach of the Israelis. Mishal was almost nonchalant in his response to a phone call in the first week of September 2007, when he was informed that Israeli jets had penetrated deep into Syrian airspace to bomb a secret target that was alleged later to be the early stage of a suspected nuclear facility.

Israel tends not to formally confirm its involvement in killings abroad, but attacks in Europe and in Amman, Tunis and Malta in the past have demonstrated that its agencies have no regard for international borders. It has a proven track record on the ground in the Syrian capital. The Hamas operative Musbah Abou-Houwaileh escaped certain death when his car exploded minutes after he alighted from the vehicle with his wife and daughter in the Mazzah quarter of Damascus on 14 December 2004. The bombing is widely believed to have been carried out by or on behalf of Israeli security. Syria blamed Israel for another device almost three months earlier, which exploded as the Hamas bomb-maker Izz al-Din Sheikh Khalil turned the key in the ignition of his car in the Zahraa neighbourhood of Damascus.

Mishal always has ready answers for questions about the attempt on his life in Amman in 1997. But when it comes to the mechanics of a likely future attack, he is reluctant to speculate. He insists that the earlier bombings in Damascus were not directed at him personally. But he knows the Israelis are already in his backyard.

'I expect martyrdom at any time. But the decision on how and when I die is for God, not Mossad,' is all he will say.

THE FREE GAZA
FLOTILLA

Istanbul, Turkey
4 June 2010

In the blackness before the rising of a burnt-orange moon, all
that could be seen of the Israelis were the pinpoints of light
around us—warships sitting a kilometre or more each side of the
flotilla were inching in, seemingly to squeeze the humanitarian
convoy bound for Gaza.

Then the noose tightened. Sneaking up and around every
boat were bullet-shaped hulks which soon became impossible
to hide as the moonlight made fluorescent tubes of their roiling
wakes. First one, then two, maybe four could be seen sneaking
in from the rear. These boats hunted like hyenas, moving up and
ahead on the flanks; pushing in, then peeling away; and finally,
lagging before lunging.

The attack was timed for dawn prayers. A good number of
those aboard the *Mavi Marmara* were assembled on the aft deck
as the big Turkish passenger ferry motored steadily through
international waters in the eastern Mediterranean Sea. The call

to prayer could be heard across the water, chords made tinny by the ship's PA system, yet haunting amid the tension sparked several hours earlier—the captains of the six ships in the Free Gaza Flotilla had each rejected a demand radioed by the Israeli navy: change course away from the Gaza Strip or be confronted with lethal force.

Pacing the *Mavi Marmara* at a steady eight knots and just 150 metres to its port side, I was aboard the 25-metre *Challenger I*, the fastest, but also the smallest, boat in the flotilla. It was a front-row seat for the opening of Israel's Operation Sky Wind, which, despite confident predictions by a gallery of Israeli officials and commentators, was about to go horribly wrong.

By the time the Israeli commandos were done with the ships—in little more than an hour—nine Turkish activists would be dead, more than 50 wounded and about 700 captured and forcibly removed from international waters to Israel, where they would be charged with entering the country illegally, and then deported. This account of what happened on the decks of the *Mavi Marmara* is based on interviews with dozens of activists while they and I, along with my photographer-colleague Kate Geraghty, who also accompanied the flotilla as a non-participating observer, were held in an Israeli prison for more than two days. Eyewitnesses were also interviewed on board one of three aircraft sent to Israel by the Turkish government to ferry the near-700 activists to a rousing 4 a.m. reception by tens of thousands of cheering Turks at Istanbul's airport.

Caught up in the excitement of the flotilla as it sailed in the last days of May were three young Australian Muslims: twenty-year-old Ahmad Luqman Talib, his eighteen-year-old sister Miryam, whose family had migrated to the Queensland Gold Coast in the mid-1990s, and the young man's blonde-haired and blue-eyed Australian wife, 21-year-old Jerry Campbell.

For this impressionable young trio the flotilla might have been a conventional Mediterranean cruise, with a twist. 'It was beautiful,' Miryam recalled of their first days at sea. 'The atmosphere was wonderful . . . there was a great sense of spiritual connection. I had never felt this kind of emotion before.'

In the hours after the warning, the *Mavi Marmara* was preparing for an engagement with the Israelis. People were distributing lifejackets and taking up positions on the rails. Others readied themselves for the precarious task of snatching Israeli sound bombs and tear-gas canisters and hurling them back from where they came. Groups had been rostered through the night to sleep or be at the ready, and the shriek of electric angle-grinders could be heard cutting steel bars from the lifeboat bays along the main decks.

Despite thoughts of what might lie ahead, there was good humour. Matthias Gardel, a key figure in the Swedish delegation, was getting used to his lifejacket, unaware that even though it was 3 a.m. back home, his twelve-year-old daughter was out of bed and watching a live-feed video from the ship on the Free Gaza Movement's website. Seeing him in the video, she shot him an email: 'Dad, take it off—you look ridiculous.' To which he fired back: 'It's past your bedtime.'

Mustafa Ahmet, a 33-year-old Londoner, is irreverent as he recollects the events. Having completed his ablutions, he joined a big group for the dawn prayer session. Minutes later a cry went up: 'They're here! They're here!'

'They' were Israeli commandos coming alongside the ferry in their assault craft. But the imam leading the session was unmoved; instead of cutting proceedings short, he continued the prayers. Unable to restrain himself, Ahmet moved to the rails, where he observed the commandos' arrival: 'It was like a scary movie—their helmets were shiny, the sea was shiny and battleships sat off on either side. But the imam just kept on, holding us in position—it was bonkers.'

Suddenly tear gas and sound bombs were exploding amid the prayer meeting on the main aft deck. The lifejacketed passengers on the rails at first seemed oblivious as those behind them donned the few gas masks that were on board; others, wearing asbestos gloves, sought to grab the devices and throw them back at the Israeli commandos before they exploded. As the assault craft pulled alongside the *Mavi Marmara*, the dozen or so masked commandos in each boat took the full force of the ferry's fire hoses and a shower of whatever its passengers found on deck or could break from the ship's fittings.

Some on the ship thought the Israelis did not put enough into their opening shots. Espen Goffeng, a Norwegian journalist, said: 'I looked over the rail and saw the zodiacs. It seemed hopeless for the Israelis—they tried to lock on their grappling hooks, but they were hit by the fire hoses and their own projectiles going back to them.'

Despite failing to get their grappling irons to hold on the rails of the five-deck ferry, the commandos continued to be an irritant. Or perhaps they were intended as a decoy to draw passengers to the rails, because at this point the Israelis opted for a critical change of plan—if they could not come up from the water, then they would drop from the sky.

On hearing the thump of helicopters, activists on the *Mavi Marmara* rushed to the upper decks, where distress flares launched from the ship cut through the spotlights on Israeli helicopters hovering overhead. The first Israeli commandos who slithered down ropes from the choppers were easy pickings for the waiting activists, who grabbed at them even before they landed. The commandos were disarmed and in some cases beaten until, according to several eyewitnesses, the activist leaders demanded that they not be harmed. In one case however, an Israeli commando was hurled from one deck of the ship to the next.

Ahmet was perplexed. 'We were a convoy of peace. But the Israeli choppers overhead, the smoke grenades . . . all the screaming, all the noise. People were running all ways and there was blood everywhere. But before we could do anything it was all over.'

But it was merely the beginning of what would become an international crisis for Israel. Two days before the Israeli assault, I had interviewed the bullet-headed Bulent Yildirim, head of the Turkish non-government relief agency IHH, which in effect ran the flotilla, as the *Mavi Marmara* steamed towards this collision with the Israelis. Quite presciently, he explained that Israel could ill afford the diplomatic disaster that he confidently predicted would ensue should the Jewish state attempt to intercept the convoy. It would add to a recent litany of tactical successes which had morphed into strategic disasters for Israel: the Gaza war and the Goldstone report; the Hamas assassination in Dubai and world anger over Mossad's abuse of the passports of several nations, including Australia, to get its hit team into the emirate. Now there was this high-seas venture on the eve of a critical meeting between President Barack Obama and the Israeli prime minister, Benjamin Netanyahu, which was intended to dilute the bad blood generated by the recent announcement of Jewish settlement expansion on Palestinian land while the US vice-president, Joe Biden, was in Israel.

The coalition of Palestinian support groups behind the flotilla—drawing funds from NGOs in Turkey, Malaysia, Ireland, Algeria, Kuwait, Greece and Sweden—was determined to reveal the Israeli blockade of Gaza as an exercise in collective punishment that was to be maintained until ordinary Gazans turned on Hamas. Tel Aviv claimed the blockade was vital to Israel's security.

Four of the flotilla ships carried 10,000 tonnes of emergency supplies for Gaza, which Israel has kept under blockade since Hamas, designated a terrorist group by Israel, the United States and the European Union, won electoral control of the Palestinian Occupied Territories in 2006. A year later Hamas retained control of Gaza in the face of a US and Israeli-backed bid to oust the Islamist movement from power by armed force.

There were conflicting accounts of the first commando's landing on the ship—some activists said he was injured and was being carried inside the ship for treatment by the flotilla doctors. However, a Serbian cameraman, Srojan Stojiljkovic, said that some of the activists had armed themselves with lengths of chain and the metal posts that cordoned off the lifeboat bays. 'Some of the people caught the first commando before he touched the deck. A few started to hit him, but a lot of people moved in to shelter him with their bodies,' the cameraman said. 'Another soldier had a bleeding nose . . . a few people threw punches, but not as many as I would have expected.'

Gardel, the Swede who had been chipped earlier in the evening by his fashion-conscious daughter, confirmed the soldiers had been beaten, but he insisted that the activists involved were unarmed and that in keeping with the ship's non-violent charter, the soldiers' weapons were thrown overboard.

After the Israeli soldiers had been treated, the injured and the dead from among the ship's passengers were brought in, according to Stojiljkovic. 'Some were not badly wounded, but then a guy was brought in with a point-blank shot between his eyes. He was dead, and I was told that another person was killed in the same way.'

The Turkish actor Sinan Albayrak said he witnessed a senior Turkish activist ordering passengers to cease beating two of the Israeli soldiers. Later, he saw a Turkish photographer who had been shot in the back of the head. And while he and others were attempting to assist an injured activist, Israeli troops had opened fire on them.

Goffeng, the Norwegian journalist, sensed, from the sound it made as it struck the ship, that the Israelis initially used paint balls as ammunition. 'But some people said there had to be glass in them, because of the wounds they caused. There was a lot of blood in the ship's stairwells, and then the sound of ammunition hitting metal changed again—I decided that was the live ammunition. People were yelling, "Live ammo! Live ammo!"'

He said the activists in the crucial television-broadcast area on the aft deck were being targeted. 'I helped to carry one of the dead down to the second deck and as I returned a man who had been shot in the leg was being carried down. When I moved to the press room, one of the men who worked there was dead, with a hole in his forehead and half his head missing.'

Gardel said the bulk of the passengers had remained in second-deck saloons and had not been involved in resisting the Israelis: 'But a bunch of people tried to protect the bridge, engine room and the point from which we streamed the live video.'

In the midst of all this, the young Australian, Ahmed Luqman Talib, made a foolhardy call to venture out on deck. 'I saw a man who nearly got shot—I could see the red dot of the laser weapon sights on his knee, but he moved in time,' Talib told me. 'Then I felt something slice through my leg—blood was squirting from my right leg and then a second bullet sliced across, just above my knee. I was still standing, but my leg jerked up in the air and it froze like that—for a time it was paralysed. With my weight on the good leg I tried to put it down—but it wouldn't move. I couldn't believe I'd been hit, but that's how it looked—bullets, holes and blood.' Talib attempted to get himself down the now-bloodied stairs to the first-aid post, which by then was chaotic. But he collapsed on the way and others carried him in for treatment.

Having slept through the drama of the Israeli warning to the ships' captains, Jerry Campbell awoke at 4 a.m. to attend dawn prayers. No sooner had she bowed her head than she was dragged off to the nursing station to which she and her sister-in-law had been assigned 24 hours earlier; Campbell was in her second year of nursing studies and Miryam was a second-year pharmacy student. Two of the dead had already been brought to the aid post and Campbell first helped to stabilise a man who had been shot five times. 'He had a lot of holes in him, but none of his main arteries had been hit.' She was then helping a wounded Indonesian when a commotion drew her eye to the door. 'I looked up and saw my husband being carried in.' She rushed to Talib's side, cutting away his blood-soaked clothes before acting on his insistent instruction that she tend to others. 'I'm okay,' he told her.

But Talib wondered if he would survive. 'I looked down and my legs were drowning in blood,' he told me a few days later, when Geraghty and I tracked him down in an Istanbul hospital, his gangly frame spread on crisp, pink bed linen. 'I was getting weaker; it was difficult to breathe.' He said that he seemed to be willing himself into a sleep from which he believed he might not wake. A devout Muslim, Talib recalled reciting the prayer for those facing death. 'I said it quietly—to myself. Then I worried maybe that was not enough, so I said it again—this time out loud.'

Reconstructing the chaos of the aid post, the women told of the constant screaming of the injured; of slipping on blood-soaked floors; and of the difficulty of identifying which of their yelling colleagues could afford to be treated from their meagre medical stocks.

'One man's stomach was opened—his intestines were out and the doctor reached inside and pulled out some bullets before pushing everything back in and wrapping him up,' Campbell told me. 'I don't know if he survived. We had no pain-killers, no instruments to extract bullets. But we had heaps of gauze so we were able to apply pressure bandages to stop or slow the bleeding. The heat was intense—we were sweating as first we had ten people to treat and then twenty. I saw two men die . . . the floor was covered in blood. The IV units were tied to the ceiling with bandages.'

Gigdem Topcuoghe, a 45-year-old Turkish woman, was another in the aid post who was shocked to discover her husband among those brought in for treatment. Shot in the forehead, he was bleeding from his mouth and nose. 'I think of first aid—I need to help him,' she told Geraghty while sharing a cell with her in the Israeli prison. 'I checked his breathing . . . he was bleeding faster. I gave him some water and started praying for him—I held him in my arms. He wasn't conscious. I held him tight, but I realised he was gone when he didn't react in any way. But my husband is not dead—he will live on with and among us.' Several witnesses have recounted in awe how Topcuoghe accepted condolences briefly, before leaving her husband's body to throw herself into helping the injured.

Another of the activists, a Turk, lifted his shirt to show me ten puncture-marks in a rough, bruised circle about the circumference of a teacup. He said the marks were inflicted by an Israeli security dog while he was assisting the Israelis as a translator to consolidate control of the ship.

The dead include a Turkish journalist, Chetin Genghis, whose head wounds suggest he was shot from above, possibly from one of the helicopters. After witnessing his dying moments, his colleague Hisham Goruney said, 'I want to forget—I still don't believe that I saw it.' Also among the dead was a Malaysian doctor who, activists said, was shot while treating the wounded—among them, an Indonesian cameraman, Sura Fachrizaz, who was shot in the chest.

All up, it took the Israelis 85 minutes to capture the *Mavi Marmara*. Espen Goffeng said: 'Then there was an announcement on the PA system telling us, *Keep calm; it's over . . . They have taken the ship and we have lost.*'

The Israelis assembled their hundreds of prisoners first on an open deck and later in one of the big cabin areas on a lower deck. Jerry Campbell accused them of denying their captives food and barring the women from giving water to the male prisoners, whose hands were bound with plastic ties. She also witnessed the first steps of a systematic attempt to control the account of what happened at sea in the early hours of 31 May. Israeli soldiers began ripping memory cards from the cameras they found and threatening any who concealed data discs on their bodies or in their clothing—a tactic adopted by most of the media on board.

As the 100-plus reporters and bloggers, photographers and cameramen on board followed orders to return to the ship's press room, many were worried that an Israeli blanket of 'white noise' had prevented them from getting the story out. Then someone flicked the switch on a TV mounted on the wall—it burst into life with a Turkish channel running the live-feed the ship had been transmitting to websites run by the Free Gaza Movement and the flotilla's other sponsors. It showed scenes of the Israeli capture of the *Mavi Marmara*. A resounding cheer went up.

Soon after, Israeli soldiers smashed in the glass doors to the press room and ordered the media workers to come forward one at a time. 'They searched us,' said a cameraman who had unpicked the waistband of his underpants sufficiently to create a series of mini-pockets in which he successfully secreted most of his camera's discs—the strip-search revealed just one. 'They took cell phones and hard drives . . . and anything else that was capable of capturing or storing images.'

On the open decks and in the lower saloons of the ship, conditions were far less pleasant than in the press room. Gardel complained of people being forced to kneel for hours on the open deck area where prayers were held. An Israeli helicopter hovered constantly, its down-draft spraying the prisoners with wind and water—in the circumstances, a freezing combination. 'Keeping the choppers there seemed to be deliberate, as though they wanted to enfeeble us by holding us in such unpleasant conditions,' he said.

People were not allowed to go to the lavatories—they were made to soil their clothes. Gardel was especially horrified at the experience of a badly wounded man in his late fifties, who the Israeli troops forced to remain on the open deck: 'Suddenly, his right eye exploded in a gush of blood—and a blob of something fell out of it.'

Several European MPs were distressed by what they described as a clear distinction the Israelis made between their 'white' and 'brown' prisoners. The Norwegian activist, Randi Kjos, a woman of some refinement, was genuinely shocked by what she observed. 'They treated us with hatred—the old were made to kneel for long periods and women had to sit with their arms crossed. Some of the wounded were naked to the waist . . . many were in shock. But Palestinians and Arabs were treated very differently to Europeans or Westerners. Palestinians who asked for anything were belted, pushed around or treated with contempt. People warned me of the hatred I would see—but still, I was shocked.'

The Australian, Talib, said that he was put into a carry-frame in which some Israeli commandos set about dragging him, feet first, up the stairs to the next deck. He was in great pain and still bleeding, but halfway up he was tipped from the frame and told by one of the Israelis: 'You have one healthy leg—walk up.'

The challenge for Talib then was to follow a trail of blood to a point high in the ship from where the seriously wounded were to be evacuated by helicopter to Israeli hospitals. Blacking out several times as his captors forced him to drag his broken body up another flight of stairs, pushing and kicking him along the way, the twenty-year-old student finally fell through a door leading to the top deck. From there, the blood trail led to a ladder, up which Talib was made to haul himself to the medical evacuation point. He was given no assistance. Talib had found himself at the sharp end of his deferred course of study at Bond University—international relations.

With demands around the world for an inquiry into the attack on the flotilla in international waters, it seems likely that claims such as these—alongside Israeli counter-claims alleging violence by protesters—will be tested forensically. Other charges the young trio from Australia have levelled against their captors include: failing to provide early medical care for the injured; handcuffing Talib to his hospital bed, but removing the cuffs just before he was visited by Australian diplomats; for a time denying him access to a lawyer as they attempted to interrogate him; destroying the CCTV cameras on the ship to prevent their activities being recorded; parading prisoners before cameras and an 'audience' of security and other workers, who laughed as they took 'happy snaps' of them; withholding information from Campbell on her husband's whereabouts and condition; treating the prisoners in ways intended to weaken them physically and psychologically; humiliating the Islamic women prisoners by strip-searching them and mocking their undergarments and bodies; and, in the case of Campbell, calling to colleagues after her clothes had been removed to joke at her European features and mock her as a convert to Islam.

It is startling enough to have black-masked commandos hijack your boat on the high seas, but when the orders and the threat that any who resist will be shot are barked in Australian accents on the far side of the world, it becomes surreal.

Commando 1: 'Down! Sit down! Get down!'

Geraghty: 'Professional journalists!'

McGeough: 'We're with the *Sydney Morning Herald*.'

Commando 2: 'We know you're with the *Herald*.'

Geraghty: 'Bloody hell—Aussie accents!'

Commando 1: 'No worries.'

I was sitting on a bench, trying to get a line through to the *Herald* in Sydney to report the battle raging on the *Mavi Marmara* and this new assault on the *Challenger I*, but the satellite phone was snatched from my hand—and has not been seen since.

As the killing started on the *Mavi Marmara*—and it seemed just a matter of time before the other slow boats in the flotilla would be commandeered by the Israelis—the *Challenger I*'s English skipper, Dennis Healey, pushed the 25-metre cruiser to top speed, about 18 knots. Initially, four Israeli assault craft were tailing us, but they were unable to get close because of the powerful wake Healey was ploughing across the water. But then the Israelis gave Healey pause for thought. With previous protest runs to Gaza under his belt, he knew what it was like to have his vessel rammed by an Israeli boat, so he cut the motors, allowing the craft to slow to a drift.

Other veterans of earlier runs—the Palestinian lawyer and head of the Free Gaza Movement, Huwaida Arraf, and the deceptively demure Scottish postal worker, Teresa McDermott—yelled to those on the fly bridge to brace for a collision as the powerful spotlight on a bigger Israeli boat bored into all on deck while the Israeli vessel positioned its bow to *Challenger I*'s starboard side. An assault craft quickly came along each side of the boat and, before any of the commandos leapt aboard, a flash of white preceded a jolt to my photographer-colleague Geraghty's forearm as she tried to take pictures of the Israeli boarding party. The jolt, which appeared to be from a taser, threw her across the deck.

Thinking the Israelis would approach the fly bridge from the ladder-like steps beneath a hole in the deck, McDermott sat on a lid that closed over it. But the commandos—six of them—came over the side rails; when McDermott refused to move away from the lid, she had a pistol thrust in her face.

The commandos' sudden arrival on the fly bridge was accompanied by the din of sound bombs on the lower deck and the shattering of one of two big sliding glass doors between the main cabin and the aft deck.

As we were herded down from the fly bridge, the dozen activists on board resorted to passive resistance techniques—refusing to cooperate, yelling and screaming and seeking to provoke the commandos, who were identifiable only by numbers stuck on their chests.

Two of the women, including Arraf, were dragged to the foredeck, where they were handcuffed and forced to sit with bags over their heads. A young Belgian woman who had been hit by a paint pellet was bleeding from the nose.

As the crew was ordered to steer a course for the Israeli port of Ashdod, the activists and the *Herald* team—our requests to have our rights as journalists respected were ignored—were taken one at a time to the wheelhouse, where we were stripped of all electronic communications and photographic equipment, and even such innocuous items as my two wristwatches—all at gunpoint. The equipment was numbered and, we were assured, would be returned upon arrival at Ashdod along with the rest of our possessions.

The four-hour voyage to Ashdod became a taunting test of will. From time to time, shouting matches became a refusal to cooperate and those who shouted loudest were handcuffed in a bid to silence them. Some of the activists resorted to creating decoy ruckuses to interrupt the heavy or pushy Israeli questioning of their colleagues.

When Fintan Lain, an Irish anti-war activist, refused to hand over his passport, his refusal was accepted by the Israelis. But when a Dutch academic refused to hand over her documents, she was stood over by four commandos who stayed within inches of her. She kept her passport.

All those on the *Challenger I* were bundled off to Ella Prison, a two-hour ride in caged wagons, where they were held for more than 48 hours and again promised that their possessions would be returned on their release. But of all the equipment and possessions belonging to the seventeen who had sailed on the *Challenger I*, all that arrived at the baggage pick-up point in Istanbul was a single computer case of mine, which was empty save a few cables, a handful of laptop accessories and my chequebook.

It was a spectacular week in the Mediterranean, with the Israeli government the butt of intense domestic and international criticism. European diplomats in Tel Aviv openly scoffed at their claim that the flotilla organisers had ties with Al-Qaeda. One of the diplomats, who had visited the passengers in jail, argued that if such a claim was the Israeli government's best opening shot, then it had a serious credibility problem.

Each side is documenting its case against the other. The flotilla organisers accuse the Netanyahu government of hijacking six vessels in international waters—and killing and maiming their passengers in the process. The organisers in turn will face Israeli allegations that steel bars were used to beat their troops, and that weapons confiscated from captured commandos may have been used against their comrades.

The threads of an Israeli case, being leaked selectively in the Israeli media, argue that 60 to 100 'hardcore' activists had been embedded on the *Mavi Marmara*. They included Turks, Afghans, Yemenis and an Eritrean, experienced in hand-to-hand combat.

However, the flotilla crisis is not just about Israel. The virtual takeover of what was a coalition of groups from a dozen countries by Turkish non-government organisations plays into regional politics. Long an Israeli ally, Turkey is flexing its muscles, bonding with Syria, Iran, Iraq, Qatar and Hamas. At the same time it is awkwardly exposing the Arab world's about-faces on the Palestinian cause and, by its demonstrable actions, almost shaming them to do more.

Tucked in under all this is Washington's role in the region. The rest of the world was quick to criticise Israel in the aftermath of the flotilla fiasco, but the Obama White House lamely called for an Israeli inquiry—the kind of response that placates Israel but erodes US credibility in the region.

CONTROLLING THE NARRATIVE IN ISRAEL AND PALESTINE

A paper presented to the Festival of Dangerous Ideas
Sydney, Australia
3 October 2010

Tooling around suburban Washington earlier this week, my car radio began shrieking, it seemed, just a single word. National Public Radio was reporting the uncertain fate of the latest round of Middle East peace talks in light of last Sunday's expiration of what was dubbed a moratorium on Israeli settlement expansion on Palestinian land. But when quoting the president of France, the reporter did not use the word 'settlement'. Instead, she attributed to Nicolas Sarkozy the dreaded C-word: 'colony'.

Not quite as jaunty as 'settlement', is it? If 'settlement' suggests opening up an unclaimed frontier—think the fabled Jaffa orange, the taming of the wilds and something found—then 'colony' suggests dispossession, the planting of foreigners; more something lost than found.

Playing on many levels, the Middle East is the constant, treadmill struggle of our time. But within the dynamic of this conflict, the leadership on all sides has an enduring capacity to fail to surprise us. But here I want to look at a genuine element of surprise—the seeming surrender, or the loss of strategic high ground, by a key player in a critical dimension of the conflict.

Arguably, engagement takes place on three levels. There are two—weapons and diplomacy—on which Israel has been ascendant since, oh, I would say about 1948. But there is a third dimension—one that sways diplomacy and is influenced by resort to weapons. This dimension is the control over the narrative of the conflict.

Over the decades, Israelis have told the story of their enterprise brilliantly. Palestinians, by contrast, have told the story of dispossession terribly. In storytelling, words can be bullets. Sure, events happen and, as Israelis are wont to say, facts are created on the ground. But the words chosen by participants and observers shape the narrative as it resonates in the region and around the world. In this context, Sarkozy's use of the word 'colony' was a small but significant victory for Palestinians and their supporters, who only recently decided to inject the more hard-edged word 'colony' into the debate, instead of the less-specific term, 'settlement'.

I have long believed that with its supremacy in weapons and diplomacy, Israel has this conflict stitched up. It has become an exercise in crisis management, not conflict resolution, in which the United States and, frequently enough, the Palestinian leadership are also complicit.

The wrongness of the occupation has become the status quo. How else do we interpret Israeli Foreign Minister Avigdor Lieberman's take on the renewed peace talks, which he shared a few days ago with the United Nations General Assembly, telling the gathering in New York that rather than a final settlement, the talks should focus on some sort of long-term, interim arrangement. 'Something that could take a few decades,' he said.

How else do we interpret the snouts-in-the-trough corruption of the Fatah cronies, their squandering of the meagre resources of their people as they enjoy their Israeli-sanctioned special privileges? How else are we to see the callous indifference of our world leaders in their abandonment of the civilian population of Palestine? The rights of East Timorese and Bosnians mattered—but those of longer-suffering Palestinians don't?

Early this year it seemed that Israel's grip on the story was loosening. Had events caused the narrative pendulum—the impact of the story as it was heard beyond the Middle East—to swing towards the Palestinian side of the ledger? Even before the debacle of the flotilla, Israeli bungling, as measured by rising diplomatic criticism in the West, had dulled the lustre of a PR machine which, historically, had shaped the exploits of Mossad and other Israeli agencies as nerve-tingling embroidery in a national narrative that left little room for failure.

Israel's mythology is built on the likes of the stunning success of the Six-Day War and on daring, edge-of-the-seat ventures like the 1976 raid on Entebbe Airport in Uganda. Remember the abduction, halfway around the world, of Adolf Eichmann? And the surgical strike on Saddam Hussein's nuclear facility?

More recently, Israel has achieved some of its tactical objectives. But these days, each outing seemingly incurs greater strategic or diplomatic cost. Whether it was its 2006 assault on Lebanon or its 2008 invasion of Gaza, its assassination in January of a Hamas operative in Dubai or its May attack on the Gaza flotilla, usually stout allies and, in the case of the invasion of Lebanon, domestic boards of inquiry, have felt obliged to criticise.

In Gaza, Israel was accused of war crimes in the controversial Goldstone report. In Dubai, it incurred the wrath of governments around the world, including Australia, over the abuse of those countries' passports as cover for almost 30 members of the

Mossad hit team—who were held to international ridicule upon the release, by the Dubai authorities, of CCTV footage of their Inspector Clouseau antics.

In the weeks after the attack on the flotilla, the chief of Mossad, Meir Dagan, told the Knesset: 'Israel is gradually turning from an asset to the United States to a burden.' This was an analyst's call that coupled naturally with a disquieting moment of another kind for Israel early this year—the impact of which has yet to reveal itself.

The setting was an appearance in March before a Senate committee by General David Petraeus, at which he revealed a new line of Washington thought on this conflict. As the then chief of the US Central Command, Petraeus brought along a considered 12,000-word document in which he framed the Israel–Palestine conflict as a 'root cause of instability' and an 'obstacle to peace' which played into the hands of Iran and Al-Qaeda.

Ditching a cornerstone of neo-conservative dogma, Petraeus charged that perceived US favouritism for Israel fomented anti-American sentiment across the region. The general was articulating a Washington view that would have been impossible under George W. Bush; that is, the security of Israel and the urgent need to resolve the Israel–Palestine crisis are distinctly separate, core issues of US national interest. It follows that Washington can be rock-solid on the former yet still demand action on the latter—thereby robbing Israel of its default argument that its security must always comes first.

Behind these headline events, other developments show elements of the historic Israeli story playing out abroad for Palestinians and the plight of occupation garnering sympathy—or at least less hostility.

In the 1960s and 1970s, it was a rite of passage for many non-Jewish students from around the world to spend time on a kibbutz. Today the young 'internationals', as they are called, still come to the Holy Land, but a good number of them are to be found in the West Bank, helping Palestinians to replant damaged orchards and olive groves or offering themselves as human shields against harassment by Jewish settlers as Palestinian villagers harvest their crops.

This is part of a growing campaign of Palestinian civil disobedience. First in five and then twelve and now sixteen villages, locals have taken to weekly protests against aspects of the Israeli occupation—often with back-up from young internationals and young Israelis who oppose the occupation.

After five years, an international BDS campaign—boycott, divestment and sanctions—is becoming more than an irritant for Israel. Financial institutions in Scandinavia, Germany and elsewhere have succumbed to lobbying to divest from companies with ties to Israel. And there has been a spate of big-name tour cancellations—Meg Ryan, Elvis Costello, Gil Scott-Heron and the Pixies accepted bookings but then balked at performing in Israel.

The European Union now insists that the precise origin of produce and products from Jewish settlements in the Occupied Territories be identified on their labels and most recently the Dutch association of municipalities cancelled a visit to the Netherlands by a group of Israeli community leaders—because several of the Israeli delegates were from West Bank settlements.

The Gaza flotilla story is a contemporary echo of the *Exodus 1947* story, when underdog Jewish immigrants faced heavy-handed British opposition to their deliberately illegal landings in Palestine in the 1940s. Told as a potted history on the online *Jewish Virtual Library*, the role-reversal is all too apparent: 'On July 18, near the coast of Palestine but outside territorial waters, the British rammed the ship and boarded it, while the [Jewish] immigrants put up a desperate defence,' goes this account. 'Two immigrants and a crewman were killed in the battle, and 30 were wounded.' Sound familiar?

Had the Israelis pulled off a clean capture of the *Mavi Marmara*, the world would be thinking 'Entebbe'. Instead there are nine new graves in Turkish cemeteries and John J. Mearsheimer is writing of the IDF in the *American Conservative* as 'the gang that cannot shoot straight'.

After a near six-year period in which there had been just a single Hamas suicide-bomb attack, but in which thousands of erratic rockets were fired into Israel, Hamas readily acknowledges that there is much more to be gained in setting up Israel as a target of international criticism for its own actions than as a target for rockets launched by Hamas and the other factions. 'When we use violence, we help Israel win international support,' Aziz Dweik, a Hamas MP in the West Bank was quoted as saying in the *Wall Street Journal*. 'The Gaza flotilla has done more for Gaza than 10,000 rockets.'

And this takes us to another element of the Israeli bungle—the proverbial self-inflicted wound. The world had virtually ignored its siege of Gaza up to now, but Western governments could not remain silent after the flotilla: 'The status quo we have is inherently unstable,' US President Barack Obama said.

All of this, then, takes us to the wider architecture of the narrative in this conflict—how things are not quite as they seem.

Backed by Washington, Israel still believes it is entitled to select the Palestinian leadership, to choose its 'partners in peace', as it calls them in narrative-speak. So we need to go back to 2006, when Palestinians voted to sweep the remnants of Yasser Arafat's secular Fatah movement from office and to install an Islamist Hamas administration. Utterly wrong-footed, and forgetful of the years they left Fatah to the mercy of Hamas, Israel and the West said 'No, we want Fatah'—and even then, it seemed, only up to a point. They still cut the ground from under the current Fatah leader and Palestinian Authority president, Mahmoud Abbas, obstinately refusing to put on the table the kind of deal that might swing popular Palestinian support away from Hamas to Fatah.

But one must not confuse the current Palestinian leadership—groomed and shaped as it is by Israel and Washington—as even a distant relative of the democratic cure-all they claim is so vital for the region.

The 2006 Palestinian election ought to have been celebrated by all sides. A cathartic moment for Palestinians, the poll was a more consistent expression of the will of the people than most other elections in the region—and deemed to be free and fair by an army of international observers. But because they voted for Hamas, the entire Palestinian population was sin-binned and denied international funding. Half of their elected MPs were rounded up and jailed by Israel, which then embarked on a lock-down of Gaza which, over time, has been tightened, transforming the Strip into the world's biggest—and as the locals see it, the world's meanest—prison.

Four years after an election outcome that might have been embraced by Washington as the Middle Eastern democracy of its dreams, we now have a once-elected Palestinian president whose term has expired but who remains in office because he feels like it. He, in turn, appointed an unelected prime minister, whose Third Way party won a dismal 2.4 per cent of the vote in 2006. The Palestinian parliament, a rarity in the region, has been neutered. In less than a year, three tiers of Palestinian elections have been cancelled: presidential, parliamentary and local council.

Like the tin-pot dictators of the region, the Palestinian president and his prime minister rule by decree. And they have at their disposal a foreign-trained and foreign-funded security force, which, like its counterparts in the region, resorts to torture as it roots out political opposition, rounding up suspects by the hundreds and busting any gatherings that might dare to criticise. Hamas—designated as a terrorist organisation by the United States, Europe and Israel—has been driven underground in the West Bank, under the weight of an unrelenting assault by Israeli forces and Abbas's security apparatus—whose units are required to humiliate themselves before their own people by disappearing from the streets when Israeli forces choose to mount an operation on Palestinian turf.

It is hardly surprising that for many Palestinians, this amounts to collaboration with the occupiers—further undermining Abbas and his prime minister, Salam Fayad, at the same time as Israel and the West go through the motions of propping up the Palestinian leadership. This sentiment is reinforced when Palestinians read in the most recent annual report of Shin Bet, Israel's domestic intelligence agency, that combined Palestinian–Israeli operations have reduced attacks on Israelis to their lowest since 2000. A reporter from the Israeli daily *Yedioth Ahronoth* was present at a joint Israeli–Palestinian security meeting in 2008, when the head of the Palestinian delegation told his Israeli counterparts: 'We have a common enemy—we are taking care of every Hamas institution in accordance with your instructions.'

Not quite, says Hamas. In claiming responsibility for the death of settlers near Hebron late in August, the movement explained that the attack was not so much a bid to undermine the peace talks as a demonstration that the Israeli and Palestinian Authority security machines had not bottled up Hamas quite as tightly as they liked to believe.

Prime Minister Fayed continues to have difficulty garnering popular support, but he is sticking to a plan to knock Palestinian institutions into shape by next year—at which time, he says, he will simply declare an independent Palestinian state. What will the world do when he does? Fayed is opening new schools, planting trees and issuing parking tickets. He cracks down on some of the Fatah freebies—the cars and the cell phones. To some Palestinians, all this might be just another halfway house—perhaps like Israeli Prime Minister Benjamin Netanyahu's 'economic peace'. But to the World Bank it sounds like a plan. In a statement last week, it enthused: 'If the Palestinian Authority maintains its current performance in institution-building and delivery of public services, it is well-positioned for the establishment of a state at any point in the near future.'

That the Palestinian Authority has morphed to become another Western-friendly autocracy—it actually dictates the sermons to be read by imams at Friday prayers—was confirmed by a European official who in August told *The Economist*: 'We prefer division [among Palestinians] and no elections, to reconciliation [between Fatah and Hamas] and elections.'

To shoehorn it into the narrative, the security agency on which the Palestinian Authority leadership depends is dressed up as a local law-and-order exercise—cops on the beat and that kind of thing. But it is an American construct and its number-one priority is the elimination of Hamas; in the last three years, the US State Department has allocated $US392 million to the service and it has its hand out for another $US150 next year.

Bear in mind that, notionally at least, the Oslo years were the most hopeful in recent decades, before considering this assessment by Jessica Montell, executive director of B'Tselem, the Israeli watch group, and ask yourself why should Palestinians take heart from another round of talks. Montell writes: 'Since the first negotiations began in Madrid in 1991, the West Bank settlement population has tripled. The settlers are dispersed among over 121 settlements and about 100 outposts . . . their regional councils encompass vast swathes of land—fully 42 per cent of the West Bank is under settlement control.'

Since 1948, a constant in Israeli–Palestinian relations has been Israel's coveting of Palestinian land—remember David Ben Gurion's admonition to comrades that they not draw boundaries for their new state lest they deny themselves an opportunity to push eastward towards the Jordan River.

Take a helicopter-view of history and the bludgeon of reality emerges. It is this: it does not matter which party or coalition of parties is in power in Israel; whether the Israeli military, settlers or peace movement is ascendant; whether Democrats or Republicans are in the White House; whether Fatah rules in the Occupied Territories or has been routed by Hamas; it makes no difference whether there is a cold peace or a hot war, an intifada or an Oslo-induced new spring; it does not matter whether Area A is the square root of areas B and C; or whether the Arab world is spoiling for war or suing for peace. The outcome is always the same—while Israel goes through the motions of talking about returning the Occupied Territories, it takes more and more Palestinian land and the rest of the world pretty much looks the other way.

Only this week, Osamah Khalil, of the California-based Palestine Policy Network, pulled out this gem on then Prime Minister Yitzak Shamir's thinking when he agreed to the Oslo talks: 'I would have carried on autonomy talks for ten years and meanwhile we would have reached a half-million people in Judea and Samaria [as Israelis refer to the West Bank].'

How can any Palestinian believe in a two-state solution when one of those potential states is being shrunk, square metre by square metre? As Josh Ruebner, a Jew who heads the US Campaign to End the Occupation, wrote in *USA Today* of the renewed talks: 'Palestinians paradoxically will be expected to negotiate statehood with Israel, while Israel—with the full support of the United States in the form of $US3 billion per year in military aid—continues to gobble up the territory designated for a Palestinian state.'

If Hamas is such a fundamentalist threat to Israel, the region and the world, then an imperative at any point in the last decade might have been an honourable deal with Fatah, a settlement that would allow Palestinians to see the successors of Yasser Arafat as leaders worthy of their respect and loyalty. As it is, these latest talks are set to fail, further diminishing Abbas and Fatah in the eyes of Palestinians and thereby creating new political and emotional space in which Hamas will say, 'We told you so.'

There is no peace process. As Chas Freeman, former US ambassador to Saudi Arabia, puts it, the process is a handmaiden of Israeli expansion rather than a driver for peace. In an address to the staff of the Norwegian Ministry of Foreign Affairs in September, Freeman was withering: 'The perpetual processing of peace without the requirement to produce it has been especially appreciated by Israeli leaders. It has enabled them to behave like magicians, riveting foreign attention on meaningless distractions as they systematically removed Palestinians from their homes, settled half-a-million or more Jews in newly vacated areas of the Occupied Territories and annexed a widening swathe of land to a Jerusalem they insist belongs only to Israel.'

Afterword

AL-QAEDA LOST ON
THE ARAB STREET

Washington DC, USA
5 February 2011

Can you hear it? There is nothing, only stunned silence, from the wilds of the Pakistani mountains where the fugitive Osama bin Laden and his lieutenants must be assumed to be watching the revolt of Arab youth in slack-jawed disbelief.

As we near the end of what historians will call the September 11 decade, the Al-Qaeda silence is a hallelujah moment barely acknowledged in wall-to-wall media coverage of the uprisings across North Africa and the Middle East, as hundreds of thousands of over-educated and underemployed youngsters begin a life's journey—setting out as subjects and serfs, they demand to become citizens in charge of their own destiny.

In a region where life is cheap, the spark was the despair of 26-year-old Mohamed Bouazizi, who in mid-December set himself on fire to escape his numbing existence as a fruit vendor in Sidi Bouzid, in central Tunisia.

As reverberations are felt in Riyadh, Damascus, Amman and Sanaa, many in the West are confounded that these protests took off so spectacularly. More nationalist than religious, more economic than ideological, they have shredded the legitimacy implicit in the term 'Arab government'—all of it telecast live across the region and the world.

Were they not the bin Laden generation, so saturated in Islamist and terrorist bile, so hateful towards American freedom and values that their protest almost certainly would be a suicide-bomb attack on a busload of foreign tourists or a foreign diplomatic mission? When they answered the call, it would be to run violently with the Islamists—yes?

That's the stunner—instead, they walked into the streets of their towns and cities, defenceless but dignified, and simply said, 'Enough!' After all that fundamentalist nonsense about needing to revert to the pious past to get away from the shallowness of a Western-influenced life, they say 'No' to bin Laden.

In Yemen, to make sure they would not be dismissed as just another 'Allahu Akbar' battalion, protesters reportedly wore pink—instead of Islamic green.

Looking eastward, to the relative success of Islamist insurgencies in Iraq and in Afghanistan and then northward, to the cafes and campuses of Europe, they are making an informed choice, of which many beyond the region had not considered them capable. In their part of the world, at this time in history, 'More, please,' does not mean a jihadi-led retreat to seventh-century Islam as pursued by the Taliban in Afghanistan. Nope—books and iPods, Starbucks and McDonald's are, by far, more attractive.

'It's a huge defeat for Al-Qaeda in a country of central importance to its image,' says Noman Benotman, who was described by Reuters as a former organiser for a group associated with Al-Qaeda in Libya. 'It has wounded their credibility with potential supporters.'

The combustible mix of their circumstances is difficult to comprehend. Two-thirds of the population of the region is younger than 24. University numbers have rocketed but graduates are dumped into an economy that cannot employ them—in Egypt, youth unemployment runs as high as 34 per cent; in Tunisia, 31 per cent. Their pressure-cooker existence is complete, living by the whim of police thugs, obsequious state-controlled media and an over-class that rigs the legal and electoral systems to keep power and money in its pockets.

For all that, Gary Wasserman, an American analyst at George-town University's school of foreign service in Qatar, ponders aloud to the *Herald* on the extent to which Arab and Muslim youth are indoctrinated on the internet: 'I'm not sure that they have been inundated with Al-Qaeda material . . . that idea might be a Western obsession, too, [because] who wants to go to the mountains, to deprive themselves, living as a fanatic, and then to die? Some will always want that but most just want to have a good life.'

As the tempo of the uprisings rose, there were internet calls for an attack on the gas pipeline from Egypt to Israel; and in Yemen, for attacks on Shiite Muslims. But Brian Fishman, a counterterrorism analyst at the New America Foundation in Washington, said the revolt was 'a direct repudiation of Al-Qaeda's core argument, which is that the only way to create change in Arab countries is through unmitigated violence'.

When the protesters took to the streets, it was their dictatorial leader, Mubarak, who revealed himself in the bin Laden mould. A pin-striped sophisticate, to be sure, but with his back to the wall he did not hesitate in sending in knife-wielding thugs. Commenting on the absence of the usual American flag-burning and Israel-taunting by the protesters and any Islamist ugliness, Joshua Landis, the director of the centre for Middle East studies at the University of Oklahoma, told the *Herald*: 'It is the regimes that are the scary face—the violence of the Mubarak thugs is a reminder of what the people have to put up with.'

None of this is to say that bin Laden has been neutered—the experts contend that he remains a clear and present danger, for the US in particular. The CIA veteran Michael Scheuer writes in his new biography of Osama bin Laden: 'His rhetoric and his actions [still] address the current grievances Muslims have against Western intervention and the cruelty, hypocrisy, incompetence and corruption of their own regimes.'

Scheuer argues that, while the US will continue to be a key target, Al-Qaeda's priority job will be inciting Muslims to jihad— 'once America is defeated, he will turn to toppling Arab tyrannies, destroying Israel and, eventually, to fighting the Shia'.

But the new uprisings and their extraordinary success in robbing autocrats of their most powerful weapon—their own people's fear of them—are more a shining light than the Bush-led invasion of Iraq. And they are an inspiring alternative prescription for confronting the emptiness of life and the absence of a future in the region to that offered by bin Laden.

Efforts by Al-Qaeda and other terrorist groups in Egypt, Saudi Arabia and Yemen have brought only greater oppression as the regimes have been armed and aided by Washington and other Western capitals, entrenching them as they embark on tighter nationwide crackdowns. But this week, naked people power, by a generation we figured was resigned to its aimless existence, is doing what bin Laden failed to do—take those regimes to the brink.

The Lebanon-based commentator Rami Khouri ranks the uprisings as the third and most significant historical pivot in Arab historical development—after the European colonial powers made such a mess of carving out the borders of the modern Arab states in the aftermath of World War I; and later, in the 1970s and 1980s, when the Arab rulers fashioned their lands as police states in the service of the foreign governments that propped them up. He writes: 'We are witnessing an epic, historic moment of the birth of concepts that long have been denied to ordinary Arabs—the right to define ourselves and our governments; to assert our national values; to shape our governance system; and to engage with each other and the rest of the world as free human beings, with rights that cannot be denied forever.'

Scheuer and Landis argue that the critical setback for Al-Qaeda in the region was the bloodthirstiness of its leader in Iraq, Abu Musab al-Zarqawi, whose Sunni-orchestrated mass murder of Shiite Muslims during the insurgency wars in Iraq was, according to Scheuer, the most serious strategic threat to Al-Qaeda after September 11, one, he writes, that 'all but mortally wounded' Al-Qaeda.

More bullish than Scheuer, Landis says: 'In many ways bin Laden's extremist ideology has played itself out. The Islamic world is frightened—what happened in Iraq profoundly scared Muslim society because it saw the damage to itself and its relations with the world.'

And are the street protesters impressionable youth, merely being led? There can be little complaint about the wholesomeness of their calls for change, despite Hillary Clinton's early public angst about 'stability' and Tony Blair's amnesia on Britain's historic role in laying the foundations of today's cot-case Middle East, when he cautioned: 'You don't just have a government and a movement for democracy . . . You also have others, notably the Muslim Brotherhood, who would take this in a different direction.'

If the Obama administration revealed itself somewhat torn, attempting an uncomfortable crab-walk to be on the 'right side' of the Egyptian crisis before meandering back towards 'stability', Blair was like a drowning sailor, clinging to the notion that governments such as that which he once led are entitled to hold whole populations hostage. Mubarak, he said straight-faced, had been 'immensely courageous and a force for good', and change in Egypt needed to be 'stable and ordered'.

The test now for the leadership of the uprisings and for any foreign governments that might offer assistance will be measured by what they have won. So far, they have reasserted their pride and dignity, but all else, even in Tunisia from where the dictator fled, is uncertain or tenuous.

With the military in the middle and cronies trying to hang on and with foreign capitals resorting to calls for 'orderly transitions', coded references to keeping parts of the status quo, the brave ones who stood in the streets, day after day, could still be short-changed on their very reasonable expectations.

The West needs to understand that its effort to retain some kind of 'stability' could see Mubarak remaining in office for a further eight months in which to shape his legacy, at the same time as he ensures that his cronies keep a grip on the levers of power. That is the kind of stability that bin Laden wants, too.

'The best thing for Al-Qaeda would be for this uprising to raise and then to dash popular expectations,' the US counterterrorism specialist Jarret Brachman says. 'The more that Al-Qaeda can say that "the people" still haven't had their voices heard, and become a populist advocate for a "new Egypt", the better Al-Qaeda's hand will be.'

In our efforts to better understand the Muslim world in the aftermath of September 11, there has been occasional pontification on Arab societies as the unfortunates who were bypassed by the Enlightenment. Well, sit back and watch. It might be late but it has begun in the Arab world.

ACKNOWLEDGEMENTS

The chain has its essential links—a book like this does not exist without the people whose stories are told from zones of conflict around the world; without newspaper editors and media executives who dispatch reporters to get those stories; and without book publishers who discern a trend that warrants telling a succession of stories as one.

As a reporter I could choose my time and gauge my safety as I went to hellholes from the Mediterranean eastward to Pakistan in the nearly ten years since the September 11 attacks on New York and Washington. The people whose stories I tell here did not have this luxury—they were stuck, mired in circumstances not of their making, but invariably always willing to be interviewed. Similarly, it is the reporter's name that appears on the published story, but we could not get by without our local fixers—in my case, these unsung stars of journalism include Ranya Kadri in Amman, Salam Mohamadoui in Baghdad, Qais Asimy and Hashim Shukoor in Kabul, and Wafa Issa in Beirut. In the same vein, life on the road would be far less rewarding without the company of my photographer colleagues—like the ever-resourceful Ash Sweeting in Kabul and my tenacious *Sydney Morning Herald* colleague Kate Geraghty.

At Fairfax Media, I'm indebted to a succession of *Herald* editors who always backed the story—Robert Whitehead, Alan Oakley, Peter Fray and Amanda Wilson. When I embarked on this remarkable journey, Greg Hywood was there as *Herald* publisher; now, as the September 11 decade closes, he is back at Fairfax as chief executive. In particular, I thank Peter Fray for his permission to reproduce much of my *Herald* reports in this volume and Peter Kerr, the *Herald*'s managing editor, for his help, advice and assistance when I have been on the road.

In each book project that I have undertaken, a mainstay in the process has been the inimitable Richard Walsh, Allen & Unwin's consultant publisher who sits on my left shoulder throughout. He was perched there again this time—rounding-up, straightening out and, as required, doing a fine line in panelbeating. Thank you, Richard.

Allen & Unwin executive chairman Patrick Gallagher, editorial manager Angela Handley and copyeditor Adam Shaw also deserve thanks for their tireless efforts.